THE NEW CHAUCER SOCIETY

Studies in the Age of Chaucer, the yearbook of The New Chaucer Society, is published annually. Each issue contains a limited number of substantial articles, reviews of books on Chaucer and related topics, and an annotated Chaucer bibliography. Articles explore such concerns as the efficacy of various critical approaches to the art of Chaucer and his contemporaries, their literary relationships and reputations, and the artistic, economic, intellectual, religious, scientific, and social and historical backgrounds to their work.

Manuscripts, in duplicate, accompanied by return postage, should follow the *Chicago Manual of Style*, thirteenth edition. Unsolicited reviews are not accepted. Authors receive free twenty offprints of articles and ten of reviews. All correspondence concerning manuscript submissions for Volume 6 of *Studies in the Age of Chaucer* should be directed to the Editor. Subscriptions to the New Chaucer Society and information about the Society's activities should be directed to John H. Fisher, Department of English, University of Tennessee, Knoxville, Tennessee 37996–0430.

Studies in the Age of Chaucer

Studies in the Age of Chaucer

Volume 5
1983

EDITED BY THOMAS J. HEFFERNAN · PUBLISHED
ANNUALLY BY THE NEW CHAUCER SOCIETY
THE UNIVERSITY OF TENNESSEE, KNOXVILLE

The frontispiece design, showing the Pilgrims at the Tabard Inn, is adapted from the woodcut in Caxton's second edition of *The Canterbury Tales*.

Copyright © 1983 by The New Chaucer Society, the University of Tennessee, Knoxville. Manufactured by Pilgrim Books, Norman, Oklahoma. First edition.

ISBN 0–937664–64–2

ISSN 0190–2407

CONTENTS

ARTICLES

REVIEWS

Studies in the Age of Chaucer

Chaucer's Prescience
The Presidential Address, 1982

John H. Fisher
University of Tennessee

ONE OF THE most important developments in Chaucer criticism since World War II has been the development of "historical criticism." Teachers and scholars have always recognized that much of our task is to interpret older and foreign literatures for contemporary readers. But this task was not erected into a critical principle until D. W. Robertson, Bernard Huppé, and others had to defend their exegetical interpretations of Old and Middle English literature.[1] Their argument was that to understand medieval literature we must become aware of the full range of its medieval social and aesthetic connotations. Following upon C. S. Lewis's *Allegory of Love*, which had pointed out the figurative, psychological character of medieval poetry, the Robertsonian emphasis on its dualistic symbolism has taught us that medieval poetry can be as indirect and evocative as any other, ancient or modern. We have come a long way from the simple narrative readings of the 1920s. Yet just as the hermeneutic preoccupations of the 1920s seemed limited to the critics of the 1960s, so the historicity of the 1960s seems limited today. Interest has begun to shift from the text itself to the reaction of the reader to the text. The text comes to be regarded as merely a stimulus that activates elements of the reader's own experience. The poem is no longer an entity but "an event in time," "a compenetration of a reader and a text."[2]

---

[1] There is a good discussion of the differences among the literary historians, the new critics, and the recent historical critics in the introduction to William R. Crawford, *Bibliography of Chaucer 1954–63* (Seattle: University of Washington Press, 1967), pp. xiv–xl. D. W. Robertson, Jr., "Some Observations on Method in Literary Studies," *NLH* 1(1969):21–33; and "Historical Criticism," *English Institute Essays* (1950), pp. 3–31, discuss the theory.

[2] Louise M. Rosenblatt, *The Reader, the Text, the Poem* (Carbondale: Southern Illinois University Press, 1978), pp. 11–14.

From this point of view the historical axiom as most recently expressed by D. W. Robertson seems inadequate: "Chaucer did not write 'for all humanity,' or 'for all time,' but for a specific audience that had immediate, everyday concerns."[3] This is, of course, true, but if it were the whole truth, who today would want to read the poetry of Geoffrey Chaucer? There must be other elements that have acted to bring two hundred "sondry folk" together here in San Francisco nearly six hundred years after April 17, 1387, Skeat's date for the first day of the Canterbury pilgrimage. One of these elements I like to think of as Chaucer's *prescience*, that is, the appearance in Chaucer's poems of words, topics, and patterns that activate elements in the reader's own experience — that produce the event in time that the psychological critics identify as poetry.

Harold Bloom has treated this experience in relation to poetic creativity. In his *A Map of Misreading* he suggests that modern concern for historicity is caused by what he calls the Romantic guilt of "belatedness."[4] The Romantic energizer was revisionism, in poetry as well as in politics, and Bloom sees modern literary critics — particularly American critics — forever treading guiltily in their reinterpretation, with a sense of violating daemonic ground. The historical critics are peculiarly aware of this transgression and would reveal to us the ancient mysteries. But it is too late for that. We can never see charity or cupidity, or even a summoner or a pardoner exactly as Chaucer's audience did. Since the time of Nietzsche and Freud, says Bloom, it is not possible to return wholly to a mode of interpretation that seeks to restore the meaning of the text.[5]

I am not today going to devote myself to the central thesis of Bloom's "map" — that interpretation is always misreading — though his argument provides a fruitful method for discussing Chaucerian irony. He finds the chief defense of later poets against the oppressive influence of their predecessors to be the employment of tropes — that is, the application of words and phrases that they have learned from previous poems in a new

---

[3] D. W. Robertson, Jr., "Simple Signs of Everyday Life in Chaucer," in John P. Hermann and John J. Burke, Jr., eds., *Signs and Symbols in Chaucer's Poetry* (University: University of Alabama Press, 1981), p. 15.

[4] Harold Bloom, *A Map of Misreading* (New York: Oxford University Press, 1975), pp. 35–36.

[5] Ibid., p. 85.

way—as intentional errors.[6] Think how the description of the Prioress ("And al was conscience and tendre herte") or of the Monk ("And I seyde his opinioun was good") or the Wife of Bath's patristic argument could be interpreted as deliberate misreadings of traditional sentiments. Chaucer's ironic revision of his own sources must be taken into account in any historical interpretation, as has been done by Robert Kaske in his articles on Chaucer's aubes, by E. T. Donaldson in his discussion of the idiom of *The Miller's Tale*, and by Robertson himself in connection with Andreas Capellanus.[7]

But my concern today is not the interpretation of Chaucer's poetry in historical context. It is, rather, to consider some examples of reader response. I am increasingly aware as I try to elucidate the mysteries of realism and nominalism or the complexities of the English civil service in the fourteenth century that these are not the reasons that twenty-five or thirty undergraduates have elected to read him. The reason that they are there is that Chaucer, like Homer and Shakespeare, *did* write for all humanity and all time. Even though we do not have reeves and manciples, we do have foremen and managers who terrorize their underlings and steal from their superiors. Sometimes they are even detected and prosecuted. Although the students know nothing about the Platonic distinctions between the earthly and heavenly Aphrodites, they do recognize that *The Miller's Tale* and *The Man of Law's Tale* present very different kinds of love.

What I would like to do for the next few minutes, then, is to turn the discussion around and focus not on the obscurities of Chaucer's text but on the recognizances. These recognizances are not historical but pragmatic. I will begin with some words and ideas and work up to characters and narrative techniques.

Each time I read *The Canterbury Tales* or *Troilus*, I am struck by the modern connotations that have developed for certain terms. For example,

---

[6] Ibid., p. 93.

[7] Robert Kaske, "The Aube in Chaucer's *Troilus*," in R. J. Schoeck and Jerome Taylor, eds., *Chaucer Criticism II* (Notre Dame, Ind.: Notre Dame University Press, 1961), pp. 167–79, and his other articles on the aube; E. T. Donaldson, "Idiom and Popular Poetry in the Miller's Tale," in W. K. Wimsatt, Jr., ed., *Selected Papers of the English Institute, 1941–52* (New York: Columbia University Press, 1963); D. W. Robertson, Jr., "The Subject of *De amore* of Andreas Capellanus," *MP* 50(1953):154–61.

it delights me when I read that the Prioress fed her little dogs "wastel bred" to recall that "wastel" is the Germanic form of the French *gâteau* — *w* becoming *gu* as in *Guillaume*; *as*, *â* as in *bâtard*, and *el*, *eau* as in *beau*. This association reminds me of the canard attributed to another woman just as far removed from the poverty in her society as the Prioress. Marie Antoinette never did say, "Let them eat cake."[8] Rousseau in 1740 in his *Confessions* attributed the thoughtless remark to a nameless great princess, who, on being informed that the country people had no bread, replied, "Qu'ils mangent de la brioche." In 1823, Louis XVIII attributed the remark to Marie Therêse, who had died in 1683, as "Que ne mangent-ils de la croûte de pâte" (*croûte* = crust, *pâte* = pastry). So the "wastel-gâteau-cake" association turns out to be purely serendipitous, but that does not deter the modern reader from enjoying Chaucer's use of the same figure to exhibit the Prioress's insulation from reality as that attributed to Marie Antoinette.

I have the same pleasure in observing how the "not heed" of the Yeoman presages the "roundheads" of the Puritan wars. By calling attention to the "lokkes crulle" of the Squire and the "not heed" of the Yeoman, Chaucer has fixed upon exactly the distinctions that would emblemize the Cavaliers and the Roundheads 250 years later.

The talents of the Sergeant of the Law as a "purchasour" to whom all was "fee symple in effect" look ahead in the same way. Both "purchasour" and "fee symple" are legal terms from Latin and Anglo-Norman. The first citation for "purchaser" in the *OED* is to Robert Mannyng's *Handlyng Synne* (ca. 1303). The second citation, however, is to the Man of Law, and the first citations for "fee simple" in both the *OED* and the *MED* are to Chaucer's lawyer. I am mindful of Jürgen Schäfer's recent study of *Documentation in the O.E.D.*, which points out how overrepresented Shakespeare is in the citation and lemmatization policy of the *OED*.[9] Everything written by Shakespeare was excerpted much more thoroughly than were writings of less prestigious authors like Wyatt or Nashe, with the result that first citations from Shakespeare are markedly overrepresented. Shäfer does

---

[8] See *The Oxford Book of English Quotations*, 2d ed. (Oxford: Oxford University Press, 1953), p. 329.18. The *Times* (London), April 30, 1959, has a Latin version of the same quotation attributed to John Peckham, Archbishop of Canterbury, 1225–92.

[9] Jürgen Schäfer, *Documentation in the O.E.D.* (Oxford: Clarendon Press, 1980).

not extend his investigation back into the fourteenth century, but the probability is that Chaucer is likewise overrepresented in first citations in his period. The *MED* is making a wider search. Hence it is significant that it has not been able to antedate "fee simple."

When one considers how since Chaucer's time — particularly in the United States — nearly all transfer of property has changed from entailment to absolute ownership, Chaucer's terminology takes on prophetic overtones. Both *OED* and *MED* likewise cite Chaucer's five (or six with the *Romaunt of the Rose*) uses of "chevisaunce," i.e., borrowing money or purchasing on credit, as the earliest in English. Although unlike the first two terms this term has not come down into Modern English, Chaucer's usage again looks forward to modern business practice.

I have never known whether the Clerk of Oxenford's being stuck at logic should be taken as a joke. The trivium of grammar, rhetoric, and logic was commonly the preparatory curriculum for the bachelor of arts, which the student had to complete before proceeding on to metaphysics and philosophy for the master of arts. Charles Haskins takes the reference to Chaucer's clerk as evidence of how completely logic had come to dominate the curriculum of the medieval university, but Paul Abelson is at pains to distinguish the propaedeutic place of logic in the medieval university as a tool for more advanced study.[10] After the thirteenth century the quadrivium was absorbed into the general course in philosophy, but specific references to arithmetic are found only in connection with the requirements for the M.A.[11] — a detail that may throw light on the academic status of Nicholas, with his Almagest and augrim stones. Could it be that, for all

---

[10] Charles Homer Haskins, *The Rise of the Universities* (1923) (Ithaca, N.Y.: Cornell University Press, 1957), p. 30; Paul Abelson, *The Seven Liberal Arts*, Columbia University, Teachers College Contributions to Education (1906), pp. 72–87; Jerome J. Murphy, "Rhetoric in Fourteenth-Century Oxford," *MÆ* 34(1965):14, quotes an Oxford statute of 1431 requiring that students incepting in arts and philosophy must have read in grammar, rhetoric, and logic.

[11] Hastings Rashdall, *The Universities in Europe in the Middle Ages*, ed. F. M. Powicke and A. B. Emden (Oxford: Oxford University Press, 1936), 1.441, comments on the absorption of the quadrivium into moral and natural philosophy at the University of Paris; p. 444 cites the curriculum at Paris as grammar, logic, and psychology for the B.A.; natural philosophy and metaphysics for the license of arts; and continuation of natural philosophy and moral philosophy for the M.A. Abelson, *The Seven Liberal Arts*, pp. 106–108, discusses mathematics in connection with the M.A. requirements at various universities.

his pretensions, the Clerk could not pass out of logic into philosophy and mathematics? The selection of the term "logic" is itself another example of Chaucer's prescience. The reference to the Clerk is his only use of the term, which was comparatively rare in the Middle Ages. Augustine, Cassiodorus, Isidore of Seville, Marcianus de Capella, Alcuin, and Abelard all titled their treatises on the subject *De dialectica* (or *dialecticae*) and focused on the pedagogical exercises of disputation and persuasion.[12] The term "logic" connoted for Chaucer deductive reasoning and the mysteries of the syllogism. Since the Renaissance it has come to connote inference and scientific method. Through the accident of this semantic shift the Clerk becomes a sympathetic figure to students in our post–John Dewey era, when the classroom is thought of not as a courtroom where truth is argued dialectically but as a laboratory where it is proved empirically.

This sort of verbal association can become purely serendipitous when we read about those "good felawes" the Shipman and the Summoner during a presidential administration celebrated for the "good old boys" in its sept or in the winter of our discontent with Poland and Russia that even the Knight had to fight "in Pruce, . . . in Lettow, . . . and in Ruce." These are American recognizances. Each community will have its own associations. I do not mean to imply that when Chaucer chose his words he was consciously looking ahead. I accept Robertson's dictum that he was writing at a specific time for a specific audience. What I do mean to imply is that one reason why we continue to enjoy his poetry is the magical way that his specific *parole* (to use the distinction made by de Saussure) illuminates our generalized *langue* — the way that his contemporary reference reverberates in the sphere of our experience six hundred years later.

The same sort of prescience that we find in Chaucer's choice of words we find also in his patterns of characterization and organization. For example, the catalogue of pilgrims in *The General Prologue* begins with the Knight and the Squire. In Chaucer's time the clergy were still regarded as more important than the laity, and appeared first in nearly all lists of the estates. In the summaries of the orders in which the estates are presented in various medieval treatments that Jill Mann appends to her *Chaucer and Medieval Estates Satire*, the clergy precede the laity in every listing that includes both

---

[12] The exact titles are given in the bibliography of original sources in Abelson, *The Seven Liberal Arts*, pp. 137–41.

except in Étienne de Fougère's *Livre des manières* and Chaucer's *General Prologue*.[13] The precedence of the Knight and the Squire over the Prioress and the Monk, which strikes the modern reader as perfectly natural, was anything but natural in Chaucer's time. Chaucer never did assert the superiority of civil to canon law (as Gower did in *In Praise of Peace*),[14] but he placed the courtly and civil ideals of *The Knight's Tale* as the benchmarks against which to measure the moral and legal implications of the tales that follow. Furthermore, most other lists of the estates include many more ecclesiastical categories than the *Prologue* — for example, pope, cardinals, patriarchs, bishops, prelates, monks, crusaders, lay brothers, wandering monks, secular priests, and nuns — more than half the estates in the *Sermones nulli parcentes*,[15] compared with six religious pilgrims out of twenty-four in *The General Prologue* (counting all the artisans as one). The secularism of putting the Knight first is reinforced by making a "loud, crude, hardswearing publican master of ceremonies of a pilgrimage to the foremost shrine in England," as R. W. V. Elliott puts it, and by making what Chesterton called that "great professional widow of literature" a kind of marriage counselor on the trip.[16]

The feminism of the Wife of Bath, the voyeurism of Pandarus, the complaisance of Criseyde, these and other characterizations no doubt delighted Chaucer's sophisticated audience, but they have taken on an added dimension as we have moved toward more individualistic and more psychological interpretations of character. In the light of these realistic characterizations the problem of the patient Griselda is especially interesting. What could possibly have led three of the principal authors in the fourteenth century, and several whose names we do not know, to tell this improbable and unpleasant tale? I believe that it was because the Griselda story is one of the few exemplifications in literature (until we get to the Horatio Alger rags-to-riches vulgarizations at the end of the nineteenth century)[17] of the doctrine of natural nobility. The unpromising-hero or

[13] Jill Mann, *Chaucer and Medieval Estates Satire* (Cambridge: Cambridge University Press, 1973), pp. 203–206.

[14] John Gower, *In Praise of Peace*, in *Complete Works*, ed. G. C. Macaulay (Oxford: Clarendon Press, 1901), 3.488, lines 225–31.

[15] Mann, *Chaucer and Medieval Estates Satire*, p. 204.

[16] R. W. V. Elliott, *Chaucer's English* (London: Deutsch, 1974), p. 103.

[17] See Russel Nye, *The Unembarrassed Muse: The Popular Arts in America* (New York: Dial Press, 1970), pp. 62–72.

9

heroine motif is a favorite in literature, but from Perceval to Tom Jones, or Enide in Chrètien de Troyes's *Erec et Enide* to Perdita in *The Winter's Tale*, they nearly all turn out in the end to be gently born. It is nearly inconceivable in fiction even today for a true hero to be base-born. The only example I know in medieval literature is the peasant's daughter in Hartman von Aue's *Der arme Heinrich*, who is willing to sacrifice herself to cure the nobleman's leprosy.[18]

The initial insight was not Chaucer's, but placing the Griselda story so soon after the Wife of Bath's curtain lecture on the nature of true nobility points up the motif. Chaucer's sensitivity to the theme is borne out by his subtle changes in the language. Boccaccio has no imagery at the beginning of his version that calls attention to the theme of natural nobility, but Petrarch begins with references to Versullus, ". . . mons unus altissimus. . . mons suapte nobilis natura," whose contrast with the "grata planicie" of Saluzzo emphasizes the differences between the high and low stations of Walter and Griselda.[19] Chaucer points up this contrast by adding to Vesullus "the colde," which sets sterile cold against the warmth of the "lusty playne." Petrarch speaks of the "vicis et castellis satis frequens" on the plain, but Chaucer introduces the notion of heredity by adding, "That founded were in tyme of fadres olde," and he reinforces it by expanding "marchionum. . .nobilium" with "as were his worthy eldres hym bifore."

In the next stanza Chaucer makes more specific Petrarch's description of Walter as "nec minus moribus quam sanguine nobilis" ("no less noble in behavior than in blood"), which is rendered in the French prose "moult noble de ligniage," by introducing the Wife of Bath's term "gentilesse": "Therwith he was, to speke of lynage, / The gentilleste yborn of Lombardye," and in line 96, when the people urge Walter to marry, Chaucer again introduces "gentilesse" where it is not found in the Latin or the French. Comparison of Petrarch's version with Boccaccio's shows Petrarch repeatedly pointing up the references to Walter's noble blood in contrast to Griselda's low birth. Comparison of Chaucer with Petrarch shows Chaucer further heightening this motif. He renders the generalized "ut pauperum

---

[18] Erich Gierach, ed., *Der arme Heinrich* (Heidelberg, Winter, 1913).

[19] Quotations from Petrarch and the French are from W. F. Bryan and G. Dempster, eds., *Sources and Analogues of Chaucer's Canterbury Tales* (Chicago: University of Chicago Press, 1941), p. 194. Quotations from Boccaccio are from F. J. Furnivall et al., eds., *Originals and Analogues of Some of Chaucer's Canterbury Tales* (London: Chaucer Society, 1872–87).

quoque tuguria non numquam gratia celestis invisit" ("Mais comme aucune foiz la grace de Dieu descent en un petit hostel") as "But hye God somtyme senden kan / His grace into a litel oxes stalle" (line 206), thereby heightening the parallel with the humble birth of Jesus as the supreme proof that nobility is the gift of God and not an inherited trait. This parallel is reinforced by the icons of the Annunciation that he introduces into the wedding scene. Petrarch had sharpened Boccaccio's matter-of-fact account by introducing suspense about the identity of the bride. But Griselda's moving soliloquy beginning, "I wole with othere maydens stonde" (line 281), her setting down her water pot "Biside the thresshfold, in an oxes stalle" (line 291), and her reply to the Markys, "Lord, he is al redy heere" (line 298) so reminiscent of Mary's reply to the angel in the Annunciation (I quote from the Douay): "Behold the handmaid of the Lord; be it done to me according to thy word" (Luke 1.38)—these are Chaucer's additions, revealing his sensitivity to the Christological precedent for the idea of the divine origin of nobility. He shows the same sensitivity when he renders Griselda's being clothed in her nuptual robes ("transformatum" in Petrarch; "transmuee" in the French) as "translated," with its mystical connotation of being conveyed into sainthood.

All three versions fix upon Griselda's low birth as the excuse for the removal of her children and eventually for her own banishment. Perhaps it is only Chaucer idolatry that makes me prefer Chaucer's musical "that born art of a low lynage" (line 483) to Petrarch's "plebeie domine" or Boccaccio's "bassa condizione"; "Thanne shal the blood of Janicle succede" (line 632) over "Ianicule nepos" or "un nepote di Giannuculo"; or "Noght for youre lynage ne for youre richesse" (line 795) over "mores tuos non originem respiciens" or "miei passati sono stati gran gentili uomini e signori... dove i tuo i stati son sempre lavoratori" ("my ancestors were all great gentlemen and lords while yours were always laborers"), neither of which makes the Wife of Bath's connection between "gentilesse" and "old richesse." Chaucer handles more sensitively the wretched clothes in which Griselda welcomes Walter's new bride: "Right noght was she abayst of hire clothyng, / Thogh it were rude and somdeel eek torent" (line 1011). Petrarch described her merely as "obsolete vestris," and Boccaccio, "così come era" ("clad as she was"). It is interesting that Petrarch and Chaucer after him omitted Boccaccio's parenthesis in which the ladies implore Walter to have Griselda either dressed more presentably or kept out of sight.

Although Petrarch and Chaucer pointed up the idea of the divine origin of nobility throughout their versions, it was Boccaccio who drew the moral at the end: "Che si potrà dir qui, se non che anche nelle povere casa piovono dal cielo de divini spiriti, come nelle reali di quegli che sarien più degni di guardar porci, che d'avera sopra uomini signoria?" ("What more can be said except divine spirits can rain down on a poor dwelling, just as in a royal one there may be a person more worthy to tend pigs than to rule over men?"). This conclusion may be what called Petrarch's attention to the importance of the theme of the story. I take it as an indication of the prescience of all three authors that they recognized in it the antihereditary view of virtuous character that has come to dominate the thinking of our modern egalitarian society.

The final example I want to cite of Chaucer's prescience is the structure of *The Canterbury Tales*. I cast my lot with Northrop Frye in believing that "the primary understanding of any work of literature has to be based on an assumption of its unity,"[20] and I am not solipsistic enough to be able to agree with some modern critics that the principle of unity pertains only to our way of seeing, not to anything inherent in the object to be seen.[21] Yet there is little doubt that since the advent of Impressionism we perceive unity in a different way. Completeness of action is not what is sought in the novels of Dorothy Richardson or Virginia Woolf but unity of effect. In this light the inchoate, evolving pattern of *The Canterbury Tales* is especially attractive. The finished symmetry of *Troilus and Criseyde* shows that Chaucer was capable of formal perfection. We are therefore entitled to suppose that the ambiguous structure of *The Canterbury Tales* is not accidental. And it is the ambiguous structure of *The Canterbury Tales* that has proved most interesting to critics in the twentieth century, not the finished structure of *Troilus and Criseyde*. The *Canterbury* collection has come down to us with all the movement and variety of an Alexander Calder mobile. How different it appears when we see it in the Hengwrt order in Norman Blake's new edition and the *Variorum Chaucer* or in the Chaucer

---

[20] Northrop Frye, "Literary Criticism," in James Thorpe, ed., *The Aims and Methods of Scholarship in Modern Languages and Literatures* (New York: Modern Language Association, 1963), p. 63.

[21] Lawrence Lipking, "Literary Criticism," in Joseph Gibaldi, ed., *Introduction to Scholarship in Modern Languages and Literatures* (New York: Modern Language Association, 1951), p. 93.

Society order in Skeat and Baugh or in the Ellesmere order in Robinson's edition and my own.

In all the manuscripts the frame is the same. No one has questioned its firmness except Norman Blake and Charles Owen. Blake finds no Chaucerian conception of unity among the parts.[22] He argues that the Hengwrt scribe put them together pragmatically, beginning with the tales without links and following these with the tales that had links. Some "editor" took the material in hand and produced from it the more coherent Ellesmere order. But it is significant that both the Hengwrt and the Ellesmere manuscripts begin with *The General Prologue* and end with *The Parson's Tale*. Owen goes further than Blake.[23] Despite the uniformity of the manuscript evidence, he argues that Chaucer was continuing to work toward the completion of the plan proposed in the *Prologue*, a supper back at the Tabard Inn. Both Blake's and Owen's arguments fly in the face of the cohesiveness that editors and readers have always recognized in *The Canterbury Tales* as they stand. As J. S. P. Tatlock pointed out in 1935, and Owen himself has observed as recently as the March, 1982, issue of *PMLA*, most of the scribal editing in the fifteenth century was intended to point up the completeness of the book. Ralph Baldwin was the first to discuss the signs of commencement and completion in *The General Prologue* and *The Parson's Tale* as a conceptual frame.[24] Donald Howard has gone a step further and proposed a highly impressionistic unity for the collection.[25] He finds this unity in the moderating memory of the narrator. In support he points to a parallel between the structure of *The Canterbury Tales* and Proust's *À la recherche du temps perdu*, whose "Overture" serves as a structuring principle just as *The General Prologue* does. He says:

---

[22] Norman Blake, *The Canterbury Tales, Edited from the Hengwrt Manuscript* (London: Arnold, 1980). The introduction to this edition should be read in connection with Blake's "The Relationship between the Hengwrt and Ellesmere Manuscripts of the 'Canterbury Tales,'" *E&S* 32(1979):1–18.

[23] Charles A. Owen, Jr., *Pilgrimage and Storytelling in the Canterbury Tales* (Norman: University of Oklahoma Press, 1977); Charles A. Owen, Jr. "The Alternative Reading of *The Canterbury Tales*: Chaucer's Text and the Early Manuscripts," *PMLA* 97(1982):237–50.

[24] Ralph Baldwin, *The Unity of the Canterbury Tales* (New York: AMS Press, 1971; originally published 1955).

[25] Donald R. Howard, *The Idea of the Canterbury Tales* (Berkeley: University of California Press, 1976).

In it the characters, the circumstances, the social structure of the day, the character of the narrator's mind, the form of the whole and its major themes are introduced. Everything that is to follow harkens back to this passage — the whole cannot be read without it because it imposes unity; like the *Canterbury Tales* it even permits us to read the sections out of order, to "choose another tale," without losing our awareness of its formal integrity.[26]

Howard observes that Proust said that the opening of the first novel of his cycle and the ending of the last were written on the same day — that the structure of the whole was thus a unified idea. This is exactly the impression created by the resonances of language and imagery in *The General Prologue*, the *Man of Law Headlink* and the *Parson Headlink*.

Nowhere in Howard's book do I find the terms "Impressionism" or "stream of consciousness," but it seems to me that his analysis strengthens our awareness that the arrangement of materials between the beginning and ending of *The Canterbury Tales* is more associative than logical. Paul Ruggiers has described the arrangement as "medley," Robert Jordan as "multiple unity,"[27] Ralph Baldwin as "the life of the medieval Christian...framed by Creation and Doomsday,"[28] and Donald Howard as "memory." Memory is the organizing principle of the modern stream-of-consciousness novel. From this point of view the tales can be read not as a "state" but as a "process of becoming," the "flowing river of memories," the "flux of human experience." These are phrases that have been used to describe the novels of Dorothy Richardson, Virginia Woolf, and James Joyce.[29] Their appropriateness to modern critics' analysis of the unity of *The Canterbury Tales* as thematic rather than as temporal or topographic or operative appears to me to represent Chaucer's most prescient achievement. From this point of view there can be no fixed, logical order for the tales but only an associative, aesthetic preference. Chaucer's reason for not

[26] Ibid., p. 157.

[27] Paul G. Ruggiers, *The Art of the Canterbury Tales* (Madison: University of Wisconsin Press, 1965), p. 15; Robert M. Jordan, *Chaucer and the Shape of Creation* (Cambridge, Mass.: Harvard University Press, 1967), p. 137. Jordan acknowledges Heinrich Wölfflin and Wylie Sypher.

[28] Baldwin, *The Unity of the Canterbury Tales*, p. 27.

[29] Shiv K. Kumar, *Bergson and the Stream of Consciousness Novel* (New York: New York University Press, 1963), uses these phrases in an analysis based on Bergson's theory of memory; see esp. pp. 25–26.

completing the collection with the formal perfection of *Troilus* or of Gower's *Confessio Amantis* was not incapacity but a subliminal awareness that the work is complete as it stands, like a Degas painting or a Henry Moore sculpture. The same sort of argument can be made about *The House of Fame* and the three incomplete tales in the *Canterbury* collection. By moving toward an impressionistic technique, Chaucer created works that require the participation of the reader to a much fuller degree than does a formally completed structure. And this technique is, of course, what is so particularly attractive to the modern reader.

In his *Map of Misreading*, Bloom observes that part of Milton's preternatural strength as a poet, his uncanny blend of poetic earliness and cultural lateness, is the creation of his admirers.[30] The same could no doubt be said about Chaucer. We find in him what we want to find. But *provision of the possibility* — the selection of words and characters and plots and patterns that produce a shock of recognition in audiences so very different from the poet's own — is an attribute of what De Quincy called the "literature of power." In this regard no poet in English has demonstrated more lasting power than Geoffrey Chaucer.

---

[30] Bloom, *A Map of Misreading*, p. 78.

Satisfaction and Payment in Middle English Literature

Jill Mann
Girton College, Cambridge

I N THE DEBATE between the Four Daughters of God in passus 18 of *Piers Plowman*, Peace, in the course of justifying the redemption of man, describes the need for opposites to define each other. Without woe, we should not know the meaning of "weal"; without night, we should not be able to understand the meaning of "day." Just so, she concludes (lines 216–17):[1]

---

[1] All quotations of *Piers Plowman* are from George Kane and E. Talbot Donaldson, eds., *Piers Plowman: The B Version* (London: Athlone, 1975). Quotations of Chaucer are from F. N. Robinson, *The Works of Geoffrey Chaucer*, 2d ed. (Boston: Houghton Mifflin, 1957). John Livingston Lowes, "Chaucer's 'Etik,'" *MLN* 25(1910):87–88, claimed that Chaucer's reference below is not to the Aristotelian *Ethics*; he drew attention to John of Salisbury's use of the term "ethicus" for writers of sententious tendency in general, and among them, for Horace, one of whose recommendations to moderation is cited by John with the preface "ut enim ait ethicus" (*Policraticus* 8.13). Interesting as this suggestion is, it is a perhaps unnecessarily complicated way of accounting for the line in the *Legend*, particularly since Lowes does not discuss the evidence for Chaucer's knowledge of the *Policraticus*, and other studies of this question have not been able to demonstrate more than a very limited indebtedness to this work; see W. W. Woollcombe, in *Essays on Chaucer* (London: N. Trübner, 1896), pp. 295–98; Eleanor Prescott Hammond, *Chaucer: A Bibliographical Manual* (New York: Macmillan, 1908), p. 93; and Thomas R. Lounsbury, *Studies in Chaucer*, 3 vols. (London: James R. Osgood, McIlvaine & C., 1892), 2:362–64. A further parallel with the *Policraticus* suggested more recently by John Fleming, in "Chaucer's Clerk and John of Salisbury," *ELN* 2(1964):5–6, is not, again, conclusive. As for the *Ethics*, on the other hand, although no complete translation into Latin was available before Grosseteste's version (produced in 1240–49), Latin versions of books 2 and 3 (known as the *Ethica vetus*), and of book 1 (known as the *Ethica nova*), were already circulating widely in the thirteenth century (see *Aristoteles latinus, pars prior*, ed. Georges Lacombe, 2d ed. [Bruges and Paris: Desclée de Brouwer, 1957], pp. 67–71). I have, therefore, thought it worthwhile to quote some passages of the *Ethics* at relevant points in the following discussion. I quote from the edition of R.-A. Gauthier, *Ethica Nichomachea, Aristoteles Latinus* (Leiden and Brussels: E. J. Brill and Desclée de Brouwer, 1972) XXVI.1-3, 2. I have also used the four manuscripts of the Latin *Ethics* preserved in the library of Gonville and Caius College, Cambridge, to whose Librarian I am grateful for permission to consult them.

> "...til *modicum* mete with vs, I may it wel auowe,
> Woot no wight, as I wene, what is ynogh to mene."

It is the meaning of "enough"—more specifically, the meaning attached to the word in Middle English poetry— that I should like to explore in this paper. "Enough" is a simple, everyday word that is easily passed over, a prosaic word for a rather prosaic concept, we probably feel, thinking of the cautious, commonsense attitude expressed in proverbial phrases like "Moderation in all things," or "Enough is enough." But in late-medieval literature—in Chaucer, in the *Pearl* poet, in Julian of Norwich—it becomes a poetic word, a word that vibrates with emotional and intellectual connotations. A close examination of two texts in particular, *Pearl* and *The Clerk's Tale*, will help show this.

The term "enough," as the words of Peace have already reminded us, makes sense only in relation to other terms, and setting out some of them will provide an appropriate framework for the analysis of these texts and a guide to what is important in their own language. In the first place, "enough" is, by definition, the midpoint between "too much" and "too little," or between "more" and "less." To locate and to adhere to this midpoint is, according to the *Nicomachean Ethics* of Aristotle, to achieve virtue; "vertu is the mene, / As Etik seith," as Chaucer puts it in *The Legend of Good Women* (lines 165–66). Obvious enough in itself, this observation is worth making because it alerts us to the less obvious need to bring other words into relation to the word "enough" by virtue of their grammatical forms, as well as by virtue of their meanings. The comparative forms of adjectives and adverbs assume importance, that is, because they represent a movement along the scale from "too little" to "too much"; they can serve as markers of an increase that may be an approach to satisfaction or an urge toward excess, and they likewise serve as markers of a decrease that may be a retreat to moderation or a lapse into deficiency. Superlatives too take on a special interest and have a particular ambivalence of their own. On the one hand, they seem to imply excess, in that they represent a movement beyond the midpoint represented by "enough." On the other hand, they share the stability of the mean, in that they represent a limit, a termination of the increase signified by the comparative "more."[2]

---

[2] Cf. *Nicomachean Ethics* 2.6: "Est igitur virtus, habitus voluntarius in medietate existens que ad nos determinata, racione; et ut sapiens determinabit. Medietas autem,

If we were to look for the Middle English nouns corresponding to these points on the scale, we would find that corresponding to the idea of "too little," for example, were the nouns "defaute" and "nede." It is need that stimulates the drive toward satisfaction, and it is the fulfilling of primary need that marks the boundary line of "mesure" or "temperaunce" — the nouns corresponding to "enough"; to carry on taking more beyond the point where need is satisfied is to turn satisfaction into excess (the function of need in determining what constitutes temperance is clearly explained in passus 20 of *Piers Plowman* by the personified figure of Need himself). To put it the other way round, need is eradicated by enough; to quote Henryson's fable of the town mouse and the country mouse, "Quha hes aneuch, of na mair hes he neid."[3] The Middle English nouns corresponding to the idea of "too much," on the other hand, are "excesse" and "superfluitee." Less obvious but more interesting is the embodiment of the concept of "too much" in the word "outrely" (meaning "utterly, absolutely, in an extreme degree"), which I shall, for convenience in discussion, represent by the word "outrance," even though the *OED* records this noun as appearing in English texts only after the fourteenth century — it would, of course, have been familiar in medieval French. As we have already noted of superlatives, the idea of doing something "à outrance" involves an ambivalence; it seems to imply "going to excess, going too far," but it can

---

duarum maliciarum, huius quidem secundum superfluitatem, huius vero indigenciam. Et adhuc, quoniam hee quidem deficiunt, hee autem superhabundant, eius quod oportet, et in passionibus et in operacionibus, virtus autem medium et invenit et vult. Ideo secundum substanciam et racionem que quid est esse significat, medietas est virtus. Secundum autem perfectum et bonum, extremitas" ("Virtue, then, is a state of character concerned with choice, lying in a mean, i.e. the mean relative to us, this being determined by a rational principle, and by that principle by which the man of practical wisdom would determine it. Now it is a mean between two vices, that which depends on excess and that which depends on defect; and again it is a mean because the vices respectively fall short of or exceed what is right in both passions and actions, while virtue both finds and chooses that which is intermediate. Hence in respect of its substance and the definition which states its essence virtue is a mean, with regard to what is best and right it is an extreme" [trans. W. D. Ross].

[3] These references are an indication of the consistency of the vocabulary sets here described through medieval literature generally, though the prominence given to the set, and to particular elements within it, vary, of course, between one literary text and another. Langland's own emphasis is on the concept of need; for some suggestions on this, see my article "Eating and Drinking in *Piers Plowman*," *E&S* 32(1979):30–32, 41–43.

also mean simply "going to the absolute limit, to the fullest extent"[4] — the point at which a potential is most fully realized, so that all fears of deficiency, and all pressures toward future increase, fall away in the stability of perfection.

Pearl

It is the dreamer's desire for "more" that governs the development of the dream in *Pearl*. At the beginning of the poem the dreamer is represented in a state of deprivation, bereft of the pearl that was his highest treasure; he is at the "too little" end of the scale. Paradoxically, however, this first section of the poem simultaneously represents the state of deprivation as a *good* thing; to be "wythouten spot," as the pearl is, is to enjoy complete perfection. That the pearl is without defect means that the potential beauty of its form is most fully realized. Absolute deprivation is in this instance a condition of absolute perfection. The contrast between these two kinds of deprivation at the beginning of the poem is an intimation of the two extremes — human need, heavenly fulfillment — that the poem will try to bring into relation; it is also an intimation that the one may be mysteriously transformed into the other.

The dreamer's vision instantly and lavishly repairs his loss, in one sense, by offering to him not a single pearl alone but an entire landscape of jewels. He is given much *more*, that is, than he is represented as having lost. And the idea of "more" is further emphasized by the fact that the bliss to which the light and beauty of his surroundings restore him (line 123) is a bliss that is continually increasing (lines 125–28):

> Doun after a strem þat dryȝly haleȝ
> I bowed in blys, bredful my braynez;
> Þe fyrre I folȝed þose floty valez,
> Þe more strenghþe of ioye myn herte straynez.[5]

---

[4] The phrase "à outrance" is glossed by Godefroy (*Dictionnaire de l'ancienne langue française*) as "excessivement, violemment," and by Tobler-Lommatzsch (*Altfranzösisches Wörterbuch*) as "zum Äussersten."

[5] All quotations from *Pearl* are taken from the edition of E. V. Gordon (Oxford: Clarendon Press, 1953). I have distinguished between z and ȝ in quotations.

The persistent increase of riches is emphasized by the doubling of "more" (lines 129–32):

> As fortune fares þer as ho fraynez,
> Wheþer solace ho sende oþer ellez sore,
> Þe wyӡ to wham her wylle ho waynez
> Hyttez to haue ay more and more.[6]

In accordance with the complicated verse scheme of the poem, since the word "more" is here used in the last line of the stanza, it then becomes the link word in the whole stanza section, and in almost every instance it is similarly intensified by being doubled (lines 144, 156, 168, 180). The link phrases emphasize, however, not only the increase of riches but also an accompanying increase of desire: "And euer me longed ay more and more" (line 144). Mounting desire is expressed in the tripling of "more" (lines 145–48):

> More and more, and ӡet wel mare,
> Me lyste to se þe broke byӡonde;
> For if hit watz fayr þer I con fare,
> Wel loueloker watz þe fyrre londe.

As the dreamer's pleasure grows, so does his expectation, and his longing for the opposite bank, which is even *more* lovely than the side on which he finds himself. It is this focus on the opposite bank, created by the desire for "more," that leads to the dreamer's perception of the child sitting at the foot of the crystal cliff. And, once perceived, the child attracts to herself the link phrase "more and more" (lines 167–72):

> On lenghe I loked to hyr þere;
> Þe lenger, I knew hyr more and more.
>
> The more I frayste hyr fayre face,
> Her fygure fyn quen I had fonte,
> Such gladande glory con to me glace
> As lyttel byfore þerto watz wonte.

---

[6] The interpretation of the phrase "hytte to haue" given by *MED* (s.v. *hitten*, 3b) — "to happen to get (sth.), obtain by chance" — is preferable to the *OED*'s interpretation of "hytte" in this line as meaning "aim, seek, strive" (s.v. *hit*, 18).

We might expect the mounting joy to reach a simple climax and complete fulfillment in the rediscovery of the lost pearl. But this is not the case. The dreamer is, in fact, torn between "glory" and "baysment" (lines 171, 174), so that the last use of "more" in this part of the poem ironically works against the dreamer's pleasure, not for it: "More þen me lyste my drede aros..." (line 181).

"More" cannot, then, be always and simply linked with pleasure. The comparative can signal an increase of discomfort as well as an increase of joy. And it can also signal the possibility of a direct link between the two emotional states. The dreamer's joy at seeing the girl again is in proportion to the comparative closeness of their relationship (lines 233–34):

> Ho watz me nerre þen aunte or nece;
> My joy forþhy watz much þe more.

But his grief is likewise in proportion to his former joy (lines 373–74):

> "My blysse, my bale, ȝe han ben boþe,
> Bot much þe bygger ȝet was my mon...."

With this recognition that increase of happiness brings with it an increase of vulnerability, the problem of "more" is left suspended, and a new phase in the poem's movement is opened.

The new phase is initiated by the idea of "too much." The dead girl informs the dreamer that she leads the life of a queen in heaven. Rather than being pleased by this news, the dreamer is rendered puzzled and uncertain, even when she assures him that the sovereign place of the Virgin Mary is in no way diminished by her own high position. Despite his love for her, the dreamer feels that she has been given too much (lines 481–92):

> "That cortaysé is to fre of dede,
> Ȝyf hyt be soth þat þou conez saye.
> Þou lyfed not two ȝer in oure þede;
> Þou cowþez neuer God nauþer plese ne pray,
> Ne neuer nawþer Pater ne Crede;
> And quen mad on þe fyrst day!
> I may not traw, so God me spede,
> Þat God wolde wryþe so wrange away.

Of countes, damysel, par ma fay,
Wer fayr in heuen to halde asstate,
Oþer ellez a lady of lasse aray;
Bot a quene! Hit is to dere a date."

The preceding stanza has made clear that the dreamer's objection is based
on his assumption that others will have deserved more and will therefore be
treated unjustly — given too little — if allotted only the same reward that
she enjoys (lines 473–80):

"Þyself in heuen ouer hyȝ þou heue,
To make þe quen þat watz so ȝonge.
What more honour moȝte he acheue
Þat hade endured in worlde stronge,
And lyued in penaunce hys lyuez longe
Wyth bodyly bale hym blysse to byye?
What more worschyp moȝt he fonge
Þen corounde be kyng by cortaysé?"

The maiden does not attempt to solve the dreamer's difficulties directly;
instead, she relates the biblical parable of the workers in the vineyard —
which may seem to be no answer at all, since the parable has produced in its
readers the same kind of baffled protest that prompts the dreamer's
questions. Even though the workers he has hired in the course of the day
have worked for different lengths of time, when the day is over, the lord
orders his reeve to set the workers in line and give each of them "inlyche a
peny" (line 546). The reaction of the workers who have toiled all day on
seeing the latecomers receive the same payment is predictable (lines
551–52):

"Þese bot on oure hem con streny;
Vus þynk vus oȝe to take more."

These lines conclude the first stanza of a new section of the poem, and
the word "more" thus again becomes the link word for an entire section. It
is the cornerstone of the workers' complaint (lines 553–56):

"More haf we serued, vus þynk so,
Þat suffred han þe dayez hete,

> Þen þyse þat wroȝt not hourez two,
> And þou dotz hem vus to counterfete."

The complaint is answered by the lord's mild reminder that they had originally contracted for a penny; their comparatives are negated by an appeal to the limiting stability of the bargain (lines 563–64):

> "Fyrre þen couenaunde is noȝt to plete.
> Wy schalte þou þenne ask more?"

When it is used at the beginning of the next stanza, "more" means "moreover," and thereafter in the section the word is used in ways that move it out of the context of the workers' demand, yet still its insistent repetition seems to reiterate their claims with increasing urgency. And at the end of the section, when the dreamer restates the original problem, the word "more" is supported by a whole battery of other comparatives. We are told that God rewards everyone according to their deserts; if, then, the maiden comes "to payment" (line 598) before someone who has labored in God's service longer than she has, the dreamer says (lines 599–600):

> "Þenne þe lasse in werke to take more able,
> And euer þe lenger þe lasse, þe more."

The maiden's reply begins a new section of the poem, and with it a new link word makes its appearance. The word "more" is discarded, and its place is taken by "enough" (lines 601–12):

> "Of more and lasse in Godez ryche,"
> Þat gentyl sayde, "lys no joparde,
> For þer is vch mon payed inlyche,
> Wheþer lyttel oþer much be hys rewarde;
> For þe gentyl Cheuentayn is no chyche,
> Queþer-so-euer he dele nesch oþer harde:
> He lauez hys gyftez as water of dyche,
> Oþer gotez of golf þat neuer charde.
> Hys fraunchyse is large þat euer dard
> To Hym þat matz in synne rescoghe;
> No blysse betz fro hem reparde,
> For þe grace of God is gret inoghe."

Four more times, with only one slight variation in form, the maiden repeats the same refrain: "For þe grace of God is gret innoghe" (lines 624, 636, 648, 660). The apparently relentless tide of reiterations of "more" is stemmed by the firm steadiness of "enough."

Yet the shift in rhythm and mood effected by this change in link word is not in itself the answer to the dreamer's question; it is merely a key to an understanding of that answer. Full understanding comes with perception of the meaning carried by the Pearl maiden's statement that all those in God's kingdom are "payed inlyche," whether they receive little or much. The crucial word in what she says is "payed." It is a word that naturally assumes importance in the parable of the vineyard, since it is all about payment. But "pay" also assumes importance at the beginning and end of the whole poem; it appears in the very first line — "Perle, plesaunte to prynces paye" — and it is the link word of the stanzas in the last section of the poem — which means that it also links the last line of the poem to the first, forming (as has often been noted) a circular structure. If we place these uses of "pay" beside the uses of the word and its associates in the parable, what is thrown into prominence is the simple fact that the word has two main branches of meaning: in the fourteenth century, as now, it meant "payment" in the monetary sense, but there still survived also its older meaning of "satisfaction." When the poet calls the pearl "plesaunte to prynces paye" (line 1), or when at the end of the poem he says "Now al be to þat Pryncez paye" (line 1176), it is this older meaning that is uppermost. The use of the word "paye" in the sense of "satisfaction" at the beginning and end of the poem inevitably colors the use of the word "payed" in the maiden's statement that everyone is "payed inlyche" in the kingdom of heaven and makes it into a kind of pun: all are equally "paid," because all are equally "satisfied" — that is, everyone has *enough*. The earthly notion of "payment" is transformed into the heavenly notion of "satisfaction," with the emphasis on the element "satis-," that is, on the idea of "enough." The idea of "more" then becomes an absurdity; once one is satisfied, there is no need for more — indeed, there is no room for its absorption. It is no accident, I think, that in the stanzas linked by "innoghe" the maiden uses the image of water pouring out in abundance to express the copiousness of God's grace, for as we think of human beings as the receptacles of this outflowing grace, we realize that when such a receptacle is full it cannot be any fuller. It takes different amounts of water to fill a large bowl and a small bowl, but once it is poured in, they are both equally full. Accordingly, we shall see that the idea of satisfaction becomes linked with the idea of fullness.

The substitution of the idea of satisfaction for the idea of payment and the activation of the double meaning of the word "payed" are not, of course, the only means by which the poet seeks to transform the normal mundane categories of measurement into terms more suitable to the "unquantifiable" bliss of heaven. The substitution of the pearl, the central image of the poem, for the penny that is paid to the workers in the vineyard is equally important.[7] The pearl and the penny are alike in the roundness that symbolizes the eternity of the heavenly kingdom,[8] and alike also in their role as valuable objects, as indices of worth. But the difference between them can be measured by the transformation of the two-dimensional flatness of the penny into the three-dimensional roundness of the pearl. Even more important is that the pearl's value is dependent on its completeness. In the Middle Ages a penny cut in two became two half pennies, so that it retained its original value; to cut a pearl in two, on the

[7] I was first stimulated to consider the relationship between these two images by a paper on *Pearl* delivered in Cambridge some years ago by Marie Borroff (but not, to my knowledge, published), which also perceptively drew attention to the contrast between the suggestion of eternity in the circularity of the penny and the suggestion of time in the line of workers set "vpon a rawe" to receive it. Some further comments of Borroff admirably express the transcendence of earthly scales of comparison within eternity: "Having the form of a circle, the pearl...stands for eternity, the existence of God in a timeless present from the perspective of which human history is a completed, static pattern. Human beings are trapped in progressive time, looking back from the present to the past and forward to an unknown future. Eternity is not perpetual duration, 'longer than' time; it is the absence of time. So too with the worth of the heavenly pearl. It is not 'greater than' the worth of anything on earth; it is absolute, literally 'beyond measure.' Nearer and farther, earlier and later, lower and higher, less and more, all are interdependent manifestations of a dimensional mode of being in which men, under the governance of a changing fortune, move toward certain death.... The inner dissatisfaction and perpetual striving inevitable in such a world have their otherworldly counterparts in the peace of heaven. To dwell there is to possess a happiness which, again, is not 'greater than' human happiness, but perfect, without qualification." Marie Borroff, *Pearl* (New York: Norton, 1977), p. xiii.

[8] The Pearl maiden later explains that the pearl is like the kingdom of heaven because it is "endelez rounde" (line 738). See also the excellent analysis in Cary Nelson, *The Incarnate Word: Literature as Visual Space* (Urbana, Chicago and London: University of Illinois Press, 1973), "*Pearl*: The Circle as Figural Space"; and on the background to this idea in medieval thought, see Georges Poulet, *The Metamorphoses of the Circle*, trans. Carey Dawson and Elliott Coleman (Baltimore, Md.: Johns Hopkins University Press, 1966), introduction.

other hand, would be to destroy its original value.[9] The image of the penny, therefore, corresponds to the earthly notion that to share something of value involves splitting it and sharing it out in quantifiable portions. Its replacement by the image of the pearl enables the reader to understand that the kingdom of heaven is not a divisible good of this sort — that heavenly bliss can be given only in its entirety or not at all.

The image of the pearl can also help us understand the place finally found within heaven for the concept of "more." For when the Pearl maiden describes the life of the blessed in the heavenly Jerusalem, we find, contrary to our expectations, that the idea of "more" is not scorned or discarded. Quite the opposite: each of the 144,000 virgins who are brides of the Lamb wishes the company to increase (lines 847–52):

> "And þaȝ vch day a store he feche,
> Among vus commez nouþer strot ne stryf;
> Bot vchon enlé we wolde were fyf —
> Þe mo þe myryer, so God me blesse.
> In compayny gret our luf con þryf
> In honour more and neuer þe lesse."

Following on from this usage, the word "lesse" becomes the link word of this section — but in negative form: "*neuer* þe lesse." The introduction of the key word "innoghe" has negated the idea of "less," but it has not completely negated the idea of "more"; on the contrary, "the more the merrier" is the principle on which the happiness of the blessed company is founded.[10] How can this be?

It will, I think, be easier to see the answer to this question if we briefly consider the answer that Dante represents as being given to him when he

---

[9] For the medieval habit of halving pennies (illegally), see the twelfth-century Latin beast poem *Ysengrimus*, ed. Ernst Voigt (Halle: Verlag der Buchhandlung des Waisenhauses, 1884; reprint, Hildesheim and New York: Georg Oms Verlag, 1974), 7.679–84, and George C. Brooke, *English Coins from the Seventh Century to the Present Day*, 3d ed. (London: Methuen, 1950), pp. 81, 103–04. Jewelers do use "half pearls," but these are stones which were not perfect in the first place and are, therefore, set with only part of their surface visible; see George Frederick Kunz and Charles Hugh Stevenson, *The Book of the Pearl* (London: Macmillan, 1908), p. 354.

[10] On this point I differ from Marie Borroff, who sees the link word "nevertheless" as an indication of the same "habit of insatiable desire" in the dreamer that is evidenced in the use of "more" as link word in sections 3 and 10; Borroff, *Pearl*, p. xiii.

asks a similar question in canto 15 of *Purgatorio*. Virgil tells him that in the highest sphere "the more there are who say *ours*, the more of good does each possess and the more of charity burns in that cloister." Dante, understandably, then asks: "How can it be, that a good distributed among a number of possessors makes them richer in it than if it were possessed by a few?"[11] Virgil's reply (in C. S. Lewis's words) restates the "distinction between goods that are, and goods that are not, objects of competition: he uses the image of light which gives of itself in proportion as the body it falls on is more highly polished, with the consequence that the greater the number of such bodies, the more light there is for all."[12]

The *Pearl* poet, unlike Dante, does not make this idea explicit, but its relevance to his description of the heavenly Jerusalem, which is even more dominated by the image of light than that in Revelation, is clear. The light of the Lamb (lines 1046–47) is reflected by "þe borȝ al bryȝt" (line 1048), including the pearls. It is thus a light that increases continually as they increase, so that their own share of it is never diminished. As the maiden explains to the dreamer, in the City of God "glory and blysse schal euer encres" (line 959). In this continual increase the first thing to fall away is earthly need (lines 1044–45):

[11] *Purg.*, 55–64; the translation quoted is that of John D. Sinclair, *The Divine Comedy . . . with Translation and Comment*, rev. ed., 3 vols. (London: The Bodley Head, 1958).

[12] C. S. Lewis, *Studies in Medieval and Renaissance Literature* (Cambridge: Cambridge University Press, 1966), p. 71. Lewis attributes the distinction to Aristotle, but I have been unable to trace it to an Aristotelian source. Such a distinction is, however, made by Augustine (*De civitate dei* 15.5): "Nullo enim modo fit minor accedente seu permanente consorte possessio bonitatis, immo possessio bonitatis, quam tanto latius, quanto concordius individua sociorum possidet caritas. Non habebit denique istam possessionem, qui eam noluerit habere communem, et tanto eam reperiet ampliorem, quanto amplius ibi potuerit amare consortem" ("goodness is not diminished when it is shared, either momentarily or permanently, with others, but expands, and, in fact, the more heartily each of the lovers of goodness enjoys the possession the more does goodness grow. What is more, goodness is not merely a possession that no one can maintain who is unwilling to share it, but it is one that increases the more its possessor loves to share it"; trans. Gerald G. Walsh, S.J., M.A., and Mother Grace Monahan, O.S.U.). The following comments of Georges Poulet (*Metamorphoses*, p. xxiv) are also of interest in this connection: "All medieval philosophy of light is a long commentary on the spherical diffusion of every luminous point. (*Omne agens multiplicat suam virtutem sphaerice* ['Every force diffuses its strength spherically'].) This phrase of Grosseteste is applicable to all activity, but first of all, to God. God is a light propagating Itself, a force that multiplies and diffuses itself." The image of light is thus naturally linked with the image of the circle. It may also be noted that Dante's response to Virgil's explanation is "Tu m'appaghe" (*Purg.*, 82), which is of interest here since the Italian word *appagare*, like the ME "paye," means "to satisfy" as well as "to content, please."

> Hem nedde nawþer sunne ne mone.

> Of sunne ne mone had þay no nede....

But this transcendence of earthly need can be expressed only by the use of comparatives; the heavenly city is "schyrrer þen sunne" (line 982), the river flowing from God's throne is "bryȝter þen boþe þe sunne and mone" (line 1056). The increasing excitement of the description culminates in the superlatives lavished on the description of the Lamb: "Best watz he, blyþest, and moste to pryse" (line 1131); the heavenly increase is terminated and fully realized in Him. Yet, again, the superlatives are not used to imply a ranking order, a hierarchy in which more and less can be measured along a scale: "Tor to knaw þe gladdest chere" (line 1109). In this context "too much" no longer indicates the dreamer's indignant sense of unmerited reward but conveys his humble sense of inadequacy in describing the joys of the heavenly kingdom (lines 1117–18):

> Delyt þat hys come encroched
> To much hit were of for to melle.

The superlatives indicate not the last point on a linear scale but a perfect fullness corresponding to the perfection of the circle (lines 1097–98):

> Þis noble cite of ryche enpryse
> Watz sodanly ful wythouten sommoun....

The crowd of virgins, "Hundreth þowsandez" strong, makes up the superabundant fullness of the heavenly city, a fullness that is itself a source of joy.[13]

The image of "innoghe" in this poem, then, involves no renunciation, no settling for second-best, but rather an endlessly sufficient abundance. As the dreamer says of the pearl on the young girl's breast (lines 223–24):

---

[13] Thus in the first three (interconnected) definitions of God in the pseudohermetic *Book of the Twenty-Four Philosophers* discussed by Poulet (*Metamorphoses*, p. xi), the first conceives God in terms of light, the second conceives him in terms of a sphere, and the third conceives him in terms of fullness ("*Deus est totus in quolibet sui*" ["God is entirely complete in every part of himself"]). Cf. Col. 2.9–10: "quia in ipso [sc. Christo] inhabitat omnis plenitudo divinitatis corporaliter, et estis in illo repleti" ("for in him dwelleth all the fullness of the Godhead bodily, and ye are complete in him").

> A mannez dom moȝt dryȝly demme,
> Er mynde moȝt malte in hit mesure.

In this abundance of bliss human capacity will founder before it even approaches the midterm of "enough"; even "mesure" is beyond a man's wildest imaginings. "Vrþely herte" cannot "suffyse" for the extent of heavenly happiness (lines 135–36). The dreamer's human insufficiency means that the "melting" of his mind at the sight of heavenly bliss (lines 1153–54) leads him to overstep the boundaries of "mesure," imposed by his still-human existence. Impatient for his own satisfaction, and careless of that of his "Prince," he wants to see more than is allowed him and tries to cross the stream that separates him from the heavenly company. The result is the loss of his dream—as if in illustration of the principle earlier enunciated by the maiden that "ofte mony mon forgos þe mo" through the inability to suffer "lurez lesse" (lines 339–40). In confirmation of this we are told at the end of the poem that had the dreamer not grasped after more he would have received it; "more" is not a right to be claimed but an unsolicited, gratuitous experience of increase (lines 1189–94):

> To þat Pryncez paye hade I ay bente,
> And ȝerned no more þen watz me gyuen,
> And halden me þer in trwe entent,
> As þe perle me prayed þat watz so þryuen,
> As helde, drawen to Goddez present,
> To mo of his mysterys I hade ben dryuen.

In the heavenly kingdom renunciation is paradoxically rewarded with satisfaction. In its fullness the desire for "more" falls away, not because one prudently settles for "less" but because that endless desire is endlessly satisfied, and it is the completeness of that satisfaction that constitutes "enough."

This identification of "enough" with both moderation and superlative completeness is, however, no idiosyncratic vision of the *Pearl* poet; it is founded in the everyday English usages of the word, as I shall try to show in the following section on *The Clerk's Tale*. We shall then see that the refrain "þe grace of God is gret innoghe" draws on the double significance of "innoghe" just as the parable in which it is set draws on the double significance of "paye."

The Clerk's Tale

The vocabulary associated with "enough" appears from an early date in Chaucer's works. We can see it, for example, in his translation of Boethius. Philosophy explains to Boethius that riches do not provide "suffisance"; although rich men have "inoghe" to make them safe against hunger, thirst, and cold, the "nede" that they experience in common with all other men "mai nat al outrely be doon awey; for though this nede that is alwey gapynge and gredy, be fulfild with richesses, and axe any thyng, yit duelleth thanne a nede that myghte be fulfild. I holde me stille and telle nat how that litel thyng suffiseth to nature; but certes to avarice inowgh suffiseth nothyng" (*BO* 3, pr. 3).

It is just such a "gapynge and gredy" desire for more and still more that we can recognise in Walter in *The Clerk's Tale*, which I shall make the focus for study of the idea of "enough" in Chaucer's work. For although the complex of ideas surrounding the notion of "enough" recurs throughout the Canterbury collection, it is in *The Clerk's Tale* that it is given fullest and profoundest expression. The word "enough" appears in this tale more often than in any other; even more important than its frequency is its key placement in the structure of the narrative. It is, in the first place, used to seal the marriage compact between Walter and Griselda; Griselda's acceptance of the condition that she must be obedient to Walter's every desire and command is greeted by the immediate reply, "This is ynogh, Grisilde myn" (*CIT* 365). But, of course, the whole point of the story is that it is *not* enough — that Walter insists on testing Griselda to see whether he can make her give still more.[14] He is, in other words, insatiable. Chaucer's comments[15] on the beginning of Walter's obsession emphasize this inability to rest content with "enough" — the desire for "more" that is inexcusable because it is unprompted by need (lines 449–62):

[14] The desire for more initiates not only the testing of Griselda but also Walter's marriage (and thus the whole story); in this instance, it is his tenants' desire for the "o thyng" that could give them "moore felicitee" that leads them to request his marriage (lines 109–10).

[15] I call these comments "Chaucer's" rather than "the Clerk's" partly to avoid cumbersomeness but also because I think that the function of the pilgrim-narrator is not present to our imagination at this point — and precisely because it has no essential role to play in our response. Continuity of style throughout the *Tales* is enough to show that Chaucer fuses himself with each of his narrators in turn.

Ther fil, as it bifalleth tymes mo,
Whan that this child had souked but a throwe,
This markys in his herte longeth so
To tempte his wyf, hir sadnesse for to knowe,
That he ne myghte out of his herte throwe
This merveillous desir his wyf t'assaye;
Nedelees, God woot, he thoghte hire for t'affraye.

He hadde assayed hire ynogh bifore,
And foond hire evere good; what neded it
Hire for to tempte, and alwey moore and moore,
Though som men preise it for a subtil wit?
But as for me, I seye that yvele it sit
To assaye a wyf whan that it is no nede,
And putten hire in angwyssh and in drede.

Chaucer likewise emphasizes the needlessness of the next stage of Griselda's trial—the loss of her second child—and adds a comment on Walter's contempt for "mesure" (lines 621–23):

O nedelees was she tempted in assay!
But wedded men ne knowe no mesure,
Whan that they fynde a pacient creature.

And after the loss of this child Chaucer yet again intrudes into the narrative with similar comments on it (lines 696–700):

But now of wommen wolde I axen fayn
If thise assayes myghte nat suffise?
What koude a sturdy housbonde moore devyse
To preeve hir wyfhod and hire stedfastnesse
And he continuynge evere in sturdinesse?

And yet at the close of the story Walter's obsessive urge to test Griselda *does* miraculously come to an end—and what is striking is that he brings her trials to a close with exactly the same words that he had used to initiate them (lines 1051–57):

"This is ynogh, Grisilde myn," quod he;
"Be now namoore agast ne yvele apayed.
I have thy feith and thy benyngnytee,
As wel as evere womman was, assayed,
In gret estaat, and povreliche arrayed.
Now knowe I, dere wyf, thy stedfastnesse," —
And hire in armes took and gan hire kesse.

The question is, How is it that Walter's insatiability is finally satisfied? How is it that enough finally *is* enough for him — that his obsessive desire for more does not lead him on to devise yet further torments and humiliations?

In repeating the word "ynogh" at the beginning and end of the tale in such a way as to raise this question, Chaucer is following the lead given in Petrarch's Latin prose version of the Griselda story, which he identifies in *The Clerk's Prologue* as his main source for the tale. That Chaucer probably also knew *Le livre Griseldis*, one of the French prose translations of Petrarch, is of less concern to us,[16] since it was the artistic shaping of Petrarch's version to which Chaucer responded, as becomes evident from the sensitive re-creation of it in his own tale.[17] In Petrarch, as in Chaucer, Walter proclaims that he has "enough," both when Griselda makes her promise to him before marriage and when he finally brings her trials to an end. The word in the Latin text is *satis*; "Satis est," he says, in the first instance, and, in the second, "Satis. . . mea Griseldis, cognita et spectata michi fides est tua" (we can see at once that in making these speeches identical, rather than merely similar, Chaucer sharpens our sense of the

---

[16] See the detailed study of J. Burke Severs, *The Literary Relationships of Chaucer's Clerke's Tale* (New Haven, Conn.: Yale University Press, 1942), and also the shorter presentation of his conclusions in W. F. Bryan and Germaine Dempster, eds., *Sources and Analogues of Chaucer's Canterbury Tales* (New York: Humanities Press, 1941), pp. 288–331. The text of Petrarch's version is given in both works; a modern English translation is printed in Robert P. Miller, ed., *Chaucer: Sources and Backgrounds* (New York: Oxford University Press, 1977), pp. 136–52.

[17] The French translator does reproduce many elements in the complex vocabulary pattern that Petrarch builds around the word "satis," but in a haphazard fashion that suggests that he was not consciously aware of its significance. The vocabulary pattern is completely absent from Petrarch's own model, the tenth tale of the tenth day of Boccaccio's *Decameron*, ed. Vittore Branca (Florence. Le Monnier, 1965).

question they pose).[18] Petrarch repeats the word *satis* elsewhere in his narrative in ways that make it carry a deliberate weight of significance. It is, for example, used ironically by Walter in a bland pretense of satisfaction, even as he is pursuing his desire for more; he prefaces the announcement that he is going to have Griselda's daughter taken away by saying "Michi quidem cara satis ac dilecta es" ("To me you are dear and beloved enough"). He likewise introduces the news that he plans to divorce her by saying "Satis . . . tuo coniugio delectabar" ("I was happy enough to marry you").[19] Again these uses underline the fact that enough is precisely not enough for Walter.

But to translate *satis* merely as "enough" in these latter instances is of course to be guilty of inaccuracy or translationese; in such expressions the Latin *satis* does not qualify but intensifies. *Satis cara* means not "moderately dear" but "very dear" — even "wholly, completely dear."[20] The Italian *assai* and the medieval French *assez* share the same characteristics; both can mean "rather, moderately" — indicating a kind of halfway house — but can also mean "fully, completely, abundantly" — indicating the end of the line, the fullest realization of some possibility.[21] And the same is true of the Middle English "ynogh"; in adverbial use it means not only "sufficiently, moderately" but also "extremely . . . fully, completely, entirely" — "as much as well could be," as the *OED* puts it.[22] Thus the refrain in *Pearl* — "þe grace of God is gret innoghe" — means not only that God's grace is "sufficiently" great, reaching to the limit of the demand made on it, but also that it is "abundantly" great, limitless, acknowledging no boundaries but those of the radiating sphere of perfection.

Following Petrarch's practice with *satis*, Chaucer exploits this possible use of the word "ynogh" many times in his tale. We are told at the opening

---

[18] 1.62, 6.44–45. Quotations are taken from the edition of the tale in Burke Severs, *Literary Relationships*.

[19] 3.8, 5.3.

[20] This meaning is not acknowledged in the *Latin Dictionary* of Lewis and Short, but see Du Cange, *Glossarium mediae et infimae latinitatis*, and Niermeyer, *Mediae latinitatis lexicon minus*, s.v. *satis*.

[21] For medieval French, see Tobler-Lommatzsch, *Altfranzösisches Wörterbuch*, s.v. *assez* (*viel, reichlich*, as well as *genug*); for Italian, see the *Cambridge Italian Dictionary*, s.v. *assai* ("very, . . . very much; a great deal; . . . plenty," as well as "quite").

[22] Sense 2a. For the other glosses, see *MED*, s.v. "inough," adv., senses (b) and (e) for the meaning "moderately," and senses (a) and (d) for the meaning "fully."

that Walter is "Discreet ynogh his contree for to gye" (line 75). Griselda is described as "fair ynogh to sighte" (line 209), and Walter, in his married life, enjoys "outward grace ynogh" (line 424). And, as in Petrarch, it is with a blandly cruel pretense of satisfaction that he introduces his plans for divorce (lines 792–93):

> "Certes, Grisilde, I hadde ynogh plesaunce
> To han yow to my wyf for youre goodnesse."

The semantic ambivalence in the word alerts us to an ambivalence in the concept of "ynogh." In one sense it represents a point of balance between extremes. But in another sense "ynogh" is itself a superlative; it indicates "outrance" — fullness, abundance, satisfaction to the utmost limits. Walter's desire to test Griselda "to the outtreste preeve of hir corage" (line 787) is matched by her willingness to pursue obedience to its limits; "ynogh," for Griselda, is not "a moderate amount" but everything that it takes to satisfy him.

Following through the use of the word *satis* and its associates shows us that Walter's obsessive insatiability has, however, one oddly positive corollary — that is, he does *not* become "sated" with Griselda in the manner characteristic of men of rank who amuse themselves by taking up with lowborn girls. This is pointed up by the use of the word *sacietas* ("satiety") in the Latin text at the point where Walter sends Griselda back to her home; her father gloomily reflects that he had always expected such a consequence to the marriage ("semper hoc eventurum cogitaverat"), "that a man so exalted, and proud after the fashion of nobles, would at some time send her back home, satiety with so lowborn a wife having arisen" ("sacietate sponse tam humilis exorta").[23] But the father's reading of the situation is, of course, mistaken: paradoxically, Walter's very insatiability preserves him from this more usual kind of satiation. We learn to make a crucial distinction here, in recognizing that, while we want Walter to have "had enough," it is not in this cruder, more vulgar sense. We want him to be satisfied, not sated.

---

[23] 5.45–46. Chaucer's use of conventional phrases of the "bothe lasse and moore" type for the meaning "everybody" (lines 67, 940) reminds us that the scale from "more" to "less" is realized in social as well as emotional terms. The union of Walter and Griselda reconciles and mediates between the social polarities designated by the superlatives "gentilleste" (line 72) and "povrest" (line 205), achieving the point of balance that represents "enough."

The chain of significant words through which Petrarch explores the concepts of insatiability and satisfaction extends further. Prominent in it are the noun *cupiditas* (indicating a greedy, selfish desire), and its associates, the adjective *cupidus* and the verb *cupio*. *Cupiditas* is the term Petrarch applies to Walter's desire to test over and over again his wife's already proven loyalty: "Cepit, ut fit, interim Valterium. . . mirabilis . . . quedam cupiditas, sat expertam care fidem coniugis experiendi altius et iterum atque iterum retentandi" ("An amazing desire to prove further, and to test over and over again the loyalty of his wife, which had already been proved enough, seized hold of Walter").[24] Surprisingly, however, the words that denote Walter's insatiability are also used of Griselda. When Walter orders her to make ready his house for the reception of his new bride, she answers that she will, now and always, obey him "non libenter modo. . . sed cupide" ("not only willingly. . . but greedily").[25] Similarly, when the new wife and her brother arrive, we are told that Griselda "could never be sated with praising them" ("ipsa imprimis puelle pariter atque infantis laudibus saciari nullo modo posset").[26] But Griselda's "insatiability" is unlike Walter's in that it is founded on satisfaction. Walter asks her whether she finds his new wife "beautiful and noble enough" ("satis pulcra atque honesta"), to which she replies emphatically "Plane" ("Certainly"). Her rejection of any suggestion of possible increase is signaled by the negation of comparatives: "nor can any more beautiful and noble be found" ("nec pulcrior. . . nec honestior inveniri potest"). With her, if with anyone, she goes on, Walter will be happy, "and I desire [*cupio*] and hope that it may be so."[27] It is Griselda's "satisfaction," her full and wholehearted acceptance of the woman who is, she believes, to take her place, that carries its own kind of "insatiability"; her desire to do Walter's will can never reach a termination, never be sated. And so it is Walter, not Griselda, who finally reaches the limit of endurance; "ferre diucius non valens" ("able to bear no longer"), he is brought to his final acknowledgment that he has enough. As is signaled by the negation of another comparative (*diucius*), his insatiability is terminated. Or, rather, it is transformed; for, with a final deliberate use of the adjective *cupidus*,

[24] 3.1–4.
[25] 6.11–12.
[26] 6.30–31.
[27] 6.35–39.

Petrarch tells us that Walter embraced Griselda *cupidis ulnis* ("with greedy arms").[28] The *cupiditas* that drove him to send Griselda away is henceforth transformed into an insatiable desire for union.

Chaucer was fully alive to these subtleties in Petrarch. He used his own network of vocabulary to re-create them and even, I think, to go beyond Petrarch in subtlety. We have seen already that the central position in this network of words is occupied by the word "ynogh." The adverb "outrely" also belongs to it; it is used several times in connection with Walter, emphasizing his "extremism," his urge to go to the limits (lines 639, 768, 953).[29] The words "ful," "fulliche," and "fulfild" fit into the pattern too; for example, at the point when Walter sends Griselda back home, Chaucer uses the word "fulfild" to do the work of Petrarch's *sacietas*, saying that Griselda's father believed she would be sent back home "whan the lord fulfild hadde his corage" (line 907). The deliberate debasement of the richer, more satisfying possibilities in the word "fulfild" here is paralleled in the use of the adverb "fulliche" in the lines telling us that Walter "fulliche hath purposed / To tempte his wyf as he was first disposed" (lines 706–07) or of his desire "his wyf to tempte moore / . . . Fully to han experience and loore / If that she were as stidefast as bifoore" (lines 786–89). Petrarch's structuring of the final scene of the tale is likewise imitated by Chaucer; when Walter asks whether his new wife pleases her, Griselda negates a comparative — "A fairer saugh I never noon than she" — to indicate the fullness of her appreciation and wishes that God may send to her and to Walter "plesance *ynogh* unto youre lyves ende" (lines 1033, 1036, italics added). The only place for "more" in Griselda's mind here is the consideration that the new bride has been brought up "moore tendrely" than she has and therefore could not bear the same harsh treatment (lines 1040–42); when Griselda asks for more, it is not for herself but for her supplanter.

This scene also includes, however, another, crucially important word that needs to be linked into the pattern, and that is the adjective "sad," the word that Chaucer constantly associates with Griselda. Derek Brewer has drawn attention to the importance of the word in this tale and to its

---

[28] 6.44, 49.

[29] *OED* glosses the word (sense 1) as meaning "In an utter or extreme degree; entirely, absolutely; in an unqualified manner."

dissociations from any of the modern connotations linking it to the visible expression of emotion; here, on the contrary, it implies the suppression of emotion, meaning "steadfast, firm, constant."[30] When Petrarch talks about Griselda's steadfastness, he uses words like *constancia, robur, paciencia, equanimitas.* Chaucer too uses words like "constance" and "pacience," but he much prefers "sad" and "sadnesse." Walter's urge to tempt Griselda "moore and moore" arises from the desire "hir sadnesse for to knowe" (lines 451–59). And it is her "sadnesse" that finally conquers him (lines 1044–50):

> And whan this Walter saugh hire pacience,
> Hire glade chiere, and no malice at al,
> And he so ofte had doon to hire offence,
> And she ay sad and constant as a wal,
> Continuynge evere hire innocence overal,
> This sturdy markys gan his herte dresse
> To rewen upon hire wyfly stedfastnesse.

Chaucer's use of the word "sad" offers a minor puzzle. For the word goes back etymologically, as the *OED* testifies, to a root that means "sated, satisfied"; it is, in fact, a distant cousin of the Latin *satis* and likewise of "satur," "satiated." Are we to imagine that Chaucer had — among his other bookish dreams — a prophetic vision of the *OED* entry for "sad"? Or should we see it as no more than a bizarre coincidence that he builds his poem on the word "sad" as Petrarch builds his prose version on the word *satis*? Neither of these desperate hypotheses is, in fact, necessary. For the earliest meaning of "sad" in English was, of course, "satisfied, sated, full," and it had not completely lost that meaning in late Middle English.[31] Chaucer himself uses the word in this sense on one occasion, saying in *The Canon's Yeoman's Tale* of the practitioners of alchemy that "of that art they kan nat wexen sadde" (line 877). Chaucer could also have found reinforcement for the idea of a connection between steadfastness and satisfaction, had he needed it, in the word "suffisaunce" — a word common to medieval French and Middle English — and this too is a word that assumes importance in the vocabulary patterns of *The Clerk's Tale*. In Chaucer's usage the word

---

[30] "Some Metonymic Relationships in Chaucer's Poetry," *Poetica* 1(1974):1–20.
[31] See *OED*, s.v., sense 1 (current from OE up to mid-fifteenth century).

"suffisaunce" has a wide range of applications. There is, first, the concrete sense of "enough to eat and drink," exemplified in the "hoomly suffisaunce" of the friar of *The Summoner's Tale* (line 1843). The word can also denote the quality that monitors the amount necessary for bodily sufficiency — "moderation" or "temperance"; the Parson, who himself "koude in litel thyng have suffisaunce" (*GP* 490), tells us that "suffisance . . . seketh no riche metes ne drynkes, ne dooth no fors of to outrageous apparailynge of mete" (*PT* 833). But the word also stands, as has been well demonstrated by J. D. Burnley, for the grander, more comprehensive ideal of Stoic self-sufficiency.[32] As Chaucer's *Balade of Fortune* tells us (lines 25–26):

> No man is wrecched, but himself it wene,
> And he that hath himself hath suffisaunce.

Griselda's "sadnesse" is clearly a version of this kind of "suffisaunce"; at the lexical level it acts as an English equivalent of the French term. Last, we may note that "suffisaunce" is also a word that Chaucer uses in describing relationships between men and women as an indicator of what we would probably term in modern English "fulfillment." In the consummation scene of *Troilus and Criseyde*, Criseyde says to Troilus, "Welcome, my knyght, my pees, my suffisaunce!" (*TC* 3.1309). Burnley finds this use by

[32] J. D. Burnley, *Chaucer's Language and the Philosophers' Tradition* (Cambridge: D. S. Brewer; Totowa, N.J.: Rowman & Littlefield, 1979), pp. 72–73, 78–79. Burnley emphasizes that the Stoic notion naturally took on a Christian coloring in medieval writings. The definition of "felicitas" as "sufficientia" in the *Nicomachean Ethics* (1.5) is also relevant here: "Videtur autem et ex autarchia [gloss: .i. per se sufficiencia] idem contingere; perfectum enim bonum per se sufficiens esse videtur. Per se sufficiens enim dicimus non se solo vivente vitam solitarem, set et parentibus et filiis et uxori et universis amicis et civibus, quoniam natura civilis homo. . . . Set per se sufficiens ponimus quod solum effectum eligibilem facit ⟨vitam⟩, et nullo indigentem. Tale autem felicitatem existimamus esse. . . . Perfectum utique quid et per se sufficiens videtur felicitas, operatorum existens finis" ("From the point of view of self-sufficiency the same result seems to follow; for the final good is thought to be self-sufficient. Now by self-sufficient we do not mean that which is sufficient for a man by himself, for one who lives a solitary life, but also for parents, children, wife, and in general for his friends and fellow citizens, since man is born for citizenship. . . . The self-sufficient we now define as that which when isolated makes life desirable and lacking in nothing; and such we think happiness to be. . . . Happiness, then, is something final and self-sufficient, and is the end of action" [trans. W. D. Ross]. Following the alternative manuscript readings given by Gauthier, and also those of the Caius College manuscripts, I read *uxori* for *uxore*, and alter the punctuation of the last sentence.) The insistence that "sufficiency" means sufficiency for friends and family as well as oneself is of special interest in connection with Griselda.

Criseyde a perverted one; the "philosophical significance" of the word is lost, since it no longer denotes self-sufficiency but means "a kind of dependence."[33] My own feeling is that Burnley is too harsh here, and not quite alive to the complexity of the love experience that Chaucer delicately suggests — that is, that in love there *is* a kind of self-sufficiency, a steadiness of self, a sense of the fulfillment of one's own identity for the first time, achieved through the mirroring of that identity in the other person's love. At any rate, it is significant that Burnley does not disapprove when Chaucer uses the word in a similar way to describe Griselda's love for Walter (lines 754–59):

> But she, ylike sad for everemo,
> Disposed was, this humble creature,
> The adversitee of Fortune al t'endure.
>
> Abidynge evere his lust and his plesance,
> To whom that she was yeven herte and al,
> As to hire verray worldly suffisance.[34]

These lines link "suffisaunce" with "sadnesse," and more, they show us Griselda's apparently unemotional "sadnesse" as linked with her emotional "suffisaunce," the fulfillment that she finds in her love. "Sadnesse" arises from emotional "suffisaunce," and it also concludes in it; Griselda's steadfastness, arising from her love, leads to the satisfaction of that love in Walter's final change of heart. To return to the question of how it is that Walter finally "has enough," I think that Chaucer saw the answer in the concept of "sadnesse"; denoting "steadfastness," in this tale "sadnesse" takes on connotations of "satisfaction." The lines I quoted earlier on Walter's final surrender to pity for Griselda's "stedfastnesse," with his full realization that she is "ay sad and constant as a wal," are followed immediately by his second and last "This is ynogh, Grisilde myn."[35] It is Griselda's "sadnesse" that is finally "ynogh" for Walter. This may seem paradoxical —

---

[33] Burnley, *Chaucer's Language*, pp. 95–96.

[34] Ibid., p. 88. We may note at this point that the word "sad" is also associated with Walter's love for Griselda; he contemplates the humble peasant girl "noght with wanton lookyng of folye" but in "sad wyse" (lines 235–38).

[35] It may be noted at this point that *MED*, s.v. "inough," n., sense (f), classifies this phrase with the use of "inough" to mean "no more of this matter, that will do." In my view this is

even impossible — since "sadnesse," strictly interpreted, would have passive, rather than active, force — would signify "being satisfied," rather than "power to satisfy." But what Chaucer's delicate linking of words and concepts perhaps suggests is that "sadnesse" in this story comes to participate in the strange kind of "transferability" characterizing "suffisaunce" in love relationships; matching the paradoxical ability of a lover to derive "self-sufficiency" from the "satisfaction-fulfillment" offered by a mutual love, is the paradoxical ability, demonstrated in this tale, for one partner's stoical self-sufficiency to issue in the other's emotional satisfaction and hence in mutual fulfillment.

At any rate, by perceiving that Chaucer grasped the connections between "sad" and "ynogh," we can see that it is entirely appropriate that it is the "unsad" people of the city who welcome Walter's new wife in a greedy desire for "more" — marked by a battery of comparatives (lines 988–91; italics added):

> For she is *fairer*, as they deemen alle,
> Than is Grisilde, and *moore* tendre of age,
> And *fairer* fruyt bitwene hem sholde falle,
> And *moore* plesant, for hire heigh lynage.

The true function of "more" is to be found not in such greedy yearnings, or in Walter's desire continually to "tempte moore" (line 786) but in its quasimagical growth out of the acceptance of "ynogh." This growth can be seen in the description of Griselda's at first apparently static constancy (lines 708–14; italics added):

> He waiteth if by word or contenance
> That she to hym was changed of corage;
> But nevere koude he fynde variance.
> She was ay oon in herte and in visage;
> And ay the forther that she was in age,
> The *moore* trewe, if that it were possible,
> She was to hym in love and *moore* penyble.

---

incorrect. First, the citations given in the *MED* show that in this sense the more usual expression is the simple word "enough." Second, the narrative context of *The Clerk's Tale* gives Walter's words full lexical weight in both instances.

41

It is this spontaneous generation of increase that finally finds its counterpart and its reward in the increased splendor of the feast that celebrates the reunion of Walter and his wife (lines 1125–27; italics added):

> . . . *moore* solempne in every mannes syght
> This feeste was, and *gretter* of costage
> Than was the revel of hire mariage.

Chaucer's last use of the idea of "sadnesse" shows a subtlety that marks one of the points at which he goes beyond even Petrarch. Readers over the centuries have found it tempting to take Griselda's "sadnesse," the calmness with which she relinquishes her children, as due to the absence, rather than the control, of emotion. But Chaucer shows the mistakenness of this interpretation by the way he uses the word "sad" in the reconciliation scene. When she is reunited with her children, Griselda's feelings at last find expression (lines 1093–1103):

> "O tendre, o deere, o yonge children myne!
> Youre woful mooder wende stedfastly
> That crueel houndes or som foul vermyne
> Hadde eten yow; but God, of his mercy,
> And youre benyngne fader tendrely
> Hath doon yow kept,"—and in that same stounde
> Al sodeynly she swapte adoun to grounde.
>
> And in hire swough so sadly holdeth she
> Hire children two, whan she gan hem t'embrace
> That with greet sleighte and greet difficultee
> The children from hire arm they gonne arace.

We may note, first, the poignancy given to the idea of "stedfastnesse" by the application of the adverb "stedfastly" to Griselda's belief that her children are dead; the deep conviction of loss has a numbing steadfastness of its own. But even more striking is the use of the adverb "sadly." In the swoon that marks the overwhelming deliverance from her steadfast belief in the death of her children, Griselda holds them "sadly"—firmly, tightly, closely, so closely that they can barely be torn from her grasp. Griselda's love for her children has the same steadiness and depth as her acceptance of their loss. Chaucer, I think, took the hint from Petrarch's paradoxical idea of Walter embracing his wife *cupidis ulnis* and transformed it into something that is even more profound and subtle, precisely because it brings us closest to the mysterious ability of "suffisaunce" to encompass both steadfast self-sufficiency and the ecstatic fulfillment of reciprocated love.

No account of *The Clerk's Tale* could be complete if it did not at some point follow its final move on to the plane of divine-human relationships, and I want to end, therefore, with some comments on what happens in this context to the complex of words and ideas that I have been discussing. Chaucer repeats Petrarch's comment that the tale is told not as an inducement to wifely obedience but to encourage human "suffraunce" of whatever God sends us—and Chaucer offers us this encouragement, we may note, in terms of a movement from positive to comparative (lines 1149–51; italics added):

> For, sith a womman was so pacient
> Unto a mortal man, wel *moore* us oghte
> Receyven al in gre that God us sent.

Readers have often wanted, naturally but mistakenly, to make these comments a basis for equating God's role with Walter's. The emphasis is, however, all on Griselda; it is the nature of the suffering, not the nature of the testing, that forms the basis of the transition into allegorical meaning. And for that reason, and others besides, I have argued elsewhere that it is in fact Griselda, not Walter, who gives us the truer image of the God who suffers not only the cruelty that men inflict on him but also the cruelty that they inflict on each other.[36] And it is precisely in the "insatiability" of her willingness to suffer that Griselda offers an image of this aspect of the divine.

---

[36] See my "Parents and Children in the *Canterbury Tales*," to be published as part of the first series of J. A. W. Bennett Memorial Lectures, ed. Piero Boitani and Anna Torti (Tübingen: Gunter-Narr Verlag). As this article demonstrates a close relationship between *The Clerk's Tale* and the Ugolino episode in *The Monk's Tale*, the pathos of parental resignation in the first being matched by the pathos of filial resignation in the second, it is worth noting here that the word "ynough" is also of importance in the brief Ugolino story. Ugolino's children beg him to save himself from starvation by eating them: "Oure flessh thou

I would like to bring this out more clearly by quoting Julian of Norwich. In Julian's work we are first shown the insatiability of the human longing to be satisfied by the divine — a satisfaction that will meet every need:

This saw I bodely, swemly and darkely, and I desyred mor bodely light to haue seen more clerly. And I was answeryde in my reason: If god will shew thee more, he shal be thy light; thou nedyth none but him. For I saw him and sought him, for we be now so blynde and so vnwyse that we can never seke god till what tyme þat he of his goodnes shewyth hym to vs. And whan we see owght of hym graciously, then are we steryd by the same grace to seke with great desyer to see hym more blessedfully. And thus I saw him and sought him, and I had hym and wantyd hym; and this is and should be our comyn workyng in this life, as to my syght.[37]

Just as in *The Clerk's Tale*, this insatiability is met by the endless offer of more, until the acknowledgment of satisfaction is made — as we can see in the words Julian later attributes to the suffering Christ:

Then seide oure good lorde askyng: Arte thou well apayd that I sufferyd for thee? I seyde: ȝe, good lorde, gramercy; ye, good lorde, blessyd moet þow be. Then seyde Jhesu our good lord: If thou arte apayde, I am apayde. It is a joy, an endlesse lyking to me that evyr I sufferd passion for the; and if I myght suffer more, I wolde suffer more.

. . . And in these wordes: If I myght suffer more I wolde suffer more, I saw truly þat as often as he myght dye, as often he wolde, and loue shulde nevyr lett hym

---

yaf us, take oure flessh us fro, / And ete ynogh" (lines 2451–52). The poignancy comes partly from the double meaning of "ynogh" — the clash between the surface suggestion of moderation, belied by the measurelessness of the filial sacrifice. Chaucer's use of the word here may have been prompted by Dante's use of the word *assai* at the corresponding point in *Inferno* 33.61, though Dante uses it in a different way.

[37] Edmund Colledge and James Walsh, eds., *A Book of Showings to the Anchoress Julian of Norwich* (Toronto: Pontifical Institute of Medieval Studies, 1978), Long text, chap. 10, pp. 11–20. On the "insatiable" appetite for God, cf. Augustine, *Confessions* 10.6.8: ". . . ubi fulget animae meae, quod non capit locus, et ubi sonat, quod non rapit tempus, et ubi olet, quod non sparget flatus, et ubi sapit, quod non minuit edacitas, et ubi haeret, quod non diuellit satietas. Hoc est quod amo, cum deum meum amo" (". . . wherein for my soul a light shines, and place does not encompass it, where there is a sound which time does not sweep away, where there is a fragrance which the breeze does not disperse, where there is a flavor which eating does not diminish, and where there is a clinging which satiety does not disentwine. This is what I love, when I love my God" [trans. Vernon J. Bourke]).

haue rest tille he hath done it. And I behelde with grete dyligence for to wet how often he wolde dye yf he myght. And truly the nomber passyd my understandyng and my wittes so ferre that my reson myght nott nor cold not comprehende it ne take it.[38]

Like Griselda, Christ not only is willing to suffer more and more, to unimaginable limits, but is also willing to suffer "nedelees":

He seyde nott: yf it were nedfulle to suffer more, but if I myght suffer more; for though it were nott nedfulle, and he myght suffer more he wolde. This dede and thys werke abowt oure saluation was ordeyned as wele as god myght ordeyne it; and heer in I sawe a fulle blysse in Crist, for his blysse shuld nott haue ben fulle yf it myght ony better haue ben done than it was done.[39]

It is the willingness to suffer "outrely" that creates satisfaction, the "fulnesse" of bliss, in the divine vision of Julian as in the human tale of Griselda. And the emotions aroused by the tale of Griselda, the fullness of satisfaction that is created in us by Walter's final "This is ynogh, Grisilde myn," can help us understand why Julian can imagine God as having no more eloquent appeal than the words "Lett me aloone, my derwurdy chylde, intende to me. I am inogh to þe, and enjoy in thy sauiour and in thy saluation."[40] In her sufficiency, as in the miraculous power of her suffering, Griselda is God-like.

Coda

In the complex panorama of *The Canterbury Tales*, all serious concepts undergo comic transformations, and the concept of "ynogh" is no exception. A brief glance at *The Shipman's Tale*, which provides the richest example of such a transformation, will indicate the range of possible variations on this theme.

Like *Pearl*, *The Shipman's Tale* links the idea of "ynogh" with the idea of "payment"—but it does so, needless to say, in a quite unspiritual context. The opening of the tale puts the emphasis on payment (lines 10–18):

---

[38] Ibid., chap. 22, pp. 1–7, 25–31.
[39] Ibid., pp. 51–58.
[40] Ibid., chap. 36, pp. 47–48.

> But wo is hym that payen moot for al!
> The sely housbonde, algate he moot paye,
> He moot us clothe, and he moot us arraye,
> Al for his owene worshipe richely,
> In which array we daunce jolily.
> And if that he noght may, par aventure,
> Or ellis list no swich dispence endure,
> But thynketh it is wasted and ylost,
> Thanne moot another payen for oure cost...

The other elements in the now familiar lexical set duly make their appearance in this new context. Prominent among them is "nede," which is the term used of the merchant's business dealings (lines 75–76, 302–303):

> The thridde day, this marchant up ariseth,
> And on his nedes sadly hym avyseth,
>
> . . . .
>
> Now gooth this marchant faste and bisily
> Aboute his nede, and byeth and creaunceth.

"Incres" and "fulnesse" are similarly conceived in financial terms (lines 81, 84). And "sadnesse," as line 75 shows, has here a connotation quite different from that which it bears in *The Clerk's Tale*. It stands here not for the self-sufficiency of the stoic but for the sobriety of the businessman.[41] The merchant's "sadnesse" has, however, this in common with Griselda's: it entails the suppression of private emotion, to create a serene façade for the outer world. But what was, in *The Clerk's Tale*, a supremely heroic endeavor to meet misfortune with serenity becomes in *The Shipman's Tale* an attempt to make the keeping up of appearances into a bulwark against mishap. When the merchant's wife protests impatiently at the length of time he spends on his "rekenynges," because he already has "ynough...of Goddes sonde" (lines 216–19), he reprovingly insists on the "curious bisynesse" of "us chapmen," on the fear of "hap and fortune" that must be concealed beneath "chiere and good visage," so that the financial realities may be kept "in pryvetee" (lines 224–37). His response makes the concept

---

[41] On "sadnesse" as a characteristic quality of merchants, see Gardiner Stillwell, "Chaucer's 'Sad' Merchant," *RES* 20(1944):1–18.

of "ynogh" elusive of definition in this world. It is not (as the wife assumes) what it takes to satisfy present needs, whether physical or emotional; rather, it stands for the resources that will enable one to meet the vicissitudes of "this queynte world" with resilience (and is thus something like a commercial version of Stoic "suffisaunce"). And because they have a crucial role to play in maintaining one's credit, appearances constitute just such resources. Hence the merchant's parting charge to his wife (lines 245–48):

> ". . . for to kepe oure good be curious,
> And honestly governe wel oure house.
> Thou hast ynough, in every maner wise,
> That to a thrifty houshold may suffise.
> Thee lakketh noon array ne no vitaille;
> Of silver in thy purs shaltow nat faille."

The role played here by "ynough" is played by "payment" in the opening passage already quoted; the husband's "owene worship" is established by the "aray" for which he pays, because it testifies to the solidity of his credit.

It is perhaps fortunate for the merchant that his wife and her lover are every bit as committed to the world of appearances, and as skilled in manipulating it, as he is. If the merchant's success depends on the concealment of his "pryvetee" behind a façade of "sadnesse," so does his wife's. Thus, for the wife and the monk, the ideas of "ynogh" and of "nede" are mainly important for the role they can play in the superficial emotional drama behind which the real hardheaded agreement between them can be reached (lines 100, 109); the pressure of real need or "defaute" never makes itself felt (lines 180–90):

> "A Sonday next I moste nedes paye
> An hundred frankes, or ellis I am lorn.
> .   .   .   .
> Pardee, I wol nat faille yow my thankes,
> If that yow list to doon that I yow praye.
> For at a certeyn day I wol yow paye . . ."

Yet, as in the serious world of *Pearl*, so here too in the fabliau universe the apparently barren canceling-out of obligation represented by "payment" is transformed into the notion of a miraculous increase represented

47

by "ynough." The Wife of Bath, in a comic version of the Pearl maiden's lesson to the dreamer (including its light imagery), spells out the power of sex to provide a never-failing satisfaction (lines 329–36):

> "Have thou ynogh, what thar thee recche or care
> How myrily that other folkes fare?
> For, certeyn, olde dotard, by youre leve,
> Ye shul have queynte right ynogh at eve.
> He is to greet a nygard that wolde werne
> A man to light a candle at his lanterne;
> He shal have never the lasse light, pardee.
> Have thou ynogh, thee thar nat pleyne thee."

The geniality of *The Shipman's Tale*, its adroit evasion of a cynical or harshly moralizing conclusion, depends not only on the smooth maintenance of the façade that keeps the adulterous affair, like the merchant's business, "in pryvetee," but also on the inexhaustible "credit" constituted by sex, its power to provide "ynough" to fill the needs created by misfortune. Just as the merchant's "chevyssaunce" magically causes barren metal to multiply itself, so that "nede," paradoxically, comes to stand for the inevitability of profit (line 371), so sexuality constitutes a source of wealth that magically replenishes itself and cancels the "dette" between husband and wife. The wife at first again protests that her husband has "ynough" (line 380), but this apparent limitation on sexual satisfaction soon gives way, as she recognizes the newly created debt, to the offer to "paye abedde" (line 424), producing the endless supply that constitutes enough. Sex has the same careless abundance, the same inexhaustible outpouring, as God's grace. With a final triumphant appeal to the double meaning of "ynogh," the Shipman cheerfully wishes for himself and his audience access to these never-failing resources (lines 433–34):

> Thus endeth now my tale, and God us sende
> Taillynge ynough unto oure lyves ende. Amen.[42]

---

[42] An earlier version of this paper was delivered as the Tucker-Cruse Lecture at Bristol University in spring, 1982, and I gratefully acknowledge comments received then. The section devoted to *The Clerk's Tale* was delivered as the Annual Chaucer Lecture to the conference of the New Chaucer Society held in San Francisco in April, 1982. I am glad to have this opportunity of expressing my gratitude to Paul Ruggiers and the society's Board of Trustees for inviting me to deliver this lecture and would also like to thank the participants in the conference for their comments and suggestions.

The Scribe of the Hengwrt and Ellesmere Manuscripts of *The Canterbury Tales*

M. L. Samuels
University of Glasgow

THE SINGULAR number of the word "scribe" in the title is intentional. Recently R. Vance Ramsey[1] has questioned the view of A. I. Doyle and M. B. Parkes[2] that on palaeographical grounds these two manuscripts are the work of a single scribe and insists that they are by separate scribes. He admits that the hands are "identical" and states that they are so because his two scribes received identical training. He quotes no parallels for such a phenomenon, and it is doubtful whether he could do so for any but Chancery-trained scribes. Suffice it here to say that he is not arguing with the palaeographers; he has conceded them their case and has chosen to argue his own purely from spelling practices. So be it. He has chosen his position, but it is a difficult one, for it places the onus on him to prove that these texts could not have been written by one man, while taking full account of, first, what is known about the spelling practices of scribes in the later Middle English period and, second, what is known and to be expected by way of variation or standardization in the London language of a particular period, 1390 to 1420.

Ramsey inherits from Manly and Rickert the notion that the early manuscripts of *The Canterbury Tales* are "standardized"[3] and assumes

---

[1] R. Vance Ramsey, "The Hengwrt and Ellesmere Manuscripts of the *Canterbury Tales*: Different Scribes," *SB* 35(1982):133–54.

[2] A. I. Doyle and M. B. Parkes, "The Production of Copies of the *Canterbury Tales* and the *Confessio Amantis* in the Early Fifteenth Century," in M. B. Parkes and A. G. Watson, eds., *Medieval Scribes, Manuscripts and Libraries: Essays presented to N. R. Ker* (London: Scolar Press, 1978).

[3] Ramsey, "The Hengwrt and Ellesmere Manuscripts," p. 134, with reference there made to John M. Manly and Edith Rickert, eds., *The Text of the Canterbury Tales* (Chicago: University of Chicago Press, 1940), 1.558.

from that that the rest of their language, apart from the points of difference that form his case, can be taken for granted. But this procedure is unjustifiable, for much more is now known about the language of London in this period than was available to Manly and Rickert. As I have shown elsewhere, there was no standardization in London to the degree that he postulates until the emergence, ca. 1430, of what I have termed Chancery Standard, or type IV.[4] Before that time there are three other types that may be considered, but of these only type I (Central Midland Standard) comes anywhere near the kind of homogeneity postulated by Ramsey, and obviously our scribe does not partake of it, whereas types II and III are terms of convenience that embrace a series of heterogeneous London texts in the period 1340 to 1420, including our scribe as one of the evidently separate and individual contributors to type III.[5] During this whole period, apart from type I, the spelling of each scribe is idiosyncratic, and can be distinguished as such from every other by application of a special questionnaire of at least one hundred common variables in spelling that was devised for the Middle English Dialect Survey at the Universities of Edinburgh and Glasgow.[6] The result, for the whole survey, is some 3,500 linguistic "profiles" of separate scribes.[7] When the questionnaire was applied to the Hengwrt and Ellesmere manuscripts, they were found to agree for all variables except a few in which there was a difference of emphasis in the proportion of variants found in each manuscript, e.g., *agayn/ayeyn*, *aske/axe*, *heighe/hye*, *hundred/hondred*, *murye/myrie*, *neigh/ny*, *noght/nought/nat*, *seigh/saw/saugh*, *thogh/though*, *thowsand/thousand*, *weere(n)/were(n)*. Since none of these forms was exclusive to one manuscript, the profiles for both manuscripts were regarded as those of a single scribe who had slightly changed his habits and/or had come under the influence of varying exemplars.

Now when Ramsey states that the usages of individual Middle English scribes could not alter in this way, he is simply ignoring a great deal of

[4] M. L. Samuels, "Some Applications of Middle English Dialectology," *ES* 44(1963):81–94.

[5] Ibid., pp. 87–88; and cf. M. L. Samuels, "Chaucer's Spelling" (forthcoming).

[6] For accounts of the survey see A. McIntosh, "A New Approach to Middle English Dialectology," *ES* 44(1963):1–11; and M. Benskin, "Local Archives and Middle English Dialects," *Journal of the Society of Archivists* 5(1977):500–14.

[7] This total does not include a large number of other Middle English manuscripts that were inspected for peculiarities of language.

evidence to the contrary. There is, first, the detailed study by M. Benskin and Margaret Laing,[8] showing that it was normal for scribes to possess repertoires of spellings, variants from which became activated under different circumstances of copying. Then, especially for the fifteenth century, Norman Davis has shown how Edmond Paston gradually changed his original Norfolk spellings in the direction of standard English, even to the extent of proceeding by intermediate stages, e.g., first from *xal* to *schal* and finally to *shall*.[9] Furthermore, writers who changed their habits in this way were not rarities: there is a large body of similar evidence for other writers in the fifteenth century.[10]

Especially relevant to the period when Hg and El were produced is Doyle's recent study of University College, Oxford, MS 97.[11] He shows the shifts of scribal habit that took place in the three separate sections written by the single scribe of folios 85–185 and, after careful consideration of all the possible factors involved, concludes that the changes are "intelligible as adaptation to the fashions of a metropolitan milieu about 1400" and that "a contrary hypothesis is not easily tenable."

The principle of changes in scribal habits is thus a well-established one, and Ramsey's denial of it cannot be justified. Such changes could, however, be brought about by two different kinds of pressure, and since in what follows both will be found to apply, they must first be distinguished.

II

A frequent cause of variations in spelling in the work of a single scribe is the influence of his exemplar. For Ramsey this matter is cut and dried: either the scribe takes over the form of the exemplar exactly, or he uses his own, single and monolithically fixed, form. But the matter is by no means as

---

[8] M. Benskin and Margaret Laing, "Translations and *Mischsprachen* in Middle English Manuscripts," in M. Benskin and M. L. Samuels, eds., *So Meny People, Longages and Tonges: Philological Essays in Scots and Medieval English Presented to Angus McIntosh* (Edinburgh: Editors, 1981), 55–106.

[9] Norman Davis, "A Scribal Problem in the Paston Letters," *English and Germanic Studies* 4(1951–52):31–64; Norman Davis, "A Paston Hand," *RES* 3(1952):209–21.

[10] M. L. Samuels, "Spelling and Dialect in the Late and Post-Middle English Periods," in Benskin and Samuels, eds., *So Meny People*, pp. 43–54.

[11] A. I. Doyle, "University College, Oxford, MS. 97 and Its Relationship to the Simeon Manuscript (British Library Add. 22283)," ibid., pp. 265–82.

simple as that. For some items a scribe's usage *always* admitted of variants. For example, a Norwich scribe might normally use *swych*, *sweche*, and *swylk* in free or conditioned variation (his "active" repertoire), but be quite prepared to use other forms he was familiar with like *such* or *sich* (his "passive" repertoire).[12] It can be proved from manuscripts in which the same scribe copied several works from different exemplars that he would select the variant that was nearer that of his exemplar (though not necessarily the identical form), and the same applies to different manuscripts in the hand of a single scribe. As an example I choose here two manuscripts not used by Benskin and Laing in their article: British Library Additional 34779 of *Piers Plowman* (C version) and Manchester Rylands English 90 of *The Prick of Conscience*, both so outstanding in their common idiosyncrasy of script, duct, and spelling as to leave no doubt that they are in the same hand. In the Rylands manuscript there are several extra variants conditioned by the Northern exemplar; e.g., the scribe writes here *mekel* as well as his normal *meche*, *ilk* as well as his normal *uche*/*vche*; but otherwise the spelling is reasonably consistent throughout both manuscripts. There are, however, two notable exceptions:

1. For "are" the scribe uses three forms, *ben*, *arn*, and *ar*, throughout both works but with opposite proportions in each: in *Piers Plowman*, *ben* is predominant; in *The Prick of Conscience*, *ar(n)*. In other words, the forms are the scribe's own, but the proportions of them are influenced by those of the exemplars, though these were not necessarily the same forms.

2. For "through" he writes exclusively *þruȝ* in *Piers Plowman*, but *þurgh* and *þurȝ* (and variants) in *The Prick of Conscience*, with only a very rare *þruȝ*. There is thus no indication of the scribe's own preference; all we know is that he had both forms in his repertoire and could use either, consistently and for long stretches of text, according to circumstances.

The conclusion to be drawn from this, and from many other similar examples,[13] is that, under the influence of an exemplar, certain of a scribe's own forms can vary in their proportions or even undergo a virtually 100 percent shift, while the remainder of his usage remains constant throughout.

[12] Benskin and Laing, "Translations and Mischsprachen," p. 59.
[13] Ibid., pp. 99–101.

The second kind of pressure toward change in spelling belongs especially to the later Middle English period (i.e., the late fourteenth century onwards) and amounts simply to this: if changes in practice are taking place, or if there is oscillation from competing practices, scribes observe this in their exemplars and shift some of their own practices accordingly. As pointed out above, in London ca. 1400 there was as yet no specific standard for scribes to aim at, but there were pressures on them to alter their habits nevertheless. The spelling practices current in London had only recently undergone a complete metamorphosis in the change from type II to type III;[14] in addition, the period from 1400 to 1420 was crucial for the development of Standard English, for it was from the competing and changing fashions in spelling at this time that the new written standard was to evolve. Some typical changes in train at this time are the replacement of þ and ȝ by *th*, *y* and *gh*, of *e* and *o* by *ee* and *oo* when denoting long vowels, of *þeigh* by *þough* and *though*, and of *say/seigh*, "saw," by *saw* and *saugh*. As I have attempted to show elsewhere,[15] these changes were due largely to immigration from the Central Midlands, and it was midlanders who were setting the pace in the changing spelling of the capital. Besides these, there were two other tiers of scribes who would start from different thresholds of spellings and therefore achieve different repertoires, depending on how far they adapted to change: the native Londoners, and immigrants from parts other than the Central Midlands, notably the North, the Northwest Midlands, and the Southwest Midlands. The immigrant scribes might react in two ways: they might continue to use their regional spellings in London, thus contributing to the confusion by wholly exotic forms, or they might attempt to adapt their own regional spelling systems to what they conceived to be more acceptable in London, thus contributing more subtly to the confusion. That there were northerners of the former type at work in London ca. 1400 is shown by some curious relict northern strata in certain manuscripts in which such contaminations are the last thing that would be expected (e.g., British Library Harley 7334 of *The Canterbury Tales*, the Lansdowne manuscript of the same, and British Library Additional 27944 of Trevisa's *De proprietatibus rerum*); while the continuing use of þ and ȝ is especially noticeable in the work of scribes who had migrated from the

---

[14] Samuels, "Some Applications of Middle English Dialectology," p. 88.
[15] Ibid., pp. 89–91.

Southwest Midlands (the Petworth manuscript of *The Canterbury Tales* and the upper stratum of the Lansdowne manuscript are examples of this).

There is, therefore, much evidence from manuscripts copied in London in the early decades of the fifteenth century of a variety of conflicting spellings, local and regional.[16] That there still existed scribes who wrote consistently and conservatively is not, of course, to be denied, but it cannot be too strongly emphasized that the preconditions for changes in scribal habits existed in full force. In particular, the lack of a common currency of spellings at which immigrant scribes might aim leads to some extraordinary shifts and vacillations. An outstanding example is the scribe who wrote British Library Harley 7334 and Corpus Christi, Oxford, 198 of *The Canterbury Tales*, as well as nine other manuscripts (including seven of Gower's *Confessio Amantis*).[17] Basically this scribe was attempting to adapt his regional Southwest Midland orthography to London use; however, when copying Chaucer, Trevisa and *Piers Plowman*, he would for some stretches use Gowerian forms that he had learned and added to his repertoire from copying Gower, whereas for other stints within the same manuscripts he returned, quite unpredictably, to his earlier repertoires of Southwest Midland and London forms.[18]

III

As has been shown above, there are scribes who show great versatility in learning new forms in midcareer. Even if it is conceded that these are the exception rather than the rule, enough has also been said to show that a mere shift in the proportion of variants used within a scribal repertoire is not only commonplace but, especially at this period, to be expected in all

[16] Further evidence is available from the earlier MSS of Chaucer's *Troilus*, for which cf. Samuels, "Chaucer's Spelling."

[17] Doyle and Parkes, "The Production of Copies," pp. 164, 174ff. He is also the fourth scribe in Trinity College, Cambridge, MS R.3.2, and is therefore referred to by Doyle and Parkes as "Scribe D."

[18] For a fuller account of this scribe see J. J. Smith, "*Studies in the Language of Some Manuscripts of Gower's Confessio Amantis*" (Ph.D. diss., University of Glasgow [forthcoming]). A preliminary sketch is to be found in Smith's "The Language of the Gower Manuscripts," part of a volume on various aspects of the manuscripts of Gower under the general editorship of Derek A. Pearsall (also forthcoming).

but the most doggedly conservative of scribes.[19] And what else is our Hengwrt-Ellesmere scribe but a straightforward example of such a shift? Of all the variables quoted by Ramsey, none is exclusive to one text; there is merely a shift in emphasis, not a change of repertoire. The scribe has not had to *learn* a new form. Ramsey quotes two so-called exceptions, but one is of a form that the scribe gives up (Hg *down*/*doun*, El *doun* only), and that leaves only *elles* as his one new form that partly replaces *ellis*; but both these cases are merely parts of the larger shifts of *ow* to *ou* and *-is* to *-es*; they are extensions of existing habits to further contexts, not genuine innovations (a fact that Ramsey concedes when he combines all the different sequences with *ow*/*ou* into a single list). If these manuscripts were by separate scribes, we should expect at least a few substantive differences of spelling exclusive to each manuscript; but there are none.

Next: Is the size of the shifts as great as Ramsey makes out? He presents a superficially impressive table of so-called dominant contrasts between the two manuscripts, ranging from 60 to 99 percent. Now, although I showed above that there are proved cases of 100 percent shift in scribal habit, that was for the purposes of the argument only. In fact, Ramsey's method of counting and presentation has inflated the figures for each shift, in some cases to the extent of doubling or even trebling them. As he points out, his count is restricted to those cases where the two manuscripts differ and wholly omits the many cases where they agree.[20]

Let us take his column 7 ($þ^t$/*that*) as an example. For this he shows a "dominant contrast" of 81.95 percent, from which the average reader might justifiably assume that $þ^t$ is the predominant form in Hg, *that* in El. Such an assumption would be entirely mistaken, however, as can be shown quite simply by counting *all* the cases of $þ^t$/*that* in a representative stretch of the texts. For this purpose I chose *The General Prologue* and the *Knight's*, *Miller's*, *Reeve's* and *Cook's Tales*, which must be admitted as a fair sample because, according to Ramsey's method of calculation, it would yield a "dominant contrast" of 88 percent, not the 82 percent of his overall

[19] Further evidence of such shifts can be found in other cases where one scribe wrote two MSS that survive, e.g., (1) Cambridge University Library Gg.4.27 and Bodleian E Museo 116 and (2) Bodley 423, fols. 244–351, and St. John's College, Cambridge 29 (B.7).

[20] As even his own first set of figures shows (pp. 135–36), he is omitting residues of 46 percent for *town*/*toun* and *at the*/*atte*, 37 percent for *thogh*/*though*, and 21 percent for *thow*/*thou*.

figure. In this stretch the total number of instances for comparison is 688, which shows that Ramsey, in restricting himself to 199 of them, has ignored 71 percent of the usage. The distribution of the 688 instances is as follows:

	Hg	El
$\flat^t$	334 (49%)	181 (26%)
that	354 (51%)	507 (74%)

The resulting shift is thus in reality no more than 23 percent, not 88 percent. Then, even if one were to discount all cases of line-initial *That* (and it is by no means certain that that would be methodologically preferable), the shift is still only 32 percent, not 88 percent. Admittedly, $\flat^t$/*that* may be a rather extreme case of the discrepancy between Ramsey's figures and reality, but anyone considering his arguments would do well to bear in mind what his table of figures really represents: not a series of radical contrasts that must prove separate scribes but merely a series of shifts that is perfectly compatible with the work of a single scribe.

So much, then, for Ramsey's "balance of probability." He ignores a whole dimension of the subject: a large body of evidence for changes in scribal habits and, in particular, the special reasons for such changes in the period 1390 to 1420; and he compounds this omission by presenting figures that misleadingly exaggerate the differences in question. Of the total orthography of this scribe, only a minor part is affected, and then only by shifts of existing variants, not change of form; the rest remains the same idiosyncratic set of forms. Obviously, if one compares the same work in two copies word for word, the differences will be highlighted; but that is to lose sight of the way they agree when compared with the great bulk of other surviving Middle English texts. Add to this the identity of handwriting, and the balance of probability is clearly against Ramsey's view. There remains, however, a second whole dimension that he has ignored. When that is examined, it will be seen that this case is, in reality, very different, and no longer a mere matter of balancing probabilities.

IV

There is a peculiar mystery about Ramsey's article: Why, when he professes to challenge the view of Doyle and Parkes (and has presumably read their article), does he ignore the third text that they show to be also in the same hand, namely, hand B of Trinity College, Cambridge, R.3.2? I cannot credit that he has deliberately shut his eyes to it, and I can therefore only surmise that he has tacitly dismissed it as irrelevant, perhaps because he sees further spelling differences in it that would lead him to claim that it is by yet a third scribe, writing, again, in an identical hand (he could hardly deny the identity since he has already conceded it for the other two manuscripts). If this is so, he is evidently unaware that, when due account is taken of the constraints of the Gower exemplar, the linguistic profile for this text is identical with the profiles for Hg and El referred to in section I above. It so happens that we are now in a strong position to judge this, for the Fairfax and Stafford manuscripts of Gower's *Confessio Amantis* have been authenticated to an extent never hitherto thought possible for any medieval text other than autograph: they have been proved to be in language and spelling that is an entirely idiosyncratic mixture of two quite separate dialects, which in turn can be isolated and pinpointed exactly as those of two places in Kent and Suffolk that were associated with the Gower family.[21] That our scribe's Gower exemplar was in the same language can be proved from relicts in his version,[22] but it is his own treatment of the Gower text that stands out; for, whereas most of the early manuscripts of Gower attempt to reproduce the idiosyncrasies of their exemplars, this scribe has imposed on the Gower text the normal spelling familiar to us from Hg and El, and his concessions to Gowerian spelling are wholly transparent and therefore easily discounted. Thus, in addition to his normally consistent *they*, he also writes *thei* (or even *þei*) under the influence of Gower's *þei*; he consistently writes *ayein* (Gower *aȝein*), though that is his rarer variant elsewhere; and he is faithful throughout to Gower's *tofore*, which he must have regarded as quite distinct from Chaucer's *bifore/biforn*.

---

[21] M. L. Samuels and J. J. Smith, "The Language of Gower," *NM* 82(1981):295–304.
[22] Samuels, "Chaucer's Spelling."

Since it can be shown that our scribe is influenced by his Gower exemplar, the next question that arises is: Could the differences between Hg and El stem from differences in his exemplars for those manuscripts? That explanation is not the main one proposed here, but it must be pointed out that Ramsey has too easily dismissed it as a possibility. His main objection, that the features in question should show an uneven distribution when the stemma affiliations change, will not bear examination, for one could postulate any number of intermediate exemplars, all of which preserved the same stemma confusions, but which — at least in the copy antecedent to El — had had all their inconsistencies in spelling homogenized by the translation process so frequent in Middle English. That explanation cannot, therefore, be ruled out, at least as a secondary source of variation; but obviously the more important hypothesis, and the one to which all our indications point, is that Hg and El represent stages of a progression in the career of our single scribe, the differences being due to changes in habit brought about by the second type of pressure defined in section II above. Here the evidence of the Trinity Gower is crucial, for, if the hypothesis is correct, this manuscript should fall into place as part of the progression. To test this, it is necessary to do what Ramsey has declined or omitted to do: to apply his differential criteria to hand B of the Trinity manuscript.

The result is everything that we might hope for from this accession of extra evidence: *the Trinity manuscript stands somewhat more than midway in a progression from Hg to El*. At the time when the Trinity manuscript was written, six of the shifts in emphasis had already taken place, three were in progress, and three had yet to come, as follows:

1. The shifts in proportion from & to *and*, *y* to *i*, *ay* to *ey*, single to double vowel, *-er-* to abbreviated *-er-*, and *-ow-* to *-ou-* had taken place.

2. The shifts from *h* to crossed *h*, *þᵗ* to *that*, and *d* to tailed *d* were in progress.

3. The shifts from *-on* to *-oun*, *-ogh* to *-ough*, and *with* to *wᵗ* had not yet taken place.

There remain two points (the addition of final *-e* or *-n*) on which a statistical comparison with the Trinity manuscript is not practicable because of the differing metrical practices of Chaucer and Gower; but in any event, as will be shown in section VI below, these two features do not form part of the progression proper and are more probably due to a different cause. Of the points listed above, two call for further comment:

1. The distribution of -*ow*- and -*ou*- is the same as in El, with *doun* and *toun* as the regular forms but *thow* still occurring as a minority variant to *thou*.

2. The distribution of *þᵗ* and *that* is of especial interest. It changes twice, so that the text of Trinity must be considered in three sections (section 1, 3.793 to 3.1916; section 2, 3.1917 to 3.2708; section 3, 3.2709 to 4.2142). In section 1 the proportions are similar to those of Hg, with perhaps a suggestion that the shift has begun (41/59 percent compared with 49/51 percent in Hg). In section 2 the scribe succumbs to the influence of his exemplar and, reverting to what was certainly an earlier habit of his of using *þ* in words other than *þᵗ*, takes over the Gowerian *þat* in addition to increasing his proportion of *þᵗ*; but in section 3, the proportion of *that* greatly increases, almost reaching the level seen in El. The intrusion of *þat* in section 2 (26 percent) complicates the issue, but it drops to 14 percent in section 3, and, since all cases of it are due to the exemplar and do not form part of the scribe's normal usage, it is reasonable to draw up a table of percentages of the majority *þᵗ*/*that* usage only (the percentage figures for Hg and El are included for comparison):

	Hg	Trinity Section 1	Trinity Section 2 (influenced by exemplar)	Trinity Section 3	El
þᵗ	49	41	48	29	26
that	51	59	52	71	74

These percentages are obviously significant, but their exact interpretation requires care, depending as it does on the following three factors: (1) that the choice of *þᵗ* would save space and/or labor, (2) that the distributions could be inherited from, or influenced by, those present in the exemplar, and (3) that *þ* was obsolescent in London by this period and being replaced by *th*.

At first sight the fact that *that* is favored in El, the more lavish production, might seem to favor (1), but that is counterbalanced by exactly the opposite shift from *with* in Hg to abbreviated *wt* in El. Although, therefore, the scribe may well have shifted his preference from *with* to *wt* in order to save labor (irrespective of the scale of production), there remains the obvious fact that neither *with* nor *wt* involves *þ*, and we are therefore left with a very strong pointer towards (3) as the cause of the progression from *þt* to *that* as seen in Hg, Trinity and El overall.

There is, in addition, a further argument that tells against (1)—that the choice of *þt* or *that* is primarily grammatical, not codicological. Throughout, in Hg, Trinity, and El, the scribe distinguishes in midline between the "heavier" form *that*, which he regularly uses for the demonstrative, and the "lighter" form *þt* in "pleonastic" uses such as *when þt*, *whil þt*, *if þt*. It is only for the middle category of independent relative that he shows variation, and, in effect, practically the whole of his shift is due to his "upgrading" of a proportion of the relative category from *þt* to *that*. Hence, if (1) were the primary factor, it would surely affect all three categories, and since it does not, it can hardly be more than secondary.

We are left, then, with a choice between (2) and (3) as the primary reason for the choice in the Trinity manuscript. Here even if (2) were to apply, it would still be significant that the scribe started with a proportion near to that of Hg but finished with a proportion nearer to that of El; at the very least it would prove that he was capable of the change, whatever the influence. Nevertheless, there are some indications against (2): first, if the different distributions in sections 1, 2, and 3 stem from the exemplar, they ought to be confirmed by other linguistic differences between these three sections, but they are not; second, this scribe's normal habit of distinguishing between different grammatical categories of *þt*/*that* should, if (2) applies, be disrupted, but it is not.

There are thus strong grounds for believing that what we see in the Trinity manuscript is the actual shift in the scribe's preference from *þt* to *that* and that it takes place as a result of the conflicting pressures of the exemplar and of factor (3): in section 2, the influence of the exemplar induces a high proportion of *þ*,[23] but in section 3 it is in reaction to that,

---

[23] From the Gowerian relics in this hand, and from the greater prevalence of them in hands C, D, and E, it is reasonable to assume that the exemplar was of the normal Fairfax-

and under the renewed influence of (3), that the scribe swings to the later distribution found in El. This is an attractive hypothesis and, if accepted, shows that the shift took place suddenly as a result of conflicting pressures. If, however, factor (2) is preferred as the explanation, the argument is not affected.

V

Whichever of the above explanations is favored, the Trinity manuscript constitutes an important link in the progression from Hg to El: not only does it show the identical choice of both constants and variables, but it shows how far the shifts had proceeded, and possibly even the working of the scribe's mind (whether conscious or subconscious) when one of the shifts took place. Since the shifts seem to have taken place in consecutive batches rather than simultaneously and more gradually, it would even be possible to use the progression as a time scale: we might hazard dates of ca. 1402–1404 for Hg, 1407–1409 for Trinity, and 1410–12 for El. However, at this point in the inquiry one looks rather for some other sample of this scribe's work — even if it is only a single leaf — in the hope that it might tell us more about the order of those six earlier shifts. And that is precisely what we have, in the shape of the Cecil fragment of *Troilus*, a single defective leaf in this same scribe's hand.[24] On its own, with no progression established, such a fragment would be regarded as statistically negligible and discounted, but as corroboration of an already established progression, it is invaluable. It clearly precedes Trinity, since it shows five cases of *thow* but none of *thou* and six cases of midline *þᵗ* to only one of *that*; but equally clearly it is after Hg, since *i* outnumbers *y*,[25] and *and* is unabbreviated. Then, when placed in order between Hg and Trinity, it suggests a refinement in the ordering of the shift from -*ow*- to -*ou*: whereas in both Trinity and El the shift from *thow* to *thou* is shown to have lagged behind those of *doun* and *toun*, here it has not yet even begun, in contrast to the single

---

Stafford kind; i.e., it had midline *þat* throughout (hand A is more modern in both language and script; cf. Doyle and Parkes, "The Production of Copies," p. 168).

[24] Ibid., p. 170.

[25] For this estimate only those words that show variation in Hg and El are considered (typical examples are *lif/lyf* and the ending *io/yo*).

instance of *toun*, which has thus preceded it. Representation of the remaining features is naturally scanty in such a fragment, but there are probably enough cases of doubled vowels to suggest that that shift has begun; the single cases of full and abbreviated *-er-* at least do not contradict the view that that shift was then in progress; and similarly its other forms do not tell against the view that the remaining changes were later: *noght* and *thoght*, crossed *h* and tailed *d* in a minority of possible instances, and *-on* three times compared with *-oun* in a single rhyme.

It is surely significant that this fragment, so far as its evidence goes, not only fits automatically at a new point (say, 1405–1406) in the progression already established but can even suggest a refinement of our knowledge of that progression. It provides the ideal corroboration that would be expected from new evidence and suggests strongly that if yet a fifth text or fragment by this scribe were discovered it too could be expected to fall readily into place and provide still further refinements of the progression. Its significance is thus out of all proportion to its size, and it is for that reason that it is included in the following table summarizing the sequence of the shifts (in this table A denotes a distribution before the shift has taken place, AB that the shift is in progress, and B that the shift has already taken place).

	Hg	Cecil Fragment	Trinity	El
y/i	A	B	B	B
ay/ey	A	B	B	B
&/and	A	B	B	B
town/toun	A	B	B	B
-er-/-er-	A	A B	B	B
Doubled vowels	A	AB	B	B
thow/thou	A	A	B	B
h/crossed h	A	A	AB	B
þᵗ/that	A	A	A B	B
d/tailed d	A	A	AB	B
-on/-oun	A	A	A	B
ogh/ough	A	A	A	B
with/wᵗ	A	A	A	B

It must be stressed that the arguments here presented do not depend on the inclusion of the Cécil fragment, which is an extra bonus that we may accept or reject as we please. Since it does not carry the same statistical weight as the other three, its column above may be regarded as more hypothetical, but not necessarily in proportion to its small coverage, in view of the startling degree of corroboration and refinement that it provides.

VI

The evidence for a progression during a period of this scribe's life is thus dramatic, and, in the face of it, Ramsey's other objections lack cogency.[26] There remain his other two criteria, which relate to the greater use of final -e and -n in El. Here, as often elsewhere, Ramsey's figures for "contrast" between Hg and El give a misleading impression, since they ignore the fact that in most cases these endings agree in both manuscripts. Then, if we are to concentrate only on the differences, it can nevertheless be shown that this scribe has the same tendency throughout: to add final -e and -n when they contravene the meter and are not present in his exemplars. This latter can be proved from the Trinity Gower, which at 4.375 reads "Abouen alle othere men as tho": the meter clearly requires *abou*[e] with final -e elided, and the Fairfax manuscript has *Aboue*.

The scribe's habitual practice can be shown by his treatment of the words for "own" (adjective) and "these." It can be established statistically that his normal forms for these words throughout are *owene* and *thise*, in spite of the fact that the meter always requires *owen* and *this*.[27] It follows that when he does write *owen* and *this* in Hg he is simply taking over the metrically intended forms from his exemplar; in Trinity and El he uses his own forms in final -e, and there is even an instance of *owene* in the *Troilus* fragment.

[26] For example, he makes much of the unique textual alterations in El but cannot prove that our scribe is to blame for them. As Doyle and Parkes point out (ibid., p. 186), the accuracy of copying in Hg and Trinity tells heavily against such an assumption.

[27] Ramsey refers to the work of J. G. Southworth as if there were still uncertainty in the matter of Chaucerian metrics, but there is not. See M. L. Samuels, "Chaucerian Final -e," *N&Q* 217(1972):445–48; D. Burnley, "Inflexion in Chaucer's Adjectives," *NM* 83(1982): 169–77; and a forthcoming article by G. V. Smithers.

In the cases of final -*e* and -*n*, therefore, it cannot be said that there is any shift in scribal practice. The difference between Hg and El here is that in Hg the scribe is likely to preserve more of Chaucer's metrically intended forms but in El to spell words according to his own habitual practice. This difference, however, is not restricted to the endings -*e* and -*n*. There are other features, of no metrical significance, for which Hg often shows relict forms from its exemplar when El has the scribe's own normal form. A typical example is the past tense of the verb *see*: there are good reasons for believing that Chaucer's own forms were *say* and *saw*,[28] and these are commoner in Hg; but the scribe's own normal form is *saugh* (with *seigh* as his earlier variant), and these, though also common in Hg, are usual in Trinity and El.

As was emphasized above, none of these cases, in aggregate, constitutes any great difference between Hg and El; overall, the scribe's practice remains the same. However, there was a considerable period—perhaps almost a decade—between the copying of the two manuscripts, and each was produced for a very different purpose, Hg being a cheaper and more makeshift volume, El a larger, more carefully planned and expensively produced one. It is not at all surprising, therefore, that the scribe should have set about each task differently, in Hg occasionally mixing the exemplar's forms with his own, in El taking more care to present his own orthography consistently. To this, however, there was the paradoxical result that, being no metrist, he more often added his own unmetrical final -*e* and -*n* in the more expensive El than he had earlier done when copying Hg.

And so we return to the great array of correspondences with which we started. There are no other known Middle English texts with these linguistic profiles, and the hands are identical. If Ramsey were to insist, in spite of the progression shown here, on his theory of separate scribes, it would be logical for him to insist on four scribes for these four texts rather than two or three, for the latter course would commit him to at least some part of the progression. Let us suppose, then, for argument's sake, that they are by four separate scribes. That four men, however closely connected, should agree on the same items of spelling and show the same sets of variables, that three of them should choose to alter their proportions of

---

[28] Samuels, "Chaucer's Spelling."

variables in ascending order, and that all four of them should then fit precisely into the progression expected for a single scribe is beyond all bounds of coincidence. This is no mere example of the "balance of probability" to which Ramsey appeals. The Trinity manuscript has provided us with evidence as near to proof as we are ever likely to get that these four texts were all written by the same scribe.[29]

[29] My thanks are due to A. I. Doyle, M. B. Parkes, and J. J. Smith for helpful criticisms of an earlier draft of this article.

Text and Context: Chaucer's *Friar's Tale*[1]

Thomas Hahn
Richard W. Kaeuper
University of Rochester

ALTHOUGH MEDIEVAL STUDIES have emphasized the need for interdisciplinary cooperation and approaches, even in the most intensively cultivated fields, like English social and institutional history and Middle English literature, there has been little systematic or extensive cross fertilization.[2] The present essay suggests some ways of exploring the necessary connections between medieval society and its literature by taking one text, Chaucer's *Friar's Tale*, as an artifact of interest to scholars trained in both literary and historical disciplines. Throughout the essay the central contention is that a reading of society helps us understand the tale and that a reading of the tale helps us understand society.[3]

---

[1] Although this article is a joint venture, T. G. Hahn is primarily responsible for sections I and III, R. W. Kaeuper for section II. Kaeuper is grateful for the assistance of a grant from the Harry Frank Guggenheim Foundation. Both authors wish to acknowledge the helpful criticism of Russell Peck.

[2] Recent studies illustrating the connection between history and literature include R. Howard Bloch, *Medieval French Literature and Law* (Berkeley: University of California Press, 1977); John A. Alford, "Literature and Law in Medieval England," *PMLA* 92(1977):941–51; J. R. Maddicott, "The Birth and Setting of the Ballads of Robin Hood," *EHR* 93(1978):276–99; John Barnie, *War in Medieval English Society: Social Values in the Hundred Years War* (Ithaca, N.Y.: Cornell University Press, 1974); John Benton, "Clio and Venus: An Historical View of Medieval Love," in F. X. Newman, ed., *The Meaning of Courtly Love* (Albany: State University of New York Press, 1968), pp. 19–42; Janet Coleman, *English Literature in History, 1350–1400: Medieval Readers and Writers* (London: Hutchinson, 1981); R. W. Kaeuper, "An Historian's Reading of the *Tale of Gamelyn*," forthcoming in *MÆ*; Laura J. Kendrick, "Criticism of the Ruler, 1100–1400, in Provençal, Old French, and Middle English Verse," (Ph.D. diss., Columbia University, 1978); Charles Muscatine, *Poetry and Crisis in the Age of Chaucer* (Notre Dame, Ind.: University of Notre Dame Press, 1972).

[3] The aim of the present article, like that of Bloch, is "to redirect the recent detour away from history — the tendency on the part of specialists either to be overly formalistic (concerned

I

Recent criticism—and especially approaches to literature through reader response, semiotics, and deconstruction—have emphasized the primacy of the text. Moreover, although he has only lately begun to attract this sort of attention, Chaucer is a writer who especially invites criticism that emphasizes the arbitrariness of epistemological systems and the ultimate importance of individual interpretative strategies.[4] It is not simply that we do not know what to think when we finish reading; we feel we *should not* know what to think, if we consider reality, external and internal, in its full complexity. These features of the poetry and of the current critical scene indeed tend to drive out external reality as a consideration in understanding the poetry. The relationship between the text and the interpreter becomes all; external reality itself becomes a text to be read by the informing mind.

In those writings where Chaucer openly depicts social and institutional realities—*The Canterbury Tales* in general, and for our purposes *The Friar's Tale*—readers have largely acknowledged the need for recourse to backgrounds and sources in order to assess his purposes and effects. But even historical criticism of this sort has tended to rely almost exclusively on intellectual traditions, whether these be exegetical and instructional works, sermons, or estates satire.[5] This body of writings certainly provides us a graphic sense of what people thought, though at the same time these traditions are so full, so diverse, and, indeed, so contradictory that, again,

---

with literature as a . . . self-referential system) or to minimize the relation between the literary text and its historical context." Bloch, *Literature and Law*, pp. 5–6. Cf. the comments of Muscatine, *Poetry and Crisis*, pp. 3–7. A highly theoretical treatment of the issue is provided by Stephen G. Nichols, Jr., "A Poetics of Historicism? Recent Trends in Medieval Literary Study," *M&H*, n.s. 8(1977):77–101.

[4] For a general introduction to these critical approaches, see Terence Hawkes, *Structuralism and Semiotics* (Berkeley and Los Angeles: University of California Press, 1977) and Jonathan D. Culler, *The Pursuit of Signs: Semiotics, Literature, Deconstruction* (Ithaca, N.Y.: Cornell University Press, 1981).

[5] See, for example, R. E. Kaske, "The Summoner's Garlick, Oynons, and Eek Lekes," *MLN* 74(1959):481–84; Przemyslaw Mroczkowski, "The *Friar's Tale* and Its Pulpit Background," in *English Studies Today* (Berne, 1961), pp. 107–20; J. L. Lowes, "Chaucer and the Seven Deadly Sins," *PMLA* 30(1915):237–371; Jill Mann, *Chaucer and Medieval Estates Satire* (Cambridge: Cambridge University Press, 1973).

it is often hard to say what we are to think, let alone how Chaucer's audience might have reacted. Scholars have shown with impressive thoroughness the variety of materials that Chaucer might have used in composing his portraits, but it seems quite likely that his listeners and readers would have measured his intent and success in these less by literary tradition than by their own experience.

All readers of Chaucer agree that *The Friar's Tale* is somehow a satire, though agreement on the tale's purpose and effect comes less readily. In part, the confusion of voices arises from the lack of agreement concerning the nature of satire. Even the minimal definition of E. W. Rosenheim, Jr. — "Satire consists of an attack by means of a manifest fiction upon discernible historical particulars" — helps point up the sources of divergent readings of the poem: all critics affirm that the tale is both an attack and a manifest fiction, but the question of "discernible historical particulars" remains open.[6] Is the Summoner of the tale (with his counterpart, the Summoner-Pilgrim) himself a "particular," that is, an actual figure known to Chaucer's audience? Is he a type, the representative of a class of officials whose practices would be familiar to fourteenth-century Christians, but a character who combines and exaggerates such traits as no living individual could? Is he an emblem whose actions in society are significant only insofar as they evince the moral and psychological "particulars" of sin. Or is the Friar's portrayal of the Summoner indeed an accurate representation of the "discernible historical particulars" that might mark the behavior of those corrupt agents of the archdeacons' courts whom Chaucer's contemporaries might have encountered?

Even when criticism has sought particulars of this kind, it has neglected the larger patterns, the social and institutional realities, that hold such particulars together in a society. Kittredge's immensely influential dramatic theory of *The Canterbury Tales* implied that the satire in *The Friar's Tale* was personal in its motivation and its object.[7] Manly's prodigious research on archdeacons and summoners shed a strong light on the tale and its context, yet he took as his premise that "Chaucer had in mind some

---

[6] Edward W. Rosenheim, *Swift and the Satirist's Art* (Chicago: University of Chicago Press, 1963).

[7] George Lyman Kittredge, *Chaucer and His Poetry* (Cambridge, Mass.: Harvard University Press, 1915).

particular person" or "model" for his satire; for Manly, to "find the truth at the center" of the tale meant to identify the precise individual whom Chaucer was attacking through the poem.[8] Few readers have been as singleminded as Manly in seeking an actual personage as the particular behind the tale, but even critics who react against this approach and declare the tale a manifest fiction concern themselves above all with personalities.

It seems clear that Chaucer intended that many of the pilgrims impress us by their dramatic presence and by their interchanges with other pilgrims, as do the Friar and the Summoner. Moreover, Chaucer undoubtedly drew upon estates literature and other traditional portrayals in creating his pilgrims. Yet it is likely that, whatever their acquaintance with notorious ecclesiastics or literary and moral traditions, Chaucer's listeners would have responded to his satire according to their own perceptions in society. What the original audience thought of the poetry would rest in large part, therefore, on what they thought of archdeacons, summoners, and their sort, and if we wish to understand the text, we must recover as precisely as possible the cultural realities that shaped contemporary responses.

II

Students of medieval English society may easily assume that the local, cellular unit of the church was simply the parish with its incumbent of questionable competence and with the occasional presence of sóme friar to add a little spark or, from the priest's perspective, some competition. Without denying the vast importance either of the local secular clergy or of the friars, we need to pay much more attention than we have to an arm of ecclesiastical apparatus that touched every believer directly.[9] In fourteenth-century England the diocese was normally divided into a number of

---

[8] John M. Manly, *Some New Light on Chaucer* (New York: Henry Holt, 1926), pp. 102–22.

[9] Much of what follows draws on the seminal study of Jean Scammell, "The Rural Chapter in England from the Eleventh to the Fourteenth Century," *EHR* 86(1971):1–22; see also the important article by Raoul C. Van Caenegem, "Public Prosecution of Crime in Twelfth-Century England," in C. N. L. Brooke et al., eds., *Church and Government in the Middle Ages: Essays Presented to C. R. Cheney* (Cambridge: Cambridge University Press, 1976), pp. 41–76; Jane Sayers, "Monastic Archdeacons," ibid., pp. 177–203; A. Hamilton Thomp-

archdeaconries, each composed of several rural deaneries. The court associated with these units, known as the rural chapter and operated under the direction of the archdeacon, as Jean Scammel has concisely described it, "constituted the point at which the gigantic superstructure of the ecclesiastical hierarchy had contact with the residential parochial clergy and the peasantry who constituted nine-tenths of the church's subjects."[10] Because it operated at a low level in society and left very little in the way of records,[11] the rural chapter until recently has been an institution almost unseen by most scholars. Yet it was clearly and continually apparent to contemporaries and doubtless had a great impact on their conception of the authority of the church.

Given the importance of an ecclesiastical apparatus of local correction that lacks day-to-day records detailing its operation, we would welcome any indirect evidence informing us how archdeacons and their subordinates exercised their authority and, even more, how the actions of these officials were perceived by their contemporaries. Does the tale that Chaucer gives the Friar provide such information, or is it simply a wickedly clever piece of satire that most fourteenth-century Englishmen would easily recognize as hyperbole and discount accordingly? How is the historian to read *The Friar's Tale*?

---

son, "Diocesan Organization in the Middle Ages, Archdeacons, and Rural Deans," *PBA* 29(1943):153–94; Robert W. Dunning, "Rural Deans in England in the Fifteenth Century," *Bulletin of the Institute of Historical Research* 40(1967):207–13; Louis A. Haselmayer, "The Apparitor and Chaucer's Summoner," *Speculum* 12(1937):43–57. There is much useful information in Norma Adams and Charles Donahue, Jr., *Select Cases from the Ecclesiastical Courts of the Province of Canterbury c 1200–1301* (London: Selden Society, 1981).

[10] Scammell, "Rural Chapter," p. 1.

[11] See the comments of Scammell, ibid., pp. 1–2; Rosalind M. T. Hill, *The Rolls and Register of Bishop Oliver Sutton, 1280–1299* (Lincoln: Lincolnshire Record Society, 1959), pp. xxviii–xxxii; Adams and Donahue, *Select Cases*, p. 57. The best surviving body of manuscript evidence seems to be that from the archdeacons of Stow, Lincoln Diocese, for roughly 1270–1304; see especially Lincolnshire Archives Office D and C Dii/64/2. There is also a small roll relating to the Stamford area in the same diocese, from 1347, D and C A/4/8/1. These records are discussed in Lincolnshire Archives Committee, *Archivists' Report*, 1953–54, p. 61. In D and C Dii/64/2 no. L8, the file contains several cases recorded on the dorses of documents of a different character, possibly illustrating the ad hoc recording of proceedings in correctional courts.

The Friar's picture of the archdeacon and the Summoner at work, painted with vivid colors, is quickly described. He establishes at once the sheer power of the archdeacon, "a man of heigh degree." Deference to the archdeacon was appropriate, for so awesome was his power that one twelfth-century preacher marveled that "even popes and archdeacons die."[12] Although an immediate subordinate of the bishop, the archdeacon was, the Friar suggests, a very powerful and sometimes competitive subordinate.[13] Villagers who had sinned might have good reason to fear the archdeacon over the bishop (lines 1317–20):

> For er the bisshop caughte hem with his hook,
> They weren in the erchedeknes book.
> Thanne hadde he, thurgh his jurisdiccioun,
> Power to doon on hem correccioun.

Of course, the administrative territory over which his powers could be exercised was much smaller than the bishop's, since his charge was limited to the archdeaconry, usually a jurisdictional division of the diocese. In *The Friar's Tale* the action takes place in the rural deanery of Holderness, a subdivision of the archdeaconry of the East Riding of Yorkshire, one of the five archdeaconries within the Diocese of York.[14] Although limited in territorial scope, the competence of the archdeacon's court was broad. The list provided by the Friar (lines 1303–14) is wonderfully accurate; he

> . . . boldely dide execucioun
> In punysshynge of fornicacioun,
> Of wicchecraft, and eek of bawderye,
> Of diffamacioun, and avowtrye,
> Of chirche reves, and of testamentz,
> Of contractes and of lakke of sacramentz,
> Of usure, and of symonye also.
> But certes, lecchours dide he grettest wo;

---

[12] Scammell, "Rural Chapter," p. 21.

[13] Brian Woodcock, *Medieval Ecclesiastical Courts in the Diocese of Canterbury* (Oxford: Oxford University Press, 1952), chap. 1; Adams and Donahue, *Select Cases*, p. 26, and see the sources cited, ibid., p. 82 n. 4.

[14] Information kindly supplied by H. A. Kelly from a forthcoming publication; the authors are grateful to Kelly for several helpful suggestions.

> They sholde syngen if that they were hent;
> And smale tytheres weren foule yshent,
> If any persoun wolde upon hem pleyne.[15]

The Friar's list can be favorably compared with contemporary statements, such as a strictly businesslike account that appears in records from a legal dispute of 1334 between the abbot and convent of Glastonbury and the bishop of Bath and Wells in which the very issue at stake was the archdeaconal jurisdiction exercised by the religious house.[16]

Moreover, the basic distinction between two methods of initiating cases in ecclesiastical courts appears at least indirectly in the tale. The widow approached by the Summoner assumes that the charge against her involves an "instance" case (i.e., one brought by a plaintiff), rather than an "office" or ex officio case (in which the judge himself brought charges against the defendant). She requests a *libellus* used in cases initiated by the former method; only a citation would be shown if the charge were ex officio (lines 1595–97):

> "May I nat axe a libel, sire somonour,
> And answere there, by my procuratour,
> To swich thyng as men wole opposen me?"

That an old woman, living by herself in a provincial village, would possess such knowledge of the court, even to the use of specialized legal terms and legal representatives,[17] provides useful testimony to the local presence of the apparatus of correction.[18]

---

[15] All citations of Chaucer's poetry are from F. N. Robinson, ed., *The Works of Geoffrey Chaucer*, 2d ed. (Boston: Houghton Mifflin, 1957).

[16] See the register of Abbot Walter de Monington, preserved in the Bodleian Library, Oxford, Bodleian MS Wood empt 1, fols. 20–28, cited, with helpful comments in Sayers, "Monastic Archdeacons," p. 189.

[17] It is noteworthy that Chaucer reserves these words for this context: *libel* occurs nowhere else in his writings and retained its specialized meaning until the midfifteenth century; *procuratour* appears only here and in the doubtfully attributed translation of the *Roman de la Rose*. Both are obvious anglicizations of terms common in the documentary evidence.

[18] Woodcock, in *Ecclesiastical Courts*, p. 35, commenting on a later period, observes, "There could have been few people in the diocese [of Canterbury] who remained unacquainted with the cavalcades of ecclesiastical lawyers and their assistants." On "instance" and "office" cases, citation, and court appearances, see Adams and Donahue, *Select Cases*, pp. 37–72.

The range of possible judicial business thus was broad, but *The Friar's Tale* suggests a strong particular focus. To put it bluntly, the archdeacon and his men went hunting where the ducks were. Of all the wrongs that were in their power to detect, the archdeacon and his subordinates concentrated on illicit sex: "certes, lecchours dide he grettest wo" (line 1310). Moreover, the archdeacon's agents were so expert in ferreting out sexual sin that no one (lines 1371–74)

> Bet than this somnour knew a sly lecchour,
> Or an avowtier, or a paramour.
> And for that was the fruyt of al his rente,
> Therfore on it he sette al his entente.

The historian's evidence coincides with the Friar's evaluation. Granted that surviving record evidence on the practices producing this revenue amounts to only a handful of scraps and, further, that these documents come from various dioceses and various chronological periods; nevertheless, what survives presents a convincingly consistent picture. Whenever and wherever the court evidence exists, it shows the singleminded concentration on profit from sexual offenses described in *The Friar's Tale*.[19] Chaucer did not simply exaggerate a point to achieve bawdy, humorous

---

[19] On surviving records from Lincoln Diocese, see note 11 above. Lincolnshire Archives Office D and C Dii/64/2 no. 9 presents a list of sixteen names with sums collected to a total of 46s. 8d.; the charges are not specified. Cases clearly relating to illicit sex appear in D and C A/4/8/1, D and C Dii/64/2, nos. 11a, 11c, 12, 18/2. Printed records from the Archdeaconry of Sudbury (Norwich Diocese) in the late thirteenth century show at least 26 of 39 cases concerned with illicit sex; Antonia Gransden, "Some Late Thirteenth-Century Records of an Ecclesiastical Court in the Archdeaconry of Sudbury," *Bulletin of the Institute of Historical Research* 31(1959):62–69. Similar records from a court in Worcester Diocese, 1300, show the same concern in 53 of 56 cases; F. S. Pearson, "Records of a Rurideaconal Court of 1300," *Collectanea* (London: Worcestershire Historical Society, 1912), pp. 70–80; comment by R. M. Haines, *The Administration of Diocese of Worcester in the First Half of the Fourteenth Century* (London: SPCK, Church Historical Society of London, 1965), pp. 50ff. Each of the 379 charges in surviving records from the 1364 Canterbury Consistory Court concerned sexual offenses. In the period 1396–1411 more than 90 percent of the cases before this court likewise did. Although this evidence comes from a higher court, it is worth noting, especially since the Diocese of Canterbury was not divided geographically into archdeaconries; the jurisdictions of the archdeacon's court and the bishop's consistory were concurrent. See Patti Mills-McInerny, "Spiritual Correction in the Medieval Church Courts of Canterbury" (Ph.D. diss., University of Rochester, 1980), p. 8, chap. 2, passim.

effects. His suggestion (noted above) that the archdeacon rather than the bishop often secured jurisdiction over the sins of ordinary folk, no less than his identification of the particular focus of that jurisdiction, tallies well with the view of modern scholarship:

> The jurisdictional lines seem to have been quite fluid, but cases of fornication, adultery and minor moral offenses of the clergy probably were normally heard at the archdeaconal level, whereas cases involving more serious or more complicated offenses, as heresy, simony, sorcery, pluralism, as well as those of criminous clerks, probably were heard at higher levels.[20]

Significantly, the archdeacons' initial power and influence seem to have been nourished by the expansion of legal business — and profit — that came with the attempt to enforce clerical celibacy, especially from the twelfth century.[21] But they quickly discovered the possibilities inherent in correction of the laity. Given both the frailties of human nature and the complexities and uncertainties surrounding the medieval conception of marriage,[22] correction of sexual offenses among laymen and laywomen assured the officials good hunting.

Historians of English common law will find little to surprise them in the development of this jurisdiction across the first half of the twelfth century, for similar processes were at work in the legal mechanisms of church and state.[23] Archdeacons, acting on their own authority and knowledge, were prosecuting offenders, replacing the traditional methods of private accusation and "parochial presentment through the voices of synodal witnesses" (i.e., accusation delivered by sworn members of the parish before the bishop). At the same time the crown was combating crime and protecting the rights associated with crown pleas by ex officio prosecutions carried out by local officials. The trend in secular courts was halted by Henry II's creation of juries of presentment, or accusing juries, which replaced local

[20] Adams and Donahue, *Select Cases*, p. 57.

[21] Scammell, "Rural Chapter," p. 6.

[22] See especially Michael M. Sheehan, "The Formation and Stability of Marriage in Fourteenth-Century England," *MS* 3(1971):228–63. Jean Scammell, "Freedom and Marriage in Medieval England," *Economic History Review*, 2d ser. 27(1974):523–37, is also useful.

[23] For what follows, see Raoul C. Van Caenegem, "Public Prosecution of Crime in Twelfth-Century England," in Brooke et al., *Church and Government*, pp. 41–76; quotation from p. 64

justices, whose power could be troublesome to central authority. In ecclesiastical courts, however, a large ex officio jurisdiction supervised by a local official with a generous measure of independence continued to grow; the archdeacons went from strength to strength.

The archdeacon, his official, and the rural dean seem to have presided over a range of administrative and judicial meetings; but most of their corrective and disciplinary jurisdiction, as the Friar suggests, was exercised in a rural chapter, itself "an institution of amorphous constitution and multifarious functions."[24] Because of the low social level at which the court operated (in correcting the sins of local clergy and villagers) and the pragmatic tenor of proceedings and records in a court characterized by "a rather impressionistic sense of justice,"[25] historians have not always appreciated the extent and vigor of the work of archdeacons and their subordinates in rural chapters. As Jean Scammell suggests:

This is not the leisurely world of the episcopal consistory or of proceedings before papal judges delegate: the sphere of highly qualified lawyers expensively spinning out nice legal points through an infinity of notarial instruments which the successful party would cherish through the centuries. This is the operation of the Church's authority at a social level where the judge preserved only a note of convictions and punishments for strictly practical use and the judged desired only forgetfulness. To put it bluntly, the introduction of canon law appears to have largely passed the rural chapters disciplinary functions by.[26]

To this chapter the archdeacon's Summoner, in the tale a man with a "fyr-reed cherubynnes face" and fond of "garleek, oynons" and "strong wyn, reed as blood," brought the suspected sinners. The archdeacon or his official might preside over a chapter, or it might be supervised by a rural dean, with an appropriate division of profits. Solemn or common sessions were regularly scheduled and were limited in frequency by canon law; the

---

[24] Scammell, "Rural Chapter," p. 1.

[25] Sheehan, paraphrasing the official of the Bishop of Ely, "The Formation and Stability of Marriage," p. 283.

[26] Scammell, "Rural Chapter," p. 15; cf. Woodcock, *Ecclesiastical Courts*, pp. 69–70; Adams and Donahue, *Select Cases*, pp. 10–11, 57–59, 83–84. The last two writers point out (pp. 58–59) that summary procedure in contrast to long-form procedure is evident in their thirteenth-century records but makes its official appearance in the law of the church only in the decretals of Clement V at the beginning of the fourteenth century.

western deaneries of the Diocese of Canterbury, for example, were visited fourteen times a year on a schedule that seldom varied.[27] But extra circuits, more informal and unpredictable, could apparently be held at the arch-deacon's pleasure; the "private chapters" on these circuits could be "small, highly localized affairs," perhaps consisting of the parson and leading peasants of a parish or even a family group questioned about the sins they or others had committed.[28] These less formal meetings seem to have carried the greater load of judicial business. As Brian Woodcock noted:

One of the more interesting features of late medieval enforcement of canonical discipline disclosed by the Canterbury *acta* is the comparative insignificance of the regular visitations in the process of checking and punishing of crimes and misde-meanours which were answerable *in foro ecclesiastico*. The visitations of the archdeacon's Official seem to have been no more than formal annual tours, the chief object of which was the collection of procurations.... The great bulk of *Ex officio* business arose not upon presentment after detection but as the result of a continuous process of "inquisition."[29]

Regardless of the degree of formality and the composition of the chap-ter, for those found guilty corporal punishment was the rule. As Friar Hubert says of the archdeacon, "He made the peple pitously to synge" (line 1316). Such court records as survive contain references to beatings of a severity that might easily make the unfortunate sinner "sing": "five times around the market place"; "twice around the market place"; "twice around the market place and twice around the church."[30] Some records lack this

[27] Woodcock, *Ecclesiastical Courts*, p. 35.

[28] Scammell, "Rural Chapter," pp. 13, 15–16. For an example see F. S. Pearson, "Records of a Rurideaconal Court of 1300," in S. G. Hamilton, ed., *Collectanea of the Worcestershire Historical Society* (London: 1912). See the comments in Pearson's introduction concerning the short notice given to the parish in which a court was to be held and the inadequacy of places selected to provide hospitality. Four chapters are recorded in the document he prints, meeting May 13, June 15, July 5, and July 19; at the first three meetings the date and place of the next were announced; at the fourth the announcement was simply that another will be held when necessary ("et erit aliud vbi nessitur").

[29] Woodcock, *Ecclesiastical Courts*, pp. 68–69.

[30] Examples from Antonia Gransden, "Some Late Thirteenth-Century Records of an Ecclesiastical Court in the Archdeaconry of Sudbury," *Bulletin of the Institute of Historical Research* 31(1958):62–69; Mills-McInerney, in "Spiritual Correction," chap. 5, notes that beatings three times around the church and three times around the market were common.

precision of detail but simply prescribe beatings "in the usual manner."[31] By the thirteenth century penny-pinching lords were instructing their serfs to take the beating rather than pay out scarce cash that might go toward some seigneurial exaction.[32] "Unhappily," as C. Eveleigh Woodrull observed, "repeated castigations round church and market-place seem to have had little effect on the reformation of morals."[33] But the prospect of such beatings might have quite a different effect in making a victim all the more eager to pay whatever the officials demanded in order to avoid degrading public punishment.[34] So feared were the court and its penalties that in 1284 a Staffordshire man even attempted to murder the fellow who had got him summoned before a rural chapter on fornication charges.[35]

The picture of local correctional officials and courts as presented in *The Friar's Tale* has so far been completely congruent with the view of modern scholarship. But the tale also speaks to the issues of motives, and it unmistakably implies a judgment. We want to know whose judgment is here represented — the personal vituperation of a more or less imagined literary figure? The opinion of his creator, Geoffrey Chaucer? Or a view not far from that of many of Chaucer's contemporaries? When such questions are raised, the unanimity of opinion quickly dissolves. Louis Haselmayer felt "somehow impelled to conclude that Chaucer's conception is more violent than necessary." Since historical evidence failed to produce proof of such a state of affairs, he decided that behind the tale stood "an actual prototype, forgotten now except as an artistic creation."[36] Brian Woodcock thought that evidence of corruption on a scale large enough to shock the medieval conscience is lacking and concluded that officials saw in their position only duty, not opportunity for plunder.[37] R. C. Van Caenegem

---

The practice of beating disappeared in the southern province only around the mid-fifteenth century.

[31] F. S. Pearson, "Records of a Rurideaconal Court of 1300," *Collectanea* (London: Worcestershire Historical Society, 1912), pp. 69–80.

[32] Scammell, "Rural Chapter," p. 17.

[33] C. Eveleigh Woodrull, "Some Early Visitation Rolls Preserved at Canterbury," *Archaeologia Cantiana* 32(1917):144.

[34] See the comment of Sayers, "Monastic Archdeacons," p. 193.

[35] Scammell, "Rural Chapter," p. 17.

[36] Haselmayer, "The Apparitor and Chaucer's Summoner," pp. 56–57.

[37] Woodcock, *Ecclesiastical Courts*, p. 112; cf. pp. 49, 79, 99.

took a harsher view: "The archdeacons and deans, to whom the bishop delegated this unquestioned duty, were at best apt to be rash and over-zealous and at worst to turn into aggressors and blackmailers, imperiling their own souls and making people's lives hell."[38] Scammell, connecting this kind of criticism with Chaucer, argued that "the precision with which the literary and the record evidence dovetail is remarkable" and com-mented that poetic license has not marred the accuracy of Chaucer's reporting.[39]

Of course, we know that Chaucer is writing powerful satire and that the great literature devoted to the honest servants and sound practices of major institutions is decidedly slight. But perhaps we should consider, with John A. Yunck, that "literary conventions do not endure for centuries without roots in reality."[40] What fourteenth-century men and women thought about the spiritual correction associated with archdeacons would obviously depend on the choice of witnesses. Any cleric involved in archidiaconal or episcopal governance could easily provide a rationale for the jurisdiction and the form it had come to take. The discipline of the often wayward or negligent lower clergy was of obvious importance to the health of Christian society. The discipline of lay folk was equally important, and here there was special concern about clandestine marriages. Michael Sheehan's study of the consistory court of Ely and H. A. Kelly's study of the Consistory of Rochester have shown that a quarter or more of all cases heard were matrimonial, nearly nine out of ten of these cases involving clandestine marriages.[41] Judicial activity on this scale was an understandable conse-quence of the "astonishingly individualistic attitude" displayed by canon-ists and theologians who developed the consensual theory of marriage. Defending this conception of marriage against the clear interests of "fam-ily, feudal lord, and even the king,"[42] churchmen could argue forcefully that through the effort of episcopal or archidiaconal court apparatus all

---

[38] Van Caenegem, "Public Prosecution of Crime," p. 65.

[39] Scammell, "Rural Chapter," p. 19.

[40] John A. Yunck, *The Lineage of Lady Meed* (Notre Dame, Ind.: University of Notre Dame Press, 1963), p. 185.

[41] Sheehan, "Formation and Stability of Marriage," p. 234; H. A. Kelly, *Love and Marriage in the Age of Chaucer* (Ithaca, N.Y.: Cornell University Press, 1975), chap. 6, especially pp. 163-70.

[42] Sheehan, "Formation and Stability of Marriage," pp. 229, 263.

marriages would be brought into the open. Some modern historians have surveyed the system and found it good; one scholar has even praised the good sense and intelligence of English churchmen in administering the canon law "with such discretion and such humanity."[43]

That local correction can be explained in terms of rational goals, and that it has not lacked for defenders in its own time and in ours, does not, however, imply that the rationale was fully understood or accepted by the men and women whose spiritual welfare and whose sins formed its main concerns. Ultimately our interest lies in understanding the perception and reaction of those disciplined, even more than in recovering the actuality of court practice that in detail is beyond our knowing with certainty, since we lack copious record evidence.

The attack presented in *The Friar's Tale* thus seems all the more intriguing. Friar Hubert misses no chance to assert that acquisitiveness is the motive force standing behind the local chapters. In the narrative of the tale an old widow nearly has twelve pence extorted from her by the Summoner, though he admits "of hire knowe I no vice" (line 1578). Moreover, we have the Summoner's word that the archdeacon is no better. "Purs is the ercedekenes helle" is his famous dictum in *The General Prologue*, and although the pilgrim Chaucer adds hastily that this statement is obviously a lie, he later has the Friar announce that nothing can save the archdeacon's victims from "pecunyal peyne" (line 1314).[44]

That local correction was profitable to all officers involved cannot be doubted. As Scammell argues, a small-scale, localized institution operating vigorously for three centuries without significant external stimulus must have been energized by considerable profits.[45] In the twelfth century King Henry II claimed that the archdeacons of England enjoyed an income greater than his own. His sense of justice may have been stirred no less than his jealousy; a system in which one person served as both prosecutor and judge could hardly have appealed to Henry, and he must have been well

---

[43] Rosalind M. T. Hill, "Public Penance: Some Problems of a Thirteenth-Century Bishop," *History* 36(1951):274–75.

[44] On "pecunyal peyne" see Alfred L. Kellogg, "A Reading of the *Friar's Tale*, Line 1314," in *Chaucer, Langland, Arthur* (New Brunswick, N.J.: Rutgers University Press, 1972), pp. 269–72.

[45] The following discussion is based on Van Caenegem, "Public Prosecution of Crime," pp. 61–71; and Scammell, "Rural Chapter," pp. 8–9, 18.

aware of the abuses that led to scathing comments from such writers as John of Salisbury. Early in his reign Henry II prohibited the form of prosecution being practiced in the local church courts, thus paying a backhanded compliment to their efficiency and ubiquity. He repeated his prohibition in the famous Constitutions of Clarendon (clause 6) and specified that accusations were henceforth to be collected from local juries of twelve lawful men empaneled by the sheriff and put at the disposal of the bishop. But this proposal disappeared in the great quarrel with Becket, and the archdeacons were not deflected from their course. A clause in the Inquest of Sheriffs (1170) ordering all bishops to make inquiry into the extortions of archdeacons and deans seems similarly to have proved no significant deterrent.[46] By the end of the fourteenth century papal grants allowing archdeacons to farm their offices might actually specify the sizable daily takings.[47]

Over and over in his tale, the Friar not only tells his audience that acquisitiveness is the motive of the officials but suggests as well to what disreputable means their greed propels them. The Summoner— "A slyer boye nas noon in Engelond"—has assembled "his espiaille, / That taughte hym wel wher that hym myghte availle" (lines 1322-24). The Summoner spares the sinner who points the way to more sheep for shearing, maintains certain "bawdes" to lure the unwary into sin (and into court), and then reports only half the resulting profits to the archdeacon. Thus the Friar sums him up unforgettably as "a theef, and eek a somnour, and a baude." In fact, the question of actual sin fades before the prospect of profit. Even the innocent could be made by a corrupt summoner to pay simply to avoid the inconvenience, danger, and embarrassment of prosecution (lines 1346-49):[48]

---

[46] William Stubbs, *Select Charters*, 9th ed. (Oxford: Oxford University Press, 1962), pp. 165 (Clarendon), 177 (Sheriffs).

[47] *Calendar of Papal Letters*, 4.408, cited in Thompson, "Archdeacons and Rural Deans," p. 156 n. 3. George Holmes, *The Good Parliament* (Oxford: Clarendon Press, 1975), p. 14, points out that by local English custom archdeacons did not pay annates on the profits of jurisdiction.

[48] See Woodcock, *Ecclesiastical Courts*, pp. 69–70; Adams and Donahue, *Select Cases*, p. 38. William Fitzstephen, in his *Life of Becket*, provides an instance of the corruption typical among archdeacons and rural deans just after he records King Henry's comment on their income: a resident of Scarborough came to the king and complained that a rural dean had

> Withouten mandement a lewed man
> He koude somne, on peyne of Cristes curs,
> And they were glade for to fille his purs,
> And make hym grete feestes atte nale.

Had he heard the story, Chaucer might have relished the incident in 1297 in which the summoner of the deanery of Dunstable cited all secular persons dwelling in Markyate Priory to appear before the court of the dean of Dunstable on charges of incontinence. Bishop Sutton informed the local officers that they had acted with "unwarrantable lack of evidence."[49]

Archdeacons and their subordinates were seldom held on so short a lead, however. General exhortation was more common. Across the thirteenth and fourteenth centuries councils and synods repeatedly, and apparently in vain, legislated against summoners' offenses. They were, for example, to travel on foot, in order to limit the expenses inevitably passed on to the faithful.[50] Chaucer gives a hint about the effectiveness of this rule; he tells us clearly that the Summoner goes about the countryside mounted on a horse. Much more significant is the legislation directed against summoners' malicious citations and their expectation of gifts.[51] Similarly in 1378 a parliamentary petition denounced summoners' malice in the service of greed:

The said summoners make their summons to divers people maliciously as they are going along in their carts through the fields, and elsewhere, and accuse them of various wrongful crimes, and they force poor people to pay a fine called the Bishope

---

tried to exact twenty-two solidi by charging his wife with adultery — though there was no witness — and summoning her from chapter to chapter. J. C. Robertson, ed., *Materials for the History of Thomas Becket*, R.S. 67.3 (London, 1877), p. 44.

[49] Hill, *The Rolls and Register of Bishop Oliver Sutton*, p. 16.

[50] Haselmayer comments on regulations concerning horses in "The Apparitor and Chaucer's Summoner," pp. 49–50.

[51] Haines, *Administration of the Diocese of Worcester*, p. 46, cites the statutes of the Fourth Lateran Council (1215), of the Councils of Oxford (1222), and of London (1237). He also notes an entry in Bishop Giffard's Register for 1276 providing articles for an inquiry into the behavior of archdeacons, apparently as a result of complaints about injuries, molestations, heavy fines, partiality by archdeacons and their subordinates. Haselmayer, "Apparitor and Chaucer's Summoner," pp. 53–54, cites the Salisbury *constitutiones* of 1258, the synodal statutes of Winchester of 1296, and the injunctions of the Council of London in 1342.

Almois; or alternately the said summoner summons them 20 or 21 leagues away to two places on one day, to the great hurt, impoverishment, and oppression of the said poor Commons.[52]

Six years earlier Edward III had threatened that if the prelates would not check clerical extortion he would provide a remedy himself.[53] Moreover, scholars have found specific accusations of archidiaconal extortion through threats of summons scattered in royal court records from the thirteenth to the fifteenth century. The following late-thirteenth-century examples give the flavor of this evidence:

The inquest jurors say that John de Berstrete, the subdean, maliciously charged Gilbert Fitzwarin with adultery though he was innocent and had him summoned from chapter to chapter until he made fine with him in 12 d. which he took from him unjustly.

Sibil le Walesch of Norwich was caused by John le Rodeprest to be cited before John the subdean of Norwich because there was a quarrel between them over the boundary between their properties. So she was amerced 12 d. unjustly before the dean and made reasonable fine with him, 4 s. for himself (*ad opus suum proprium*) and 12 gallons of ale which she paid in a friendly way to John Rodeprest.[54]

Fifty years later the general inquests ordered during the government crisis of 1341 produced very similar accusations. A few paraphrases from entries on the Lincolnshire roll convey a sense of the charges brought by local juries:

[52] *Rotuli parliamentorum* 3, p. 43, quoted by Haselmayer, "Apparitor and Chaucer's Summoner," p. 54 (in French).

[53] Bertha Putnam, *Proceedings Before the Justices of the Peace in the Fourteenth and Fifteenth Centuries* (London: Ames Foundation Publication, 1938), p. xlvi n. 4.

[54] The two cases paraphrased are taken from a visitation in 1286 of royal itinerant justices in Norfolk: Public Record Office, Justices Itinerant, JUST 1/575m. 101; cf. mm. 101d, 102, 102d, 103, 103d, 104, 105, 105d, 107, 109d. Although the inquest emerged from unusual circumstances, there is no reason to think its evidence untypical. See, for example, the evidence cited in the following note. The background to this investigation is discussed in E. B. Graves, "Circumspecte Agatis," *EHR* 43(1928):1–20. For further cases see E. M. Elvey, *The Courts of the Archdeaconry of Buckingham, 1483–1523* (Aylesbury: Buckinghamshire Record Society, 1975), p. xii, cases from the reign of Richard III; Dorothy M. Owen, *Church and Society in Medieval Lincolnshire* (Lincoln: Lincolnshire Historical Society, 1971), p. 36, cases from 1381; Haselmayer, "Apparitor and Chaucer's Summoner," p. 53, cases from 1350, 1365.

Dennis, vicar of Cabourne, dean of Yarborough, and former clerk of the commissary of the archdeacon of Lincoln has joined with Adam parson of South Ulceby in making false and fictitious summons on the King's people and ordered them to appear before them on charges that they were outside Holy Church when they had not been summoned, and excommunicated them until they paid fines and redemptions at their will.

Henry de Ronceby, parson of Brauncewell and dean of Sleaford maliciously and without cause in order to extort money cited Robert de Cranwell to appear at divers places until Robert made fine for 13s. 4d.

Master John de Ravenser, official of the archdeacon of Lincoln and Adam Byker, chaplain and commissary of Master Thomas, archdeacon of Lincoln, cited and vexed the men and women of Stamford to appear at Boston, Sleaford, Grantham, Corby and other places outside the deaconal jurisdiction of Stamford and received more than £20 in false and malicious fines and redemptions to the great scandal and deep depauperization of the lord King's people.[55]

Simply to read through this record from one county in one inquest leaves a strong impression of the seamy side of local ecclesiastical courts and particularly of the grasping or inventive nature of more than a few officials. Men and women must pay before they are allowed compurgation regarding adultery charges; they must pay before a will can be probated. The executors of the will of John Langton claimed that only after they had paid 10s. to an archdeacon's commissary standing at the graveside could this official be convinced that Langton had not died excommunicate and might be buried in the Church.[56]

Of course, to find, at a distance of six centuries, record evidence of gangs of spies and bawds set to trap the unwary is a taller order. But if we find some expression of contemporary unrest in Chaucer's portrayal of archidiaconal power, of the concentration on one set of offenses, of the physical and pecunial punishments inflicted, and of the opportunities for extortion, then we might well imagine that stories about informers and sexual entrapment were told by villagers as they followed the plow or lifted a mug of ale.

[55] Public Record Office, Justices Itinerant JUST 1/521. The three paraphrased cases are taken from mm. 13d, 10, and 14d, respectively. The authors are grateful to Bernard McLane, who provided transcripts of all the relevant cases from this roll.

[56] Ibid., m. 13d. Extortion regarding compurgation appears on m. 14d; extortion regarding probate appears many times throughout the roll.

Chaucer's Friar tells us that abuses such as these often made the Summoner a target not merely of satire but of physical assault (lines 1283–85):

> A somonour is a rennere up and doun
> With mandementz for fornicacioun,
> And is ybet at every townes ende.

If we are tempted to dismiss the claim as simply another example of poetic license, we ought to consider a case heard before justices of oyer and terminer in 1304. Three prominent men were commissioned to do justice on those persons who

> took Richard Christien, . . . dean of Ospring at Sellings, Kent, when he was there by the order of the Archbishop to make citations and do other things pertaining to his spiritual office, put him on his horse with his face to the tail and inhumanely compelled him to hold the tail and ride, with songs and dances, through that town and afterwards cut off the tail, ears, and lips of his horse, cast the dean in a filthy place, carried away writings, muniments, and some privileges of the archbishop in his custody, and prevented him from executing his office.[57]

The view of the people of Sellings, Kent, made reasonably clear in 1304, seems remarkably similar to the view taken in *The Friar's Tale*. Here indeed is a dean acting as summoner beaten up at the town's end in a remarkable incident that seems to have become something like a village fete, complete with songs and dances, a humiliating backward ride for the victim, and ritual mutilation of his horse before the final heave-ho into the village cesspool. Since a backwards ride was in the popular imagination associated with punishing the incontinent,[58] the villagers may have been deliberately turning the tables on the dean in their mockery, criticizing what they saw as the double standard of spiritual correction in their own way.

Such a wealth of detail cannot be expected regularly, but the assault was not an isolated incident. A decade earlier Master Richard Lynol, archdeacon of Northumberland, and his subordinates were assaulted at Newcastle, and "the rolls belonging to his officer" were carried away.[59] P. Mills-

---

[57] Ibid., JUST 1/403/2, *Calendar of Patent Rolls, 1301–1307*, pp. 274–75.

[58] On this ancient motif of the backwards ride see Ruth Mellinkoff, "Riding Backwards: Theme of Humiliation and Symbol of Evil," *Viator* 4(1973):153–77.

[59] *Calendar of Patent Rolls, 1281–1292*, p. 141.

McInerny discovered many cases of assault against summoners in surviving records from the Diocese of Canterbury ca. 1340–1475. In one of these incidents Robert and Olyver of Rainham ambushed the official, beat him with a staff, stole from him the citation no doubt meant for Robert, and carried him off to the home of an accomplice, where they further abused their victim.[60] In 1340 a knight leading perhaps a score of his followers similarly abducted Master John de Bouser, archdeacon of Essex, and held him for ransom in a manor house, where he feared for his life.[61] In Hereford Diocese another knight, followed by accomplices armed to the teeth, chased Roger the Apparitor for a mile down a public highway "as if he were a thief and man of bloodshed and guile"; luckily for Roger, they vented their anger by killing only his horse.[62] Not every archidiaconal official was so fortunate. In 1377/1379 certain "sons of perdition" actually killed an apparitor who was carrying out his office in Winchester Diocese.[63] But even where the violence stopped short of murder, we can find evidence of deeply felt resentments. When a rural dean tried to hold a chapter in the church of Bredon, Worcester Diocese, in 1303, a crowd broke into the church to prevent the session. Not only did they assault the clerics, but also on their own initiative and authority they appointed a new official and apparitors.[64]

Such incidents as those at Bredon and Sellings point in the direction of two important distinctions, one involving perceptions of the justice meted out by archidiaconal and episcopal courts, the other concerned with various motives for the hostility against the rural chapters. The bishop's consistory was by no means universally accepted and admired. The text known as "A Satire on the Consistory Courts" (from the reign of Edward II) gives the vivid complaint of a humble man convicted of sexual sins before "an old

[60] Mills-McInerney, "Spiritual Correction," pp. 49–51.

[61] *Calendar of Patent Rolls, 1338–1340*, pp. 557–58. Significantly, he paid a ransom of no less than £300 to save his life.

[62] Joseph Henry Parry, ed., *Register of John Gilbert, Bishop of Hereford (1375–1389)* (London: Canterbury and York Society, 1915), pp. 13–14. This and the sources cited in the following two notes are cited by Haselmayer, "Apparitor and Chaucer's Summoner," p. 52.

[63] T. F. Kirby, ed., *Register of William of Wykeman (1366–1404)* (Hampshire Record Society, 1899), 2.186–87.

[64] J. W. Bund, *Register of Bishop William Ginsborough, 1303–1307* (Oxford: Worcestershire Historical Society, 1907), p. 43.

churl in a black robe," forty clerks eager for bribes, and a half dozen hated summoners; he is "driven like a dog" through the market and then is forced to marry the woman "covered with mold like a moor-hen."[65] But the criticism directed at courts operated by archdeacons and deans seems more common, more deeply felt, more bitterly expressed. The two courts exercised concurrent jurisdiction and shared a concern particularly for sexual sins and clandestine marriage. How can the greater animosity to the rural chapters be explained? The answer can scarcely be a denial of the right of ecclesiastical authorities to exercise spiritual correction, or even resentment against official interference with sexual activity considered, in some modern way, to be a purely private matter. Rather, the burden of complaint against rural chapters seems to stem from a sense of extortionate unfairness and a double standard that allows innocents to face malicious prosecution while their relatively better-placed, better-off neighbors can buy license to sin; the local chapters, in this view, not only fail to correct sin but actually encourage a recurring cycle of venality and fornication. Perhaps this sense of outrage at the subversion of the disciplinary apparatus, rather than the kind of sin punished or the punishment itself, stands behind the schoolboy debate topic, "Can an Archdeacon Enter Heaven?" — "one of the sick jokes of the age," as R. C. Van Caenegem has commented.[66]

Such acidic commentary was distilled across generations of discontent and minor poems and in the sermons of popular preachers.[67] In the anonymous *Sur les états du monde* (probably written in the first half of the thirteenth century), the deans are accused of prying into the affairs of simple priests "by means of spies or by [looking] through windows"; even high-ranking clerics pay for living with their concubines while grandly forgiving lesser mortals their sins.[68] A poem on the evil times of Edward II (written early in the next reign) clearly illustrates the theme:

[65] Text in Thomas Wright, ed., *Political Songs of England* (London: Camden Society, 1839), pp. 155–59; summary and comments in Rossell Hope Robbins, "Poems Dealing with Contemporary Conditions," in Albert E. Hartung, ed., *A Manual of the Writings in Middle English, 1050–1500* (Hamden, Conn.: Archon Books, 1975), 5.1406.

[66] Van Caenegem, "Public Prosecution of Crime," p. 66.

[67] G. R. Owst, *Literature and the Pulpit in Medieval England* (London: Macmillan, 1933), pp. 216ff., 224.

[68] Isabel S. T. Aspin, *Anglo-Norman Political Songs* (Oxford: Oxford University Press, 1953), pp. 116–29.

> And officials and denes that chapitles sholden holde,
> Theih sholde chastise the folk—and theih maken hem bolde.
> Mak a present to the den ther thu thenkest to dwelle,
> And have leve longe i-nouh to serve the fend of helle to queme.
> For have he silver, of sinne taketh he never ʒeme.[69]

Similar themes can be extracted from the "Complaint of the Ploughman" composed late in the reign of Richard II: one man must pay "raunsome" though he is "clene as christall," while another buys an absolution for twenty shillings: "And al the yere usen it forth he may."[70]

The complaints penned by poets were tirelessly thundered from the pulpit, as the great summation of preaching by John Bromyard in the late fourteenth century illustrates. A frequent text was the prophecy of Micah (1.7): "For they have been gathered of the hire of an harlot, and they shall return to the hire of an harlot."[71] The Austin friar John Waldeby denounced archdeacons and deans who "cite, excommunicate, and spoil the poor and simple, who are not strong enough to resist," but who, in effect, license fornicators with means to pay.[72] His contemporary Thomas Wimbledon attacked the single cure prescribed in courts of spiritual correction as "a medicine [which] deserves rather to be called a 'laxative medicine for purses,' rather than 'a medicine for souls.'"[73]

Complaint was hardly limited, however, to popular preaching or to the lesser, anonymous verse. In the twelfth century John of Salisbury warned an archdeacon not to give the impression that "you are thirsty for the money of the delinquents" and told him to keep his hands free from "the sordid gains of false accusations" so that his office might not seem to be "a sort of business." He feared that "deans and archdeacons seem to think the spoliation of a poor man to be good sport" and "eat and drink the sins of the people." He applied to these officials the remarkable epithet "ambi-

---

[69] Wright, *Political Songs of England*, p. 332: "And officials and deans who ought to convene chapters and chastise the faithful instead make them bold; give a bribe to the dean wherever you plan to stay and you will have sufficient respite to do service to the devil in hell. As long as he has silver, he takes no heed of sin."

[70] Thomas Wright, ed., *Political Poems and Songs*, Rolls Series 14 (London, 1859), 1.304–46.

[71] Owst, *Literature and Pulpit*, p. 252.

[72] Ibid., p. 266.

[73] Ibid., p. 280.

sinistrous."[74] Gower's strictures against "Archedeacnes, Officals et Deans" in his *Mirour de L'omme* (ca. 1378)[75] stand in the tradition of John of Salisbury[76] or the *Apocalypse of Golias*.[77] Moreover in Langland the anticlerical attack is even more sharply focused on the spiritual correction exercised by archdeacons, deans, subdeans, and summoners; these officials even more than venal popes or simoniacal bishops are the target of Langland's bitter wrath. Likewise they make up no small part of the train of Lady Meed in *Piers Plowman*; a summoner is one of her three diehard supporters after she has lost her case in the royal court at Westminster. The local correctional courts persecute the poor and turn fornication into graft.[78]

Moreover these strictures of poets and preachers must be placed in an even broader context of contemporary criticism. By the fourteenth century agents of administration — manorial, ecclesiastical, royal — touched men's lives more directly, regulated local events more fully, and lightened men's purses more efficiently than ever before. Chaucer reminds us of this himself by giving the Summoner and the bailiff a conversation in which they exchange the tricks of the trade. The continuum of complaint reminds us that criticism of local ecclesiastical courts of correction can scarcely be viewed as unique. Biting denunciations of venality and injustice in the courts of both church and state run like scarlet threads through the fabric of late-medieval English thought. Fourteenth-century men and women were struggling to come to grips with the cumulative force of institutions whose capacities had increased enormously over the previous two centuries. These institutions were coming forcefully over the local horizon, providing more services but also demanding more and regulating more. At the same time

---

[74] From W. J. Millor and H. E. Butler, eds., *The Letters of John of Salisbury, I: The Early Letters (1153–1161)*, rev. by C. N. L. Brooke, Nelson's Medieval Texts (London: Nelson, 1955), quoted by Van Caenegem, "Public Prosecution of Crime," pp. 66–67.

[75] G. C. Macaulay, ed., *The Complete Works of John Gower; The French Works* (Oxford: Clarendon Press, 1899), pp. 226–28. Note also Gower's general strictures against the double standard employed by the church in dealing with the sexual sins of laymen and clerics, *Vox clamantis* 2.3, 3.4, in *Complete Works; Latin Works*, pp. 87–88, 113–14.

[76] See the quotations, citations, and comments in Van Caenegem, "Public Prosecution of Crime," pp. 66–67; Yunck, *The Lineage of Lady Meed*, p. 120.

[77] Thomas Wright, ed., *The Latin Poems Commonly Attributed to Walter Mapes* (London: Camden Society, 1841), pp. 1–20, and comments by Yunck, *Lady Meed*, p. 120.

[78] Yunck, *Lady Meed*, pp. 301–303; G. R. Owst, *Literature and Pulpit*, p. 215.

the social, economic, and demographic setting was changing in ways that can only have created anxieties for men and women at a variety of social levels. Coinciding with the flowering of vernacular literature, such conditions provided the perfect medium for a literature of satire and complaint. Chaucer's contemporaries may not have shared our modern sense of freedom of sexual expression, but their sense of the injustices practiced by major institutions ordering daily life may have been more fresh and more keenly felt than our own. To some extent any agency of governance working vigorously and efficiently at the local level would attract lightning bolts of criticism; if the agency were thought not only to be vigorously efficient but also to be open to great abuse and to operate on a double standard, the lightning bolts would come in a fierce storm of criticism.

To view the criticism of archdeacons and rural deans with seriousness is not to insist that everyone associated with their courts behaved like a character from *The Friar's Tale* every day of the week. The abuses were not imaginary, however; in fact they seem to have touched nerves in enough of Chaucer's contemporaries to make the satire very effective. If the satire of the tale were not deeply rooted in reality, the worries, criticisms, and correctives put forward by kings and parliaments, popes, synods, councils, bishops, preachers, and poets were oddly off the mark. Of course, Chaucer was writing a satire rather than a reform tract. But in the humor of *The Friar's Tale* one can readily catch outbursts of the "fierce mocking laughter" which G. R. Owst proclaimed a characteristic of the literature of satire and complaint.[79] In the tale links between Chaucer the court poet and this literature of satire and complaint may be closer than we have imagined.

Earlier in the twentieth century scholars who examined any of the evidence on local correctional jurisdiction seem to have found it vaguely embarrassing; they thought the cases involving sexual misconduct were better left in the original Latin when translating records of mixed jurisdictional business;[80] they were, moreover, willing to cast aside the substance of these cases with contempt. As one writer suggested in 1929, "Nine-tenths of the cases with which these courts deal concern rustic amours and their consequences, which would be imprudent even on the part of a

---

[79] Owst, *Literature and Pulpit*, p. 215.

[80] See, for example, C. Eveleigh Woodrull, "Some Early Visitation Rolls Preserved at Canterbury," *Archaeologia Cantiana* 32(1917):143–80; 33(1918):71–90.

genealogist to investigate too closely."[81] A reading of *The Friar's Tale* in historical context suggests, to the contrary, that we must carefully study the structure and workings of ecclesiastical correction at the local level if we are to understand the Church as a force in everyday life and in great literature.

III

The surviving evidence, then, clearly indicates that Chaucer's audience would have possessed specific notions about how archdeacons and their summoners operated and shows that these expectations were not based solely on personalities or special cases. Response to the tale depended on these social and institutional realities; Chaucer has consequently shaped his story so that it vividly reflects this context. The plot turns on the identity established between the Summoner and the devil, but the Friar goes beyond mere equation to assert that such agents of the correctional courts are indeed worse than the devil. The Summoner gives himself over to the devil not because he is too stupid to escape the devil's snare but because he is too twisted and cynical, too professional, to recognize evil when he sees it.[82]

The Friar initiates his attack by appealing to his audience's sense that "summoner" is a generic equivalent for unspeakable evil (lines 1280–81):

> "Pardee, ye may wel knowe by the name
> That of a somonour may no good be sayd."

A summoner embodies the absence of good, and by the invocation of the name the Friar justifies to his listeners the vitriol that must follow. He

---

[81] G. Baskerville, *EHR* 44(1929):4 n. 1. E. R. Brinkworth described this view as still a very common misconception in 1942: "The Study and Use of Archdeacons' Court Records: Illustrated from the Oxford Records (1566–1759)," *Transactions of the Royal Historical Society*, 4th ser., 25(1943):94.

[82] Most critics have assumed that the Friar's insults are aimed chiefly at the Summoner's intelligence and so have overlooked what is clearly a satire on the fiendish professional cynicism of summoners; see, for example, Paul Beichner, "Baiting the Summoner," *MLQ* 22(1961):367–76; H. L. Hennedy, "The Friar's Summoner's Dilemma," *ChauR* 5(1971): 213–17; R. T. Lenaghan, "The Irony of the Friar's Tale," *ChauR* 7(1973):281–94; and N. R. Havely, ed., *The Friar's, Summoner's and Pardoner's Tales* (New York: Holmes & Meier, 1975), p. 14.

drives home the uniquely rich connotations of his rival's title in the famous lines that encapsulate a summoner's status (lines 1353–54):

> He was, if I shal yeven hum his laude,
> A theef, and eek a somnour, and a baude.

The Friar's point in resorting to "eek a somnour" is that he can offer no stronger denunciation of the official than to call him by his proper name; the lesser epithets surrounding "somnour" fail to measure up to this ultimate obscenity. The Friar exploits the summoner's reputation among his fellow Christians a final time when he has the official himself repudiate his title (lines 1393–94):

> He dorste nat, for verray filthe and shame,
> Seye that he was a somonour, for the name.

The Summoner of the tale thus finds his name too dirty to utter in polite society; the Friar has, in effect, set up a demonic parody of the sacred name that must not be spoken. The officer of the archdeacon's court travels in his own society as a sort of awesome incarnation of evil.

The Friar further adduces the Summoner's depravity by allying him with the devil in a variety of ways. This equation, which Chaucer introduced into his story, originated at least as early as the twelfth century in complaints that caustically refer to archdeacons as archdevils.[83] In the tale the devil is presented in one of his traditional guises: the man "fer in the north," dressed in hunter's green, on the prowl for souls. The Summoner is

---

[83] See D. W. Robertson, Jr., "Why the Devil Wears Green," *MLN* 69(1954):470–72; J. L. Baird, "The Devil in Green," *NM* 69(1968):575–78. Also relevant are P. Aiken, "Vincent of Beuvais and the Green Yeoman's Lecture on Demonology," *SP* 35(1938):1–9; Sister Mary Immaculate, "Fiends as 'Servant unto Man' in the *Friar's Tale*," *PQ* 21(1942):240–44. The identification of archdeacons and their officials with demons occurs in complaints and seems traditional. Giraldus Cambrensis says that when people hear about archdeacons they think of the devil: "Nowadays this office is so given over to extortion, beyond all others, that the name of archdeacon, as if it were archdevil, rings with horror in the ears of those who hear it. The one, after all, is a predator of souls, and the other of money." *Gemma ecclesiastica* 2.33, *Opera*, vol. 2, ed. J. S. Brewer, R.S. 21.2 (London, 1862), p. 325. Thomas Becket makes the same sarcastic equation in two letters of 1169, in which he censures an "archidiaconus" as "archidiabolus"; see J. C. Robertson and J. B. Sheppard, eds., *Materials for the History of Thomas Becket*, R.S. 67.7 (London, 1885), pp. 20, 59.

also a hunter, but a predator more ruthless and vicious than his companion, one who does indeed go hunting where the ducks are. The Summoner keeps his "bawdes," his circle of informants, "redy to his hond, / As any hauk to lure in Engelond" (lines 1339–40). Such imagery consistently represents the Summoner as a scavenger who instinctively preys upon the infirm in society and exploits the shortcomings of its members (lines 1369–72):

> For in this world nys dogge for the bowe
> That kan an hurt deer from an hool yknowe
> Bet than this somnour knew a sly lecchour,
> Or an avowtier, or a paramour.

He performs his task of spiritual correction "evere waityng on his pray" (line 1376), always alert to the chance of catching a victim unawares.[84]

The Summoner in the tale is additionally bound to the devil through the recurrent imagery of brotherhood.[85] In their initial exchange the devil immediately perceives the identity that exists between himself and the Summoner—this despite the Summoner's reluctance to acknowledge his "name": "deere broother, / Thou art a bailly, and I am another" (lines 1395–96). The Friar iterates the title "brother" seventeen times within the tale and in this way succeeds in establishing an equation between the moral nature of summoners and devils and a conviction of their alliance in the pursuit of Christian souls. The theme of brotherhood also introduces a number of ironic contrasts. There are traces of condescension and sarcasm in the use of the title by both principals, as when the Summoner proposes to teach the devil how to go about the business of fleecing souls more efficiently (lines 1572–80):

> This somonour to his brother gan to rowne:
> "Brother, . . .
>
> . . . .
>
> But for thou kanst nat, as in this contree,
> Wynne thy cost, taak heer ensample of me."

---

[84] Janette Richardson, "Hunter and Prey: Functional Imagery in the *Friar's Tale*," *EM* 12(1961):9–20, offers an extended analysis of the hunting imagery in the tale.

[85] See A. Friman, "Of Bretherhede: The Friendship Motif in Chaucer," *Innisfree* 3(1976):24–36; M. Keen, "Brotherhood in Arms," *History* 47(1962):1–17.

There is further irony in that, although they are at one in their quest for the destruction of souls, the Summoner's depredations actually render him prey to the devil.

The ultimate irony of the identity between Summoner and devil, however, is the Friar's emphatic presentation of the Summoner as one who outstrips the devil in his evil.[86] Indeed, the more-than-demonic nature of summoners is the key to the Friar's satire, and he conveys this by offering a virtual dissertation on the devil and all his works and ways. In the Friar's portrayal the tempter appears scrupulously honest and straightforward; the irony in his oaths "by my trouthe" (line 1424) and "by my fey" (line 1535) is that he indeed always does tell "a feithful tale." Although he is a hunter, his methods show that there is honor among fiends. Whereas the Summoner strives only "to wynne good, thou rekkest nevere how," the devil observes the "entente" (line 1556) of his victims in all cases; in the incident with the carter the demon upholds the spirit of the law, just as the Summoner in his materialism and misuse of institutional power always follows the letter. The devil's behavior is, at least by comparison, sporting: he does not practice gratuitous cruelty against innocent victims, but instead he suits his methods to his prey, relying upon the inbred viciousness of the Summoner, who falls victim to his own trap. In all that he does, the demon acknowledges his own subservience to God and the existence of a principle of good in the world; since "we been Goddes instrumentz" (line 1483), he sees that out of evil may come good. The Summoner, by his nature, could never grasp principles grander or more abstract than his own motive for profit. While the actions of the tempter may, in certain cases, stand as "a cause of his savacioun" (line 1498), the audience recognizes that summoners, like archdeacons, will never achieve heaven. The devil recognizes this as well and so chooses to be perfectly straightforward with his brother.

---

[86] The way in which Chaucer has adapted the traditional story to suit the special case of summoners is clarified by a reading of the analogues; see Owst, *Literature and Pulpit*, pp. 162–63, 169; Peter Nicolson, "The Analogues of Chaucer's *Friar's Tale*," *ELN* 17(1979): 93–98; "The Rypon Analogue of the *Friar's Tale*," *Chaucer Newsletter* 3, no. 1 (1981):1–2. That a medieval writer might consider church officials as worse than the devil in their evil doings is clearly the case from John Bromyard's remark in the *Summa predicantium* that some officials to whose care souls are entrusted for protection do more terrible destruction to them than the demons themselves. See Owst, *Literature and Pulpit*, p. 257.

The Friar has, then, set the background through his use of themes and images, and through his creation of a foil for the Summoner in the devil. He allows the Summoner himself, however, to occupy center stage in the tale and to demonstrate his depravity through a typical performance. The enthusiastic reception he accords his fellow "bailly" stems not from camaraderie but from the prospect of using his brother to refine his techniques for "extorcions." He hopes to learn "som subtiltee," "how do ye," advanced techniques that will further his adeptness "in myn office how that I may moost wynne" (line 1421). The Summoner's interest is above all in a value-free efficiency, for he feels no regard for social or moral disapproval (lines 1422, 1438, 1441):

> And spareth nat for conscience ne synne. . . .

> No maner conscience of that have I. . . .

> Stomak ne conscience ne knowe I noon.

In his zeal for trade secrets the Summoner puts himself entirely beyond the bounds of common morality.

The demon acknowledges the Summoner's status as a moral outlaw when he begins "a litel for to smyle" and then guilelessly reveals his own purpose and methods: " 'Brother,' quod he, 'wiltow that I thee tell?' " (line 1447). The devil in effect asks here not only "Do you really wish me to tell?" but also "And will you accept what I tell you?" In this preliminary remark he anticipates the Summoner's absolute failure of belief, his incapacity to see anything except through the filter of his own corrupt nature. The Summoner's response confirms the demon's insight (lines 1456–58):

> "A!" quod this somonour, "*benedicite!* what sey ye?
> I wende ye were a yeman trewely.
> Ye han a mannes shap as wel as I."

The conventional, unmeaning "*benedicite!*" signals the Summoner's cynicism: he sees all creatures as exactly like himself and assumes, therefore, that this demonic claim can be no more than an elaborate cover to mask his fellow extortioner's secrets or his incompetence. The Summoner's subsequent questions reinforce his cynicism: Do you have an essential shape? Why not always assume a single appearance? If you are the devil, why do you work so hard? Do you create new bodies for your apparitions? These questions do not represent an interest in demonology; they are rather the Summoner's Faustian attempt to test the devil, to taunt and trip up his yeoman-companion and expose him, as one trickster to another, for a sham.[87]

The Summoner's attentiveness to the elusive shape of the devil is ironic, for he cannot see the truth even as it confronts him. The devil makes this plain (lines 1467–68):

> "A lowsy jogelour kan deceyve thee,
> And pardee, yet kan I moore craft than he."

It is hard not to understand the devil's mention of the "lowsy jogelour" as an indirect allusion to the Summoner's tricks in corrupting his office, although he also clearly suggests that it takes no great trickster to fool a man who is already so self-deceived and self-incriminated. Even when presented with the facts of good and evil by the devil himself, a summoner is incapable of a right choice. The devil finally seems to find the Summoner's probing tiresome, for at one point he says to him (lines 1480–81):

> "For, brother myn, thy wit is al to bare
> To understonde, althogh I tolde hem thee."

The devil refers here not to the stupidity of summoners but to the way in which their inveterate evil strips them of all moral sensibility. The Summoner does himself in not through lack of intelligence but through habitual and abject cynicism.

The demon certifies the Summoner's status as a lost soul in his prediction (lines 1513–16):

> "But o thyng warne I thee, I wol nat jape, —
> Thou wolt algates wite how we been shape;

---

[87] On this episode see Aiken (note 83 above); J. L. Baird, "The Devil's *Privitee*," *NM* 70(1969):104–106.

> Thou shalt herafterward, my brother deere,
> Come there thee nedeth nat of me to leere."

The fate of summoners is sealed by their professional activities, though the devil, like his successor Mephistopheles, still allows a loophole, should "it be so that thou forsake me" (line 1522). But the Summoner, true to his kind, immediately vows that he will never abandon evil, even "though thou were the devel Sathanas" (line 1526). His conventional oath once again reveals that the Summoner does not for a minute believe in the devil or, by extension, any systematic relation of good and evil. The flinty hardness of the Summoner's moral nature emerges further in his continual testing of the yeoman-devil's identity. He immediately seizes upon the incident with the carter as a means of proving his companion a fool: "This somonour seyde, 'Heere shal we have a pley'" (line 1548). He evidently speaks these lines to himself, for it is only afterwards that he draws near the devil and whispers to him; the "pley" he expects is to see his companion fail to live up to his claimed identity, for the Summoner still cannot believe in any evil larger than himself. His elaborate injunction is, consequently, deeply sarcastic (lines 1551–54):

> "Herkne, my brother, herkne by thy feith!
> Herestow nat how that the cartere seith?
> Hent it anon, for he hath yeve it thee,
> Bothe hey and cart, and eek his caples thre."

The Summoner's remarks are a clear gibe: "I believe he's speaking to you! Why don't you do as he asks?" One imagines that the Summoner finds the devil's solemn moral explanation unconvincing and peculiarly unsatisfying — the stupid yeoman refuses to give up the joke and admit his inferiority. He cannot imagine that the devil should be more scrupulous than a summoner.

The Summoner follows this incident with his attempt to give the yeoman-devil a forceful lesson in roguery. Again, his comments drip with sarcasm (lines 1579–80):

> "But for thou kanst nat, as in this contree,
> Wynne thy cost, taak heer ensample of me."

The irony of a summoner offering himself as an exemplum to the devil was certainly not lost on Chaucer's audience. The Summoner dedicates his entire effort here to showing how a proper extortion is carried off, in contrast to the demon's failure to capture the cart. His smugness in dueling with the devil and his conviction of his superiority in this contest of evil do indeed make a summoner seem much worse than a fiend. His callous dealing with the old "rebekke" firmly reinforces this, and his casual oath— " 'Nay thanne,' quod he, 'the foule feend me fecche / If I th'excuse, though thou shul be spilt' " (lines 1610–11)—demonstrates his total remoteness from the sanction of conscience. The perfect depravity of a summoner is evinced in his willing admission that he is incapable of repentance (lines 1630–32):

> "Nay, olde stot, that is nat my entente,"
> Quod this somonour, "for to repente me
> For any thyng that I have had of thee."

It is this full declaration of his vile "entente," together with the widow's "wyl in ernest," that allows the devil to proclaim (lines 1635–36):

> "Thy body and this panne been myne by right.
> Thou shalt with me to helle yet to-nyght."[88]

The last line, a parody of Jesus' words to the Good Thief, is the Friar's final attempt to portray the Summoner as the inversion of all that is good: he is taken to hell "body and soule" presumably because such complete corruption cannot remain in human society.

The success of the satire in *The Friar's Tale* rests partly upon the outrageousness of this individual portrait and partly upon the audience's common knowledge that summoners routinely engaged in such excesses and extortions. As the Friar half-suggests at the outset, the impact of the story makes use of the stock responses of the listeners, and these responses in turn originate in the experience of members of a society who had to accept abuses of this sort on a regular basis. The vehemence of feeling that animates the tale is not merely a triumph of dramatic art; it is also the

---

[88] On this episode see T. G. Hahn, "The Devil and His Pan," forthcoming in *NM*.

verbal equivalent of the physical violence against summoners that the surviving documents record so graphically. The Friar's purpose is to show that summoners, in their professional blackmail and harlotry, go beyond simple brutality and acquisitiveness to a pitch of depravity that even the devil would not care to emulate. This literary view of summoners, which was not just tolerated but relished by Chaucer's audience, does not stem from the behavior or sins of one official; rather, it is a social response to summoners as representatives of an institution that exercised enormous power over the daily lives of fourteenth-century Christians. Our estimate of the satirical effect of *The Friar's Tale* must depend largely on our acquiring for ourselves what Chaucer and his audience knew at first hand.

IV

A dialogue between history and literary criticism thus seems useful for readers of *The Friar's Tale* from either discipline. For his part the historian must recognize that the institutional realities he can painstakingly recon- struct from the fragmentary documentary record may not reveal contempo- rary perceptions and reactions to the functioning of the institution. How a set of courts operated does not necessarily reveal how men and women regarded it.[89] Lacking the kinds of materials so useful for public opinion in later eras (newspapers, pamphlets, diaries, a wealth of personal correspon- dence), the historian of the fourteenth century can best enrich his sense of popular attitudes by a close and informed reading of the vernacular literature that has survived in significant volume. Chaucer's *Friar's Tale* offers invaluable insights into widespread reaction to one important set of historical realities by its portrayal of the local correctional courts of the church and its powerful comparison of Summoner and devil. Archdeacons'

[89] J. C. Holt provides a fascinating discussion (with full references) of the evaluation of the rule of King John as it can be reconstructed from chronicles and record evidence in *King John* (London: London Historical Association, 1963). For the problems of record evidence and late- medieval opinion on the state of public order, see R. W. Kaeuper, "Law and Order in Fourteenth-Century England: the Evidence of Special Commissions of Oyer and Terminer," *Speculum* 54(1979): 734-37. Of course, scholars must also recognize the bounds that historical context sets for the understanding of texts. John Benton provides an excellent case in point by pointing out the distortion of reality that may occur in too literal a reading of the literature of courtly love in "Clio and Venus" (see note 2 above).

courts had been in place for more than two centuries when *The Friar's Tale* was written; the historian can feel a much greater measure of confidence in judging popular reaction to these courts when the vernacular literature of the fourteenth century is added to his evidence.

In addition, such an approach gives the literary critic grounds for interpretation beyond the alternatives of personal or institutional satire, of Summoner as particular individual or suprapersonal emblem of human frailties unfortunately general in incidence. The Summoner in the tale is certainly more than any particular summoner; yet how much less interesting he would be and how much the point of the tale would be reduced if he were something other than a summoner, that especially slippery cog in the well-oiled machinery of local spiritual correction. The Summoner in the tale can scarcely have appeared to Chaucer's contemporaries (and cannot be taken by modern scholars) as a representative summoner; fourteenth-century men and women knew summoners as in many cases imperfect or vicious officials making a profit out of the imperfections and vices of ordinary Christians, not as figures of evil surpassing even the Prince of Evil. Yet the surviving evidence on the practices of local correction, and especially the embracing of a double standard by officials of the courts, shows the reasons for a depth of resentment which could make Chaucer's satire in the tale so devilishly effective.

Satire, in its amplitude and vagueness, comprehends a great number of elements and motives — ritual, personal, professional, social, moral, and so on. We cannot decide whether in the tale Chaucer intends a "criticism . . . of his contemporaries, who were departing in one way or another from ideals that he revered"[90] unless we reassemble, insofar as possible, the discernible historical particulars that lie behind the tale. The realities of courts, officials, and procedures suggest why Chaucer chose this specific character to exemplify these specific sins, and, indeed, they may help us reevaluate the ideals cherished (and satirized) by members of this society.

Contextual evidence on *The Friar's Tale* suggests that historical criticism of medieval literature cannot overlook the social realities in which a text originates. D. W. Robertson, in a widely known essay, has stated that "Historical Criticism [is] . . . that kind of literary analysis which seeks to

---

[90] D. W. Robertson, Jr., *Essays on Medieval Culture* (Princeton, N.J.: Princeton University Press, 1980), p. xix.

reconstruct the intellectual attitudes and the cultural ideals of a period in order to reach a fuller understanding of its literature."[91] Admirable (and seldom achieved) as this objective may be, it neglects the crucial point that attitudes and ideals must be assayed by comparison with actual experience in order to obtain a full and accurate understanding of a culture or a literary text. We can hardly pass judgment on the nature or effectiveness of the satire in *The Friar's Tale* if we think of literary context as entirely literary or even entirely intellectual. Recourse to documentary evidence offers readings that take us beyond complete reliance on intellectual traditions, limited as these are by the prescriptive elements inherent in aesthetic or theological writings. Although the analysis of literary intention or effect never ends in certainty, we can proceed with more confidence if we know not merely how the leading thinkers in a period say things ought to work but how they actually worked as well.

[91] Ibid., p. 3.

The Audience Illuminated, or New Light Shed on the Dream Frame of Lydgate's *Temple of Glas*

Judith M. Davidoff
University of Miami

DESPITE JOHN LYDGATE'S longstanding reputation for verbosity, the dream frame of his *Temple of Glas* is a model of compression. Beginnings were reputedly a "special problem" for him,[1] yet he provided his vision with a rhetorically restrained fourteen-line opening that not only foreshadowed the theme of the vision but also set in motion a process whereby the audience was taught how to respond to the rest of the poem.

The importance of the frame in the *Temple of Glas* has been overlooked for several reasons, but most of all because of a generally inadequate understanding of the role the dream frame plays in any Middle English dream vision. As a result modern commentators have misconstrued the dreamer's passive role as onlooker in this vision, concluding that the entire poem is seriously flawed owing to the lack of overt thematic connection between dreamer and dream.[2] One purpose of this article is to consider the *Temple of Glas* in terms of its structure; this approach will show that there is indeed a close link between frame and vision, between dreamer and dreamed.

---

[1] With specific regard to opening lines, Derek Pearsall writes that "beginnings are Lydgate's special problem; there are so many possible things to say, the furniture of his mind is so cluttered before the removal has begun, that neither he nor the reader can force any interest, or indeed any sense out of the material." Derek Pearsall, *John Lydgate* (Charlottesville: University Press of Virginia, 1970), p. 11.

[2] John Norton-Smith, ed., *John Lydgate: Poems*, Clarendon Mediaeval and Tudor Series (Oxford: Clarendon Press, 1966), p. 179; Pearsall, *John Lydgate*, p. 106; A. C. Spearing, *Medieval Dream-Poetry* (Cambridge: Cambridge University Press, 1976), p. 174. But see a persuasive overview of the dream-vision convention in Constance Hieatt, "*Un Autre Fourme*: Guillaume de Machaut and the Dream Vision Form," *ChauR* 14(1979):97–115. Although Hieatt does not discuss Lydgate, she points out that by convention "the dreamer is basically an observer rather than a participant" (p. 100).

What follows, however, is not simply a new "reading." It is an attempt to use an examination of the *Temple of Glas* to demonstrate both the usefulness and the necessity of trying to re-create (to the extent possible) late-medieval expectations about literary works. I will argue here that scholarly reconstructions of conventional but *unstated* late-medieval assumptions about literature can enrich — and make more accurate — our historical understanding especially of the relationships between the *artes poeticae* and late-medieval practice. In the case of the *Temple of Glas* we will come to see that, whereas the generally agreed upon theme of suffering is indeed present in the vision,[3] particular characteristics of the frame extend meaning considerably beyond this most conventional motif. Using recreated late-medieval expectations as a guide, I will show that the *Temple of Glas* is a poem primarily about "light" and that Lydgate used his dream frame for two ends: first, to raise the issue of how a poet can use poetic language to shed light on his own darkness and, second, to teach his audience how to "read" his poem and by extension to apply the light/darkness theme to themselves.

My observation that light/dark imagery is prominent in the work is not an original one; critics generally follow the lead of John Norton-Smith, the most recent editor of the *Temple*, who describes the suffering of the lovers in the vision in terms of the Boethian doctrine of contraries, the dominant ones being "night/day, darkness/light, and pain/pleasure."[4] I differ with previous commentators in that I view these three sets of contrasts as one complex semantic opposition between "light" and the lack of it. In this regard there is persuasive evidence that the *dream frame* establishes the range of this polysemous opposition and thus plays a central role in guiding the members of the audience through the poem, in teaching them how to think about "light." Whereas the vision itself is suffused with brightness, readers and listeners encounter a frame shrouded in darkness. This contrast is an inversion that literally runs counter to medieval rhetorical dicta that an opening should illuminate a poem. The inversion calls attention to the

---

[3] Norton-Smith, ed., *John Lydgate*, p. 178; Alain Renoir, *The Poetry of John Lydgate* (Cambridge, Mass.: Harvard University Press, 1967), pp. 93–94; Pearsall, *John Lydgate*, p. 109; Alice Miskimin, "Patterns in *The Kingis Quair* and the *Temple of Glas*," *PLL* 13(1977):356.

[4] Norton-Smith, ed., *John Lydgate*, p. 178; all citations and quotations of the *Temple of Glas* are from this edition.

frame, thereby alerting the audience to the dreamer's true problem—his "darkness." This initial insight about the dreamer's "darkness" interacted with audience expectations about the structure of a typical dream vision. As a result late-medieval listeners and readers did perceive a clear connection between the dreamer and his vision, and this led them to look past the conventional amorous situation to the real theme about a poet's power to use the "light-giving" properties of language to temper misery and to promote constructive action.

As a first step toward understanding the special role the frame plays in Lydgate's dream vision, it is necessary to consider how frames generally function in the dream-vision convention. Some of the recent work by critical theorists calls our attention to the way all audiences make sense of unfamiliar literary works. It has been widely demonstrated that a listener-reader always brings certain presuppositions to a text and that these inevitably condition the way that text is understood.

The nature of an audience's contribution to its own understanding has been characterized in various ways. Sheldon Sacks casts it in psychological terms as "intuitive formal knowledge the author or reader must in some manner possess to create or interpret literary works."[5] Walter J. Ong uses the now popular metaphor of the game all readers must master:

Readers over the ages have had to learn this game of literacy, . . . and they have to adjust when the rules change, even though no rules thus far have ever been published and even though the changes in the unpublished rules are themselves for the most part only implied.[6]

Jonathan Culler stresses the intertextual nature of the audience's literary presuppositions: because readers possess "the track or the furrow left by the experience of texts of all kinds,"[7] each new text takes on meaning from the

[5] Sheldon Sacks, "The Psychological Implications of Generic Distinctions," *Genre* 1(1968):113.

[6] Walter J. Ong, "The Writer's Audience Is Always a Fiction," *PMLA* 90(1975):12. Among theorists who are also medievalists, Hans Robert Jauss writes of an "ongoing game with known rules and still unknown surprises" in "The Alterity and Modernity of Medieval Literature," *NLH* 10(1979):189.

[7] Jonathan Culler, *Structuralist Poetics: Structuralism, Linguistics, and the Study of Literature* (Ithaca, N.Y.: Cornell University Press, 1975), p. 140; see also Culler's "Presupposition and Intertextuality," *MLN* 91(1976):1380–96. Jauss's theory also involves intertextuality.

whole tradition in which it was written. For Wolfgang Iser the reader is implied in the text, responding in a phenomenological process of interruptions:

> We look forward, we look back, we decide, we change our decisions, we form expectations, we are shocked by their nonfulfilment, we question, we muse, we accept, we reject. . . . This process is steered by two main structural components within the text: first, a repertoire of familiar literary patterns and recurrent literary themes. . . . second, techniques or strategies used to set the familiar against the unfamiliar.[8]

But whatever the theoretical stance, these critics would all agree that every audience comes to a literary work equipped in some way with a set of intuitions developed from prior experience with similar works. Although not necessarily conscious of them, the listener-reader uses these intuitions about form, structure, style, diction, and the like, first to categorize the text in some way (i.e., assign it tentatively to a genre or convention) and then, as the work progresses, to test new details to see whether or not the original decision about category was correct and, if so, whether or not the details fit prior expectations about what is appropriate and / or necessary for that particular genre or convention. The question is, then, What were a *late-medieval* audience's literary expectations like?[9]

The traditional dream-frame opening was clearly one of the recognizable Middle English conventional practices whose characteristics were "evidently well understood" even though they were never actually formulated by medieval poets or rhetoricians.[10] Accordingly, we must assume that a contemporary audience brought to each reading of a dream vision certain expectations developed from prior exposure to literary visions.

---

[8] Wolfgang Iser, "The Reading Process: A Phenomenological Approach," *NLH* 3(1972):293.

[9] Because of limited application of modern literary theories to Middle English literature, my abbreviated discussion perforce cites those who work primarily with modern literature. Work by Zumthor and others on medieval French poetics is reviewed by Stephen G. Nichols, Jr., "A Poetics of Historicism? Recent Trends in Medieval Literary Study," *M&H*, n.s. 8(1977):77–101. See also *NLH* 10, no. 2 (1979), an issue entitled "Medieval Literature and Contemporary Theory."

[10] George Kane, *The Autobiographical Fallacy in Chaucer and Langland Studies*, Chambers Memorial Lecture, University College, London (London: n.p., 1965), p. 11.

Their expectations may have been part conscious, part unconscious. The degree of literary "awareness" is obviously impossible to gauge; but just as "Once upon a time" triggers predictable expectations in a modern audience, a conventional dream frame must have affected a late-medieval audience in predictable ways. Because dream-frame characteristics were apparently never stated in formal terms in the Middle Ages, however, modern readers must extrapolate them from extant literature by examining as many dream visions as possible and inferring from them what characteristics are "necessary to account for what happens" in the works. [11] In other words, if we are to appreciate fully the way Lydgate manipulated dream-vision conventions, we must reconstruct the late-medieval presuppositions about them. This will provide an informed context within which the dream frame of the *Temple of Glas* can be assessed.

First, an obvious point: the audience recognized that a poem belonged to the dream-vision convention whenever the opening section provided details that listeners and readers had come to associate with dream frames. [12] Typically the poet's persona used his opening remarks to indicate the season, the time of day, his location, his psychological state, and his solitude. This said, he swooned in a "sweven" that brought the vision world to life. But these details did more than enable the audience to assign the poem to the vision convention: they also triggered larger expectations about theme. My examination of more than forty Middle English dream visions indicates that casting a poem as a vision within a frame had several consequences. One prominent consequence had to do with the audience's perception of the relationship between the dreamer and his dream. The presence of a dream frame itself acted as a signal that the dreamer was in a state of *need*; this led the audience to expect that need to be *fulfilled* in the vision.

This need-to-fulfillment pattern can be found in all extant Middle English visions no matter how simple or sophisticated and no matter what the dreams were about. If the vision was an amorous one, however, the audience had certain other specific expectations as well. The listener-reader would expect the frame to consist of a spring setting wherein the dreamer,

[11] Culler, "Presupposition and Intertextuality," p. 1394.

[12] Hieatt (*"Un Autre Fourme"*) characterizes the dream vision form accurately, though her concern is not at all with audience expectations or responses.

instead of prospering in the natural season for love, suffered long and painfully as an unfulfilled lover. Almost always insomnia was a major symptom; on a superficial level the sleep that brought on the dream fulfilled the dreamer's most pressing need. But on a more substantive plane the audience expected that from each dreamer's particular misery would spring a vision centered on his amorous difficulties; in other words, to be a proper member of the convention, his vision would have to explore how he might cope with his pain and/or attain his beloved.

The need-to-fulfillment pattern flourished long before Lydgate and continued after him. Chaucer's dreamer in *The Book of the Duchess* is one such example. As the poem opens, although he confesses to having suffered from a "sicknesse" for eight years, the "boote is never the ner." After this he has a vision that probes how one responds to the loss of love. The dreamer in *Pearl* similarly grieves "fordolked of luf-daungere." Then in his dream he is reunited with his beloved Pearl for a while and awakens comforted. In a less often discussed poem like Clanvowe's *Cuckoo and the Nightingale*, the dreamer has been so lovesick during the whole month of May that he has slept "but a lyte." When he falls asleep, it is a debate about love that he witnesses. Abundant examples like these occur in both the major and the obscure writings of the period.[13]

How does Lydgate's frame for the *Temple of Glas* fit this pattern? For that we must turn to the opening lines (1–14):

> For thouȝt, constreint and greuous heuines,
> For pensifhede, and for heiȝ distres,
> To bed I went nov þis oþir nyȝt
> Whan þat Lucina wiþ hir pale liȝt
> Was ioyned last wiþ Phebus in Aquarie,
> Amyd Decembre, when of Ianuarie

---

[13] Virtually all dream visions have the need-to-fulfillment pattern. In love visions the needs are amorous ones. The *Kingis Quair* and the *Assembly of Ladies* are two more examples that show that the tradition persisted well beyond the time when Lydgate wrote the *Temple*. One finds the movement from need to fulfillment in non-amorous dream visions as well. In the *Parlement of the Thre Ages*, for example, the poacher-dreamer fears being caught and losing his life. He dreams of meeting death. *Winner and Waster*'s dreamer is concerned about his place in court and how social conditions are changing; his dream is political. *Death and Liffe*'s dreamer seems to question his own mortality. He has a vision on the subject.

> Ther be kalendes of þe nwe yere,
> And derk Diane, ihorned, noþing clere,
> Had hir bemys vndir a mysty cloude:
> Wiþin my bed for sore I gan me shroude,
> Al desolate for constreint of my wo,
> The long[e] nyȝt waloing to and fro,
> Til at[te] last, er I gan taken kepe,
> Me did oppresse a sodein dedeli slepe.

This opening frame clearly provides all the details that conventionally preface a Middle English love vision: the poet's persona indicates the season, the time of day, his location, his apparently love-induced sleeplessness and misery, and his solitude. This said, he falls directly asleep and the vision commences in the next line.

Two things are unusual in this dream frame: the brevity and the imagery. First, in a 1,402-line poem the audience would have anticipated a long frame whose conventional details were developed by amplification, digression, and other rhetorical colors.[14] Instead there are only fourteen lines. And not only is this dream frame unusually terse, but it is also remarkable for its lack of "light." To an audience accustomed to bright spring mornings for love visions, the December setting would immediately suggest a dark, sober theme and perhaps a sad outcome.[15] Moreover, the frame does not simply lack light, it lacks it in several senses. Most obvious is the "visual" darkness. There is no suggestion at all that dawn might be approaching; so even though the moon has potential to shed "hir pale liȝt," on this particular night misty clouds obscure the faintest illu-

---

[14] For example, Chaucer's *Book of the Duchess* (1,334 lines) has a 290-line frame; his *Parliament of Fowls* (699 lines), a 94-line frame; *Pearl* (1,212 lines), a 60-line frame; *The Parlement of the Thre Ages* (665 lines), a 103-line frame; *The Assembly of Ladies* (756 lines), a 77-line frame; Dunbar's *Goldyn Targe* (279 lines), a 49-line frame.

[15] Derek Pearsall makes note of the *Temple's* "unconventional but weirdly effective December-opening" in "The English Chaucerians," in D. S. Brewer, ed., *Chaucer and Chaucerians: Critical Studies in Middle English Literature* (University: University of Alabama Press, 1966), p. 210. That setting, as Norton-Smith points out, reminds one of *The House of Fame* — also a variation of conventional detail; Norton-Smith, ed., *John Lydgate*, p. 177. It is of interest that Henryson, like Lydgate, developed this same correspondence between a winter setting and sorrow in *The Testament of Cresseid* ("Ane doolie sessoun to ane cairfull dyte / Suld correspond, and be equivalent" [lines 1-2]) and that in the same tradition Shakespeare has Mamillius say, "A sad tale's best for winter" (*A Winter's Tale* 2.1.25).

mination. The meteorological conditions here contrast sharply with those of the vision in which Venus, the morning star, will bring the brightness of day, dispelling "derk Diane" who here in the frame is "noþing clere." And with the coming of the day, the day/night contrast will doubtless take on additional meaning because Diana, goddess of chastity, and Venus, goddess of love, are in mythological as well as astronomical opposition.

The language of the dreamer's emotional state also reflects this "lightless" environment. Unilluminated by the light of love, he suffers "for thouȝt, constreint and greuous heuines, / For pensifhede, and for heiȝ distres" and is "al desolate for constreint of my wo."[16] Even his dream begins distressingly: "Me did oppresse a sodein dedeli slepe." Of the words used here, "constraint," "pressure," and "heaviness" contrast with free lightheartedness. "Heaviness" will in fact become a key term in the vision; it is a semantic opposite of "light(hearted)ness."

The dreamer's solitude is in a way also a consequence of the dark, for since he has not chosen to light a candle, it is too dark for him to use the distraction of reading to place himself among literary fellowship. Thus Lydgate's persona pointedly emphasizes his separation from a tradition that goes back at least as far as Deguilleville's *Pèlerinages* (part of which Lydgate translated some years later). But if perhaps the poet did not know Deguilleville's work at the time he composed the *Temple*, he was certainly familiar with the bookish lover made popular by Chaucer's vision poems. By choice, then, a dream frame too dimly lit for reading ensured the solitude of Lydgate's dreamer and at the same time suggested that he might be cut off in some way from poetic tradition. There are, then, several

---

[16] There is a long tradition of equating day/night with the joy/sorrow of love. In *Troilus and Criseyde*, which clearly served as a source not only of lines but also of ideas for the *Temple of Glas*, one finds as an example of the proverbial (and Boethian) doctrine of contraries Pandarus exclaiming, "And next the derke nyght the glade morwe; / And also joie is next the fyn of sorwe" (*TC* 1.951–52). In book 5, addressing the now empty house of Criseyde, Troilus laments: " 'O thow lanterne of which queynt is the light, / O paleys, whilom day, that now art nyght, / Wel oughtestow to falle, and I to dye, / Syn she is went that wont was us to gye!' (5.543–46)." In the *Canticus Troili*, Troilus begins: " 'O sterre, of which I lost have al the light, / With herte soor wel oughte I to biwaille, / That evere derk in torment, nyght by nyght, / Toward my deth with wynd in steere I saille' " (5.638–41). The same equation occurs in other Chaucer works and is common throughout medieval literature. All quotations of Chaucer's works are from F. N. Robinson, ed., *The Works of Geoffrey Chaucer*, 2d ed. (Boston: Houghton Mifflin, 1957).

ways in which this dream frame emphasizes an absence of light.

Before I turn my attention to the vision and to a discussion of how the frame influenced the way listeners-readers understood it, it would be well to address a potential objection to some of what I have said thus far. One might argue that mere happenstance is responsible for the presence in the frame of one pole of what I have called a polysemous contrast between light and the lack of it. After all, it would have been difficult for Lydgate's persona to talk of "night" and "sleep" in terms other than "dark" and "night." But the brevity of the passage speaks eloquently of poetic control, especially since Lydgate's mind has been repeatedly cited for its lack of selectivity.[17] It is easy to imagine embellishment or departure from the gloomy darkness of this dream frame. But Lydgate has not given us *amplificatio* and *digressio*. There is instead sustained focus on night, darkness, and oppressive heaviness. It is impressive that, even with this very "un-Lydgatian" compression, the poet has been able to follow the rhetorical dictum "multiplice forma / Dissimuletur idem; varis sis et tamen idem."[18] He has provided multiple ways to view the single contrast between light and its absence so that the audience could find in this *dream frame* a concentration of the various oppositions to light that cluster about the "dark" pole of that dichotomy.

How, then, do these images relate the dreamer to what he dreams about? Previous commentators considered the relationship between dreamer and dream obscure at best because they were unaware of the powerful control that a dream frame exerted over the direction of audience response. Thus, although the *Temple of Glas* is usually reckoned one of Lydgate's better poems, some critics have been highly critical of the dream frame and its persona. Norton-Smith levels the charge that the poet obscures the connection between his persona and the lover in the dream

---

[17] Spearing, for example, compares Lydgate's "unintelligent imitation of Chaucer" in the *Temple of Glas* to the activity of "a magpie . . . attracted by anything shiny" (*Medieval Dream-Poetry*, p. 173). Pearsall writes that "too often . . . [Lydgate] is driven by a daemon of inclusiveness. The appropriate stimulus undams a torrent of illustrations, examples, parallels and comparisons, as if some psychological congestion had to be removed before he could move on" ("The English Chaucerians," p. 211).

[18] Geoffroi de Vinsauf, *Poetria nova*, lines 224–25, in Edmond Faral, ed., *Les arts poétiques du XIIe et du XIIIe siècle: Recherches et documents sur la technique littéraire du moyen âge* (Paris, Edouard Champion, 1924), p. 204.

and has done so without "inventive subtlety."[19] Derek Pearsall believes that "Lydgate has not fully worked out his relationship to the *persona* of the poem" and that therefore "the whole frame-story could be dropped altogether. . . for all the difference it would make to the fundamental nature of the poem."[20] Along the same lines A. C. Spearing finds "no indication that the narrator's psychology influences the content of his dream."[21]

The reconstruction of conventional late-medieval expectations, however, shows that needs expressed in the frame were to be fulfilled in the vision; accordingly, any painful condition expressed in the frame implicitly belonged to the dreamer whether or not he consciously applied it to himself. Likewise, if any amelioration of that pain took place in the vision, it too implicitly applied to the dreamer even if he was not the explicit beneficiary within the plot of the vision. That is in the nature of dreams, literary or nonliterary, medieval or modern. Their contents are not strictly self-referential. What the dreamer dreams of is connected in some symbolic way to his own state before his dream.[22] There is no paradox in saying that Lydgate's dreamer did not have to dream about himself to dream about himself. Members of his audience knew of his need for light and of his inability to articulate his needs beyond that brief fourteen-line passage. They were prepared (consciously or not) to sift the contents of the vision to see how its events might improve the dreamer's condition. In short, even though what occurs in the vision is not overtly directed at him, the dreamer becomes a beneficiary by virtue of the conventional need-to-fulfillment pattern.

The vision barely has a plot. Like many French *dits amoreux*, it is composed of ballades and lyrics with just enough narrative connection to make everything cohere. What little plot there is, is formally constructed around three figures: a chaste wife, who complains to Venus that she loves another; a gentleman, who also complains to Venus that he is smitten with love; and Venus herself, who urges the two to declare their devotion to one

---

[19] Norton-Smith, ed., *John Lydgate*, p. 179.

[20] Derek Pearsall, *John Lydgate*, pp. 106, 109.

[21] Spearing, *Medieval Dream-Poetry*, p. 174.

[22] This is true whether the dream is oracular or caused by humors. In the former a force outside the dreamer brings him a vision appropriate to his needs; in the latter the vision springs directly from them.

another and wait patiently until fortune can unite them. The dreamer is simply an onlooker in his own dream. He hears the three principals, he watches the goddess bind the lovers in a glittering golden chain, and finally a ballade sung in her praise awakens him, and he decides to record his vision. In all this, light/dark images occur in nineteen passages distributed among the speeches made by the three principals and the narrative provided by the dreamer-onlooker.[23] It is the way these images are used, however, that reveals the dreamer's connection to the contents of his vision.

His enlightenment starts in the physical world. In the often-discussed passage that opens the vision,[24] the dreamer finds himself incapacitated by the brightness of the sun shining on a temple of glass (lines 24–29):

> ...the liʒt so in my face
> Bigan to smyte, so persing euer in one
> On euere part, where þat I gan gone,
> That I ne myʒt noþing, as I would,
> Abouten me considre and bihold
> The wondre hestres, the briʒtnes of þe sonne.

It seems clear that, after the darkness that had surrounded him before he fell asleep, neither perception nor understanding of "light" is possible for him. Not until the brightness is tempered by clouds can he look about (lines 30–34):

> ...at[te] last certein skyes donne,
> Wiþ wind ichaced, haue her cours iwent
> Tofore þe stremes of Titan and iblent,
> So þat I myʒt, wiþin and withoute,
> Whereso I walk, biholden me aboute.

These lines recall the pre-vision setting when "derk Diane... / Had hir

[23] Lines 24–34, 251–54, 262–64, 326–31, 373–74, 394–97, 400–401, 550–55, 609–13, 705, 715, 815, 838, 1175, 1208–11, 1215–16, 1285–87, 1341–43, 1355–61.

[24] Norton-Smith (*John Lydgate*, p. 177), Pearsall (*John Lydgate*, p. 106), and Spearing (*Medieval Dream-Poetry*, p. 173) all discuss lines 24–34 but do not connect the passage to the language of the opening frame.

bemys vndir a mysty cloude" (lines 8–9). There the darkness reflected utter misery, but in the dream world "light" and its opposite seem symbiotic: light does indeed dispel darkness, but too much of it causes pain. If, however, one moderates the other, both light and dark can be used to advantage. By implication, the dreamer's unlit surroundings and his unrestrained grief before he fell asleep were obstacles to perception and happiness in much the same way as the unrelieved brightness of the temple of glass hindered his eyesight in the dream world. Here at the beginning of the vision, then, the groundwork is laid to link the pain of the dream frame with ways that pain might be eased.

As the vision unfolds, use or withholding of the light-dark imagery directs the listener-reader's attention toward matters of thematic significance. For example, when the dreamer makes his way to Venus's temple and describes its interior and the lovers there, light does not play a part. But when he sees the beautiful lady, the imagery recurs. As with the wondrously bright temple exterior, the image of the lady's brightness adds to an implication that will grow as the vision develops, namely, that, as long as the dreamer remains bereft of light, he will be cut off from the beauty that is inextricably connected with light.

The lady, he tells us, outshines all just as the sun makes the stars seem dim or just as Lucifer has the power to "voide þe nyȝtes sorow" (line 253). (The dream, of course, is set in the daytime so the dreamer is really the only one who at that moment needs the night's sorrow voided, perhaps by her bright beauty.) In other words, the images associated with the lady contrast completely with the words the dreamer used to frame his vision. Furthermore, almost every time the light/dark imagery is applied to her—whether by the dreamer, by Venus, or by the gentleman smitten with love for her— she is characterized in terms of light and shining beauty; nothing about her is dark or oppressive.[25]

Similarly, as critics have not recognized, when the light/dark constellation of images is used to describe or address Venus, what is said seems at least as appropriate to the dreamer as to any of the principals in the vision. Note, for example, how the lady invokes Venus (lines 328–31):

---

[25] There is one exception: in lines 373–74 we learn that she feels some "heuynes" because of unrequited love. See note 27 below.

> "O blisful sterre, persant and ful of liȝt,
> Of bemys gladsome, devoider of derknes,
> Cheif recounford after þe blak nyȝt,
> To voide woful oute of her heuynes."

This, surely, is the goddess who should be invoked by a dreamer who suffers during a long, dark night both from "wo" (line 11) and from "heuines" (line 1). Furthermore, Venus's counsel to the young woman a few lines later seems again to apply to the dreamer. He is a simple observer, of course; it is the gentlewoman who overtly seeks redress for her love longing; yet the language of Venus's simile directly addresses the dreamer's needs. As he presumably slumbers through a night of foul weather, in his vision the dreamer hears Venus say (lines 394–97):

> "And oft also, aftir a dropping mone,
> The weddir clereþ, and whan þe storme is done
> The sonne shineþ in his spere briȝt,
> And ioy awakiþ whan wo is put to fliȝt."

To underscore the contrast, the goddess adds (lines 400–401):

> "And folk also reiossh[e] more of liȝt
> That þei wiþ derknes were waped and amate."

In terms of plot, then, the dreamer overhears an amorous complaint and a response to it, but there is a striking correspondence between needs the dreamer expresses through imagery in the dream frame and appropriate fulfillments of those needs expressed through imagery in the vision.

When next the dreamer comes upon the lady's lover, the connection between dreamer and dream intensifies. If until now the dreamer has been privy to the opposites of his own circumstances (a bright lady and a shining goddess), now he overhears a man remarkably like himself. The "deso*la*te" dreamer of line 11 listens to a lover "al *so/i*tarie" (line 550).[26] He too suffers from "heuines" (line 551), lamenting that he is so love-smitten "þat fro þe deþ...I mai not stert" (line 584); (the dreamer, one recalls, had been

---

[26] Note that the words have the same lexical root *sol*.

oppressed by a "dedeli" sleep). The lover compares himself to a distressed ship on a stormy sea. Dark weather hides the light that would save him, would guide him to port if he did not find himself (lines 609–13):

> Fordriue in dirknes with many a sondri wawe.
> Alas, when shal þis tempest ouerdrawe
> To clere þe skies of myn aduersite;
> The lode-ster [I wot] I may not se,
> It is so hid with cloudes þat ben blake.

This storm-tossed bark was, to be sure, a conventional metaphor for the unrequited lover, but once again how fitting to the dreamer are the references to darkness and to black, cloud-filled skies of adversity. I maintain that if the dreamer is not dreaming of himself, he is certainly dreaming of a man whose emotional situation (as it is reflected in the imagery) is very like his own. Whatever counsel or surcease from misery this man receives will be worth the dreamer's notice.

Such advice is forthcoming, and its manner of presentation strengthens the imagistic leitmotiv of the poem. The audience had already doubtless noticed that Venus's words about tempering darkness with light seem inferentially pointed at the dreamer's state of affairs. As the vision draws to a climax, this emphasis heightens. The light/dark imagery increasingly focuses on the male lover, the figure in the vision whom poetic language seems to have associated with the dreamer. The goddess joins the lovers together and gives counsel to the lady—but she does so without using the light/dark imagery. When she turns to the man, however, she evokes the diction of the dream frame, urging him to be "nouȝt to pensif for non heuynes" (line 1175) and imploring him to (lines 1208–11)

> "Thenk hou she is þis wor[l]dis sonne and liȝt,
> The sterre of beaute, flour eke of fairnes,
> Boþe crop and rote, and eke þe rubie briȝt
> Hertes to glade itroubled with derknes."

All the goddess's advice is directed toward dispelling *his* darkness and *his* heaviness. Venus instructs his mistress to take her lover's hand (lines 1215–16):

> "Vnto þis fyne þat, after al þe showres
> Of his turment, he mai be glad and liȝt."

He kneels, and Venus adds (lines 1285–87):

> "Thus is þis man to ioy and al plesaunce
> From heuynes and from his peynes old
> Ful reconsiled, ..."

A resolution of the amorous situation is reached: whereas lack of love had been equated with lack of light, now, when love flows forth, so does light. And by extension the goddess's urgings to the lover that patience will ensure love is also an implicit admonition to the dreamer that patience and devotion will dispel his sorrowful darkness.

In sum, experience with their own literary conventions led the members of Lydgate's audience to expect a need-to-fulfillment pattern in all visions; in this particular work the diction of the frame led them to anticipate a vision aimed at dispelling both the dreamer's lack of "light" and the reticence they inferred from the brevity of his opening frame. Such expectations could be fulfilled very obviously by the flow of events, but they need not be. The pattern could operate more subtly. Accordingly, it may indeed be true, as critics have charged, that on the surface Lydgate obscured the connection between the dreamer and the dream by overtly separating his persona from the principal figures of the dream. But not far below the surface of plot detail one finds the light/dark imagery in the vision connecting the dreamer and dreamed rather closely in the minds of an audience thoroughly prepared to encounter a movement from need to fulfillment.

The foregoing argument would be seriously undercut if the light/dark imagery were used indiscriminately throughout the vision, but it is not. The examples cited are characteristic: the lady and Venus are light and shining, the lady's lover is dark and brooding, he is wounded by his lady's bright beams, and advice to the lovers (especially to the man) emphasizes how necessary it is to temper both excessive lightness and excessive gloom. The way the word "heuy" is used illustrates this point. It occurs in the frame and in the vision. In the opening frame, of course, it is the dreamer's heaviness. he took to bed initially "for thouȝt, constreint and greuous heuines" (line 1); in the closing frame, when he awoke, "great þouȝt and wo / I hade in hert. . . / For heuynes" (lines 1370–72). In the vision all but two of the instances of "heuy" occur in connection with the male lover.[27] This, I maintain, fits the imagistic leitmotiv of the poem—the language of the dreamer's misery in the frame is the language of the lover's suffering in the vision.

Further, a certain empathy connects the dreamer and the lover. The dreamer seems at no loss to describe either the lady's beauty or her misery, but he does find the lover's pain inexpressible: "For rouþe of which his wo as I endite, / Mi penne I fele quaken as I write" (lines 946–47). The words may be Chaucer's,[28] but, as we have seen, Lydgate is not without the ability to manipulate his expropriations with purpose. Moreover, this difficulty with the act of writing parallels the brevity of the opening frame; in other words, the dreamer's response to the lover's pain corresponds to the dreamer's lack of expansiveness about his own suffering in the dark.

The vision climaxes with a final tie between dreamer and dream. A ballade in praise of Venus is sung by all the lovers in the temple. Its diction summarizes the light/dark imagery of the entire poem. Venus is said to "causen in loue hertes to be liȝt" (line 1343). Thus she can dispel what the audience knows to be precisely the dreamer's anguish. Her creative power is especially emphasized in the final stanza of the ballade (lines 1355–61):

> "O myȝti goddes, daister after nyȝt,
> Glading þe morov whan ȝe done appere,
> To voide derknes þuruȝ fresshnes of ȝour siȝt,
> Oonli with twinkeling of ȝoure plesaunt chere,
> To ȝov we þank, louers þat ben here,
> That ȝe þis man—and neuer forto twyn—
> Fortuned have his ladi forto wynne."

On the surface of things, then, the vision has provided the dreamer with

---

[27] Once Venus is described as having the power "to voide woful oute of her heuynes" (line 331). A few lines later the audience learns that the lover is the cause ". . . for whom all hir [the lady's] distresse / Contynued had and al hir heuynes" (lines 373–74). It is the lady's "heuynes" to be sure, but it has its roots in her lover. "Heuy" and "heuines" used in connection with the male lover occur on lines 551, 555, 1175, 1285.

[28] *TC* 4.13–14.

his lesson — it is Venus and love that can "voide derknes." His fulfillment will come if he follows her bidding, has patience, and loves faithfully. At this point one can easily imagine the members of a medieval audience well pleased in the satisfaction of their literary expectations about well-formed dream visions. Early on they had identified the dreamer's need for light; then through the medium of an amorous vision they had their initial literary judgments confirmed. As the vision built to its climax, they watched the dreamer see example after example of an inescapable lesson about tempering light with dark, using patience and unyielding commitment to achieve love.

But the noise of this "heuenli melodie" (line 1362) jolts the dreamer awake, and with that the thematic ground seems to have shifted back to the predream terrain. He finds himself (lines 1367–75)

> For sodein chaunge, oppressid so with drede,
>
> .   .   .   .
>
> For heuynes þat I hade lost þe siȝt
> Of hir þat I, all þe long[e] nyȝt,
> Had dremed of in myn auisioun.
> Whereof I made gret lamentacioun.

The words "oppressid" and "heuynes" have returned because the dreamer has lost "syȝt" of the lady who illuminated his vision. For the remainder of the poem references to "liȝt" do not recur. Thus the narrator's waking environment — both the fourteen lines at the beginning and the thirty at the end — is devoid of brightness.

This shift away from the illuminated vision back to a lightless dream frame abruptly overturns the audience expectations that just a few lines before had apparently been so well satisfied. How can the dreamer's needs be fulfilled if the darkness and oppression have returned? What has happened to the reading-listening experience? How does this shift reflect medieval poetics in general and Lydgate's in particular?

The audience is forced to reevaluate the vision in the context of a closing dream frame that reintroduces darkness and emotional heaviness. However promising the lesson of the dream may have seemed, it now appears otherwise; the brilliance of the temple of glass has proved ultimately blinding. Thus for all the verbal enmeshing of the dreamer with his vision (and especially with the successful lover), he must wake up to reality. The light is gone; the lady is gone; the fulfillment is gone; the sad promise of a winter poem is realized.

To cast the literary situation in modern critical terms: throughout the vision Lydgate had encouraged his readers to misread, to believe mistakenly that an easy fulfillment was possible. Then, at the end of the vision, just as their conventional expectations seemed most securely confirmed, he wrenched them from their "sikernes," plunging the dreamer (and his audience) back into darkness. Lydgate's manipulation of conventional expectations has in this way transformed the facile love poem into a warning about how easy it is to misconstrue.

Despite the dreamer's return to darkness, however, the *Temple of Glas* has not permanently deserted the dream-vision convention. It is simply that the context for the need-to-fulfillment pattern has changed from a narrow amorous focus to a wider one. The unusually short preface to his vision, the audience remembers, connected the dreamer's darkness to his difficulty over expanding his words. Perhaps he might dispel his darkness through more effective use of language. A rethinking of the content of the vision confirms this. Here again the audience uses its perception that the imagery throughout the dream has made Venus's advice to the lover apply convincingly to the dreamer as well. So very like that solitary lamenter, the dreamer too has heard her counsel that "specheles noþing maist thou spede" (line 905). Remembering her warning that a lover must either tell his lady of his love "or ellis deie for defaute of spech" (line 917), the dreamer puts aside the misery of the opening frame when he was so incapacitated by grief that taking to bed (without even reading words) was his only recourse. Now he avoids that kind of emotional excess and attempts moderate action. He is not overly expansive, but neither is he excessively terse. He decides that he will write a "litil tretise... / In pr[a]ise of women" (lines 1380–81) and send it to his lady to recommend himself. His decision is revealed in a closing frame more than twice the length of the opening frame, another unusual treatment for a dream frame because most visions have perfunctory closings. Even so, the dreamer's ability to limit his proposal to a modest number of lines does suggest that he has learned some measure of control and that he has chosen moderate action over his former passivity.

The final thrust of the poem, then, comes from the dreamer's ability to cast off his poetic darkness and, having apparently learned to temper it with the clarity that light brings, to write without quaking pen. The dreamer looks back over his dream to record it, and the listeners-readers reenact this remembrance to correct their first misreading. The guided audience response, the enforced construing once more, is part of the poet's lesson to them about how hard it is to achieve clarity, to reach truth. In this, the frame and its persona are indispensable, for it is the poet-dreamer who is shrouded in darkness and who must break through it to write effectively. Thus the amorous complaints and ballades in the vision function in part to express a symbolic lesson about the need for light, a lesson that is far more important than their statements as lovers' laments. Had the opening of this poem not been cast in the imagery of darkness, or had the frame been eliminated altogether, the *Temple of Glas* would leave the impression that patient suffering and obedience are rewarded by Venus at the last.[29] Instead, the rhetorically restrained opening and closing sections have put that theme in quite a different context.

Interestingly, it seems that Lydgate, in writings subsequent to the *Temple of Glas*, developed a poetic vocabulary that more and more pointedly associated poetry with light. Lois Ebin has persuasively demonstrated that the poet came to use the term "enlumyn" to "emphasize the poet's critical role in clarifying or shedding light on the significance of his content."[30] Passages added to the *Fall of Princes, IV* lead Ebin to conclude that

Lydgate indicates by means of his central metaphor of light, [that] poetry has the power to dispel the darkness of man's mind and "enlumyn" the world around him . . . . This process of "enlumynyng," of shedding light on the design of the world, Lydgate indicates, is the supreme task of the poet.[31]

Ebin finds Lydgate's work so full of passages on this subject that his writings are in effect a "prelude" to a formally articulated tradition of English poetics that begins in the sixteenth century.[32] The *Temple of Glas* does not

---

[29] This is precisely the conclusion that Derek Pearsall draws: ". . . the mode of the poem is generally optimistic" (*John Lydgate*, p. 112).

[30] Lois Ebin, "Lydgate's Views on Poetry," *AnM* 18(1977):79.

[31] Ibid., p. 94.

[32] Ibid., pp. 104 105.

overtly deal with poetics. It can be inferred, however, from the preceding discussion that I view the *Temple* as a precursor of Lydgate's later open interest in the poetics of light.

Some twentieth-century readers may object that the foregoing analysis is primarily a reading for an *au courant* audience interested in reader-response criticism or some of the other currently popular critical modes. What validity is there, skeptics might ask, in a reconstruction of a hypothetical late-medieval audience? Can the conclusions be verified, or at least corroborated by other evidence? These are legitimate questions, I think, and ones worth considering, especially since I propose that viewing a work, as I have, through reconstructed "late-medieval eyes" can be a valuable tool to add to our other approaches.

I have in the first instance asserted that dream frames function as signals to audiences about the presence and nature of dreamers' needs, that audience recognition of a frame sets in motion expectations about a movement from need to fulfillment. This assertion admittedly flows from a twentieth-century inference that I drew from my study of the opening sections of nearly all extant Middle English dream visions. Yet even if my approach reveals a modern predilection to look for literary analogues to linguistic deep structures, nevertheless there is some strength in my observation because it has the power to explain certain otherwise confusing aspects of some dream poems. The structure of Chaucer's *Book of the Duchess*, for example, makes more sense when we recognize that multiple need-to-fulfillment sequences are embedded one inside another.[33] The fifteenth-century *Assembly of Ladies*, a work that has often been considered "silly," changes its character as we discover that it is structured by means of a series of ironic plays on a need-to-fulfillment pattern.[34] Both of these works seem to presuppose audience recognition that the dream frame is a signal marker for a need-to-fulfillment pattern. Other examples could be cited as well, but irony that approaches parody (as in *The Assembly of Ladies*) is especially strong confirmation of a literary convention.

[33] I advanced this idea in "The *Book of the Duchess*: Generic Conventions and Audience Response," paper delivered to the Second International Congress of the New Chaucer Society, New Orleans, April, 1980.

[34] See my article "Flouting Literary Convention: Structural Irony in the *Assembly of Ladies*," *Mediaevalia*, forthcoming.

Medieval thoughts on how to begin poems offer further confirmation. Authors of *artes poeticae*, insofar as they discuss the structures of poems at all, emphasize the importance of beginning well. Ernest Gallo convincingly argues that such treatises encourage a poet to use an artificial opening for rhetorical ends:

The artificial opening, then, renders a mass of particular facts comprehensible. The poet can control our response to his material by starting in a way that will lead us to see the subject in just the way he wants us to see it. In short, poetry is essentially rhetorical; the poet is arguing for a certain point of view.[35]

My contention here has been that the dream frame of the *Temple of Glas* is intensely rhetorical, that it does indeed control the direction of audience response.

Lydgate's dream frame is not, strictly speaking, an artificial opening, since it purports to relate events in their natural order. It does, however, share characteristics with the artificial *in medias res* opening that begins through memory. In other words, by definition all dreams are retellings, and hence an audience cannot help but be aware that remembrance is involved. Nevertheless, however we classify it, Lydgate's opening is compatible with medieval thoughts about using the first section of a poem to control audience response. Here I am in strong agreement with Gallo's assertion that we ought to take the dicta of the *artes poeticae* not as a set of inviolable rules, but rather as "evidence of medieval attitudes toward poetry and its functions."[36]

There is an even more striking way in which Lydgate's handling of the dream frame corresponds to attitudes expressed in the *artes poeticae*: the matter of using an opening to shed light on one's work. It is important to bear in mind the long-standing metaphoric possibilities of "light." There is a rich medieval tradition of speculation on the aesthetic connection between light and creation, a tradition whose sources according to Edgar de Bruyne can be traced back beyond *Genesis* and classical authors to the

---

[35] Ernest Gallo, "The *Poetria nova* of Geoffrey of Vinsauf," in James J. Murphy, ed., *Medieval Eloquence: Studies in the Theory and Practice of Medieval Rhetoric* (Berkeley and Los Angeles: University of California Press, 1978), p. 77.

[36] Ibid., p. 83.

mythologies and cosmologies of Persia and Egypt.[37] In Lydgate's time, as P. M. Kean has shown, illuminating one's poetry was still of major concern to makers and was by no means restricted, as is often thought, to verbal ornament. It concerned ensuring that the material was both clear and fully understood by the audience.[38] This general concern for clarity reflects the medieval habit of mind one finds delineated in the *artes poeticae*. In the *Poetria nova*, for example, Geoffrey of Vinsauf offers a variety of strategies for beginning a work. Among these Geoffrey particularly recommends a proverb "*Si pars prima velit majus diffundere lumen.*"[39] Gallo calls our attention to the significance of Geoffrey's language here and demonstrates that although the *Poetria nova* is perhaps the most influential, it is but one in a line of rhetorical treatises which emphasize that the beginning of a work should infuse the rest with light.[40]

In sum, the emphasis one finds in rhetorical treatises regarding the necessity to begin a poem carefully — and especially so that it sheds light — is compatible with my proposal that the frame of a Middle English dream vision had symbolic import. Its purpose was to direct the audience to see the dreamer's needs in a certain way. As I have shown, Lydgate was operating very much within this tradition when he set forth his dreamer's needs in terms of darkness and brevity so that the audience would be disposed to pay heed to light and expansiveness in the vision. There is quite obvious irony in Lydgate's manipulation of poetic convention: using images of "darkness" to shed "light" inverts conventional expectations and hence warns the audience in an especially subtle way that things may not turn out quite as expected. And, indeed, so subtle is the warning that the audience does at first misread; but then, still drawing on its contemporary sense of literary patterns, the audience rethinks the situation and finally understands the poem's message about the light-giving property of words.

The *Temple of Glas* is one of Lydgate's earliest works. It does not have any of the overt discussion of poetics that Ebin found in the poet's later

---

[37] Edgar de Bruyne, *Études d'esthétique médiévale*, Rijksuniversiteit te Gent Werken Uitgegeven door de Faculteit van de Wijsbegeerte en Letteren, vols. 97–99 (Bruges: De Tempel, 1946), 3.3–30, passim.

[38] P. M. Kean, *Chaucer and the Making of English Poetry* (London: Routledge and Kegan Paul, 1971), 2.232–34.

[39] Line 126 in Faral, ed., *Les arts poétiques*, p. 201.

[40] Gallo, "*Poetria nova*," p. 77.

writings. On the contrary, this poem can appear to be little more than a conventional courtly love vision. Yet, as I have tried to show, at the same time that it is a rather simple amorous poem, it is also a corrective to superficial readers, a tract on the value of moderate action, and a statement about how writing poetry can dispel a dreamer's darkness. Like much other medieval literature, it operates on several levels. Some of these, I fear, will be lost to the modern reader unless scholars see the legitimacy of reconstructing the literary "horizon of expectations" of a medieval audience.[41]

---

[41] The phrase is Jauss's, pp. 182-83. Nichols explicates this "horizon" quite clearly and gives additional references to Jauss's works.

Chaucer's *Squire's Tale*
and the Rise of Chivalry

Jennifer R. Goodman
Texas A&M University

I
N *IL PENSEROSO*, Milton saw fit to acclaim Chaucer as the author
of *The Squire's Tale* and to demand more of the story (lines 109–20):

> Or call up him that left half told
> The story of *Cambuskan* bold,
> Of *Camball*, and of *Algarsife*,
> And who had *Canace* to wife,
> That own'd the virtuous Ring and Glass,
> And of the wondrous Horse of Brass,
> On which the *Tartar* King did ride;
> And if aught else great Bards beside
> In sage and solemn tunes have sung,
> Of Tourneys and of Trophies hung,
> Of Forests, and enchantments drear,
> Where more is meant than meets the ear.[1]

Few twentieth-century readers of Chaucer have echoed Milton's wish. The
Squire's interrupted romance is currently regarded as a deliberately lame
composition, tailored to display its young narrator's immature taste and

---

[1] Milton's father knew John Lane, the Elizabethan continuator of *The Squire's Tale*. See
F. J. Furnivall, ed., *John Lane's Continuation of Chaucer's Squire's Tale*, Chaucer Society, 2d
ser., 24, 26 (London, 1888–90). Lane also adapted *Guy of Warwick*; his work is preserved in
BL MS Harley 5243. Edmund Spenser's use of *The Squire's Tale* in book 4 of *The Faerie
Queene* may also have directed Milton's interest to Chaucer's tale. An earlier version of this
paper was presented at the Chaucer Division meeting at the Ninety-seventh Annual Conven-
tion of the Modern Language Association, in December, 1982. I would like to thank Alfred
David for his good counsel in its revision.

snobbery, a tale that could be admired only by that inveterate toady the Franklin.[2] Its critics have been particularly bothered by the apparent formlessness and the discordant content of the tale. This divergence of modern taste from that of the seventeenth century is important, and not merely as an illustration of how much Chaucer's readers change in the course of time. It seems vital for defenders of the Franklin — and of Milton's judgment — to examine the basis of *The Squire's Tale*'s unregenerate attraction.

In "Chaucer's *Squire's Tale* and the Decline of Chivalry," Stanley Kahrl noted major affinities between Chaucer's tale and the world of late-medieval romance. He linked the unfinished tale with Huizinga's depiction of the waning Middle Ages and with "the growing impulse toward exoticism and disorder at work in the courts of late medieval Europe."[3] For Kahrl, *The Squire's Tale* stands as Chaucer's satire on the degenerate chivalry of Richard II's youngest courtiers. Since the appearance of Kahrl's article, however, research in the late-medieval romance has extended the work of Huizinga in several directions.[4] These new studies emphatically vindicate Kahrl's insight, but they demand a radically reactionary change in his interpretation of *The Squire's Tale*.

The most recent studies of the later-medieval romance no longer describe it as a degenerate form, testifying to the decadence of chivalry. Manuscripts, book lists, and tournament records of the late fourteenth and fifteenth centuries show a rising preoccupation with details of chivalric practice, in life as in the new verse and prose romances. Analysis of these romances for themselves, rather than as reflections of their twelfth-century ancestors, has led readers to see in them not disorder but design. The fifteenth-century author of the French prose *Fierabras* saw the *chanson de geste* that he was remodeling as "a Romaunce maad of thauncyent facyon

---

[2] See Derek Pearsall, "The Squire as Story-Teller," *University of Toronto Quarterly* 34(1964):82–92.

[3] Stanley J. Kahrl, "Chaucer's *Squire's Tale* and the Decline of Chivalry," *ChauR* 7(1973):194–209. See also Morton W. Bloomfield, "Chaucer's *Squire's Tale* and the Renaissance," *Poetica* 12(1981):28–35.

[4] See, for example, Larry D. Benson and John Leyerle, eds., *Chivalric Literature: Studies in Medieval Culture XIV* (Kalamazoo, 1979); and a useful discussion of the history of chivalry in L. D. Benson, *Malory's Morte d'Arthur* (Cambridge, Mass.: Harvard University Press, 1976), pp. 137–62.

wythoute grete ordynaunce in frensshe."[5] Chaucer regarded the tail-rhyme minstrel romances of the Auchinleck Manuscript with an equally critical eye. By the late fourteenth century the works we now consider masterpieces of metrical romance were beginning to look old-fashioned and disorganized. On the other hand, the romances that most closely parallel *The Squire's Tale* were very much up to date.

The English romances closest to Chaucer's tale are those classified by Lillian Hornstein in Severs's *Manual of the Writings in Middle English* as "composites of courtly romance."[6] Lillian Hornstein describes this group of narratives as "in great part artificial composites of elements derived from sophisticated courtly romance."[7] Like *The Squire's Tale*, *Partonope of Blois*, *Valentine and Orson*, *Generides*, and the others in this group show a fondness for Oriental detail without reference to any single Oriental source. All seem to be products of the late fourteenth and fifteenth centuries. The composite romances are marked by precisely those elements that have annoyed the modern reader in *The Squire's Tale*: meticulous attention to the niceties of courtly life joined with an inexhaustible appetite for marvels. Again, *Valentine and Orson*, *Partonope*, and *Generides* exhibit this distinctive combination of effects. The flying horse, magic ring, mirror and sword, and threatened incest of Chaucer's tale appear also in the composite romances: a flying horse is prominent in *Valentine and Orson*, while averted incest of various kinds may be found in *Generides* and the final continuation of *Huon of Bordeaux*. The composite romances have been identified, in fact, by their propensity for treating segments of earlier romances as building blocks for new and more flamboyant structures. A list of Richard II's books of 1384–85 indicates that the king himself owned "vn Romance de Generides," presumably the lost French text from which derive the two Middle English versions of the late fourteenth century.[8] It seems apparent that more than one squire was at work in Chaucer's vicinity.

[5] Jean Bagnyon, *The Lyf of the Noble and Crysten Prynce Charles the Grete*, trans. William Caxton, ed. S. J. Herrtage, in *The English Charlemagne Romances*, pts. 3–4, EETS, vols. 36–37 (London, 1881), p. 38.

[6] Lillian Herlands Hornstein, in J. Burke Severs, ed., *A Manual of the Writings in Middle English, 1050–1500* (New Haven, Conn.: Yale University Press, 1967), 1.147–67.

[7] Ibid., p. 147.

[8] Edith Rickert, "King Richard II's Books," *Library*, 4th ser., 13(1932–33):144–47.

The composite romances display unexpected features of design as well as of content. In certain respects they seem to be attempts to rival in verse the complexity of the early prose romances, with their multiple plot lines and open-ended narration. The adventures of a single hero seem monotonous unless they are accompanied by those of his parents, brothers, and friends. In addition, the distinctive taste for a combination of the fantastic and minute realism joins two strands of fiction that were to separate before long in the main divisions of fifteenth-century romance. Caxton's translation of *Paris and Vienne* and Malory's *Morte d'Arthur* represent the romance of the probable in English, while the *Amadís* romances turn toward the marvelous. The composite romance brings together realistic detail and wonder with startling audacity. Spenser and Milton would have recognized elements of two familiar varieties of narrative combined in the magic and court ceremony of *The Squire's Tale*.[9]

At first sight, Chaucer might seem to provide the wildest possible example of this eclectic form. In approximately six hundred lines the Squire introduces a mechanical flying horse, a ring that allows the wearer to understand the speech of birds, a magic sword, a mirror that reveals treason, and a hysterical falcon. A great feast, dancing in the king's presence chamber, the palace garden, and the falcon's mew in the princess Canacee's room all receive their share of attention. The Squire ends, most improbably of all, by suggesting that he will go on to describe the separate adventures of five principal characters.

This profusion of detail and incident has been hailed by dazed scholars not as God's plenty but as an ungodly mess. Yet similar sketches might be made of *Generides*, *Valentine and Orson*, or even *Huon of Bordeaux* as the fourteenth century knew it. *Generides* combines an equally unlikely series of ingredients: the magic stag hunt, a combat between father and brothers, the hero's disguise as a leper, the merging of the stories of Joseph and

---

Generides appears on the list of 1384 but not on a list of 1358 of books inherited by Edward III from his mother. Compare Sir Simon Burley's booklist of 1387 in BL MS Additional 25452, fol. 206. The late-fourteenth-century *Parlement of the Thre Ages* lists Ypomadon and Generides in its catalogue of famous lovers.

[9] On the combination of realism and the fantastic in the Renaissance romantic epic see Barbara Reynolds's introduction to her translation of Ludovico Ariosto's *Orlando Furioso* (1975; reprint, Harmondsworth, Middlesex, 1977), 1.25, 41, 45.

Potiphar's wife and of Hippolytus with the Fair Unknown motif, and a final healing of the hero by the heroine. As the lady's father says at one point:

> "This aventure," quod he, "is passing new,
> And as me think a very wonder thing;"[10]

Novelty and wonder are clearly among the poet's goals. *Valentine and Orson* integrates episodes of the stolen child who becomes a wild man and is defeated by his brother, the savage brother's combat with a green knight, the omniscient head of brass, the dwarf magician and his flying horse, repeated judicial combats, parricide, and penance that reflects the influence of the legend of Saint Alexis. Beside Chaucer's elegant steed of brass, "so horsly and so quyk of ye," the horse of the later romance seems a trifle clumsy:

by enchauntemente he had made and composed a lytell hors of wodde, and in the heed there was artyfycyelly a pynne that was in suche wyse set, that euery tyme that he mounted vpon the horse for to goo somwhere, he torned the pynne toward the place that he wolde go to, and anone he founde him in the place without harme or daunger, for the hors was of suche facyon that he wente thoroughe the ayre more faster than ony byrde coude flee.[11]

Still, the same alliance of the fantastic and the meticulous is evident in each description. Both of these wild concoctions, *Valentine and Orson* and *Generides*, are eminently successful narratives; signs of their popularity, like that of *The Squire's Tale*, may be traced into the seventeenth century.

Even the potential complications of *The Squire's Tale*—who is to win Canacee, her own brother?—connect Chaucer and the composite romances. In these works combat between relatives (*Generides, Valentine and Orson*), averted incest (*Generides* and *Huon of Bordeaux*), and other prodigies of domestic life regularly bring the marvelous into conjunction

---

[10] W. A. Wright, ed., *Generydes*, EETS, vols. 55, 70 (London, 1873–78), p. 172. See also F. J. Furnivall, ed., *A Royal Historie of the Excellent Knight Generides*, Roxburghe Club, vol. 85 (London, 1865).

[11] Henry Watson, trans., A. Dickson, ed., *Valentine and Orson*, EETS, vol. 204 (London, 1937), p. 142.

with the realistic element of the narrative. At the opening of the four-teenth century the main continuator of *Huon of Bordeaux* had already recounted the adventures of Princess Ide, who fled Aragon in male disguise to avoid marriage to her father, only to be wedded to the daughter of the Roman emperor. Disaster can be averted only by a divinely ordained sex change.[12] In such a context the winning of Canacee by her brother (hinted in lines 667–69) would be an expectable rather than an unusual event.

Critical distrust of the contents of *The Squire's Tale* may have contrib-uted to the dubious view now current of the Squire's talents as a storyteller. His use of the modesty topos, *rime riche*, and puns and his digressions on the man in the street's opinion of the flying horse and on the proper construction of narratives have been taken to indicate that the Squire is a very young, nervous, and clumsy speaker whose gaffes are intended to amuse the audience.[13] As Derek Pearsall has demonstrated, the Squire's speech does give the effect of youth. Still, when the tale the Squire tells makes better sense as a romance, the questionable passages lose much of their ill effect. The manuscript and audience studies noted earlier in this paper tell against the satirical reading of *The Squire's Tale*; if Chaucer had unaccountably been inspired to mock the composite romance, he would have found few like-minded readers with whom to share it. Interpretation may still remain a matter of taste. Robert Haller and Stanley Kahrl both deplore the Squire's notorious pun in lines 105–106:

> Al be it that I kan nat sowne his stile
> Ne kan nat clymben over so heigh a style,
> Yet seye I this, as to commune entente,
> This muche amounteth al that evere he mente,
> If it so be that I have it in mynde.[14]

The momentary visual image conveyed by the lines of a little man drawn

---

[12] John Bourchier (Lord Berners), trans., S. Lee, ed., *The Boke of Duke Huon of Burdeux*, EETS, extra ser., vols. 40, 41, 43, 50 (London, 1882–87), pp. 690–729.

[13] See Pearsall, "The Squire as Story-Teller."

[14] All quotations from Chaucer in this article are taken from F. N. Robinson, ed., *The Works of Geoffrey Chaucer*, 2d ed. (Boston: Houghton Mifflin, 1957). See Robert S. Haller, "Chaucer's *Squire's Tale* and the Uses of Rhetoric," *Modern Philology* 62(1965):290; Kahrl, "Chaucer's *Squire's Tale*," p. 204.

132

climbing up the historiated initial in some manuscript presents the high style in terms of a literal obstacle and, at the same time, signals the poet's approval of the device. Chaucer's repeated use of *rime riche* leaves the reader with no doubt that he employs this device for positive aesthetic effects.[15] Those who agree that the sharpest puns are the best will doubtless share my opinion that this is a very good pun indeed.

In the same way the crowd's discussion of the flying horse and its mode of operation has been read as a snobbish aside by the Squire (lines 199–203, 220–24):

> But everemoore hir mooste wonder was
> How that it koude goon, and was of bras;
> It was of Fairye, as the peple semed.
> Diverse folk diversely they demed;
> As many heddes, as many wittes ther been,
>
> .   .   .   .
>
> Of sondry doutes thus they jangle and trete,
> As lewed peple demeth comunly
> Of thynges that been maad moore subtilly
> Than they kan in hir lewednesse comprehende;
> They demen gladly to the badder ende.[16]

This presentation of a crowd in disagreement, evidently to Chaucer a subject of continual amusement and annoyance, echoes those in *The Parliament of Fowls*, *The House of Fame*, *Troilus and Criseyde*; that of the spectators at the tournament in *The Knight's Tale*; and the great council scene in *The Tale of Melibee*. Chaucer may find mobs amusing or sinister, but he rarely shows much respect for their judgment. The speaker's attitude here seems to combine Chaucer's distrust of the democratic process with his usual bias in favor of science and technology.[17] Every marvel,

---

[15] For further examples of *rime riche* see *The Squire's Tale*, lines 203–204, 255–56. See also Masayoshi Ito's study of *rime riche* in *Studies in English Literature* 46 (Tokyo, 1969).

[16] See Pearsall, "The Squire as Story-Teller," pp. 87–88; Kahrl, "Chaucer's *Squire's Tale*," p. 203.

[17] Compare especially *The Knight's Tale*, lines 2513–22, and *Melibee*, lines 1233–68. See also Bloomfield, "Chaucer's *Squire's Tale* and the Renaissance." Ariosto's insistence on the natural origin of his flying horse (the hippogriff) in *Orlando Furioso* 4.18.i–viii is also of interest in this connection.

natural or artificial, ought to have a reasonable scientific explanation.

The Squire's Tale as a whole suffers from a lack of precedent elsewhere in Chaucer's work. It stands alone as his only known experiment with a long romance of such intricacy. Acquaintance with contemporary composite romance enables the modern reader to see that in fact *The Squire's Tale* possesses both a recognizable genre and a coherent form. The romance moves logically from its opening evocation of Cambuskan as the ideal chivalric ruler (except in the matter of faith) and the formal presentation of marvels at his feast in the manner of an interlude to the first branching of its multiple plot, the meeting of Canacee and the lovesick falcon.[18]

The plot summary of lines 651–70 identifies the romance as a composite and enables the reader to estimate the size and shape of the projected narrative. Indeed, the summary seems to have been included for precisely this reason (lines 661–70):

> First wol I telle yow of Cambyuskan,
> That in his tyme many a citee wan;
> And after wol I speke of Algarsif,
> How that he wan Theodora to his wif,
> For whom ful ofte in greet peril he was,
> Ne hadde he ben holpen by the steede of bras;
> And after wol I speke of Cambalo,
> That faught in lystes with the bretheren two
> For Canacee er that he myghte hire wynne,
> And ther I lefte I wol ayeyn bigynne.

Chaucer's plan is definite enough to be reduced to an outline. First, the narrator will tell of Cambuskan the conqueror. Next, he will recount how Algarsif his son won Theodora with the aid of the brazen horse. After this

---

[18] The virtues of Cambuskan correspond to those recommended in Ramón Llull's *Libre del orde de cavayleria*, a work that Chaucer might have known in its fourteenth-century French translation. See William Caxton's translation, *The Boke of the Ordre of Chyualry*, ed. A. T. P. Byles, EETS, vol. 168 (London, 1926), pp. 27–65. On the importance and implications of the feast in late-medieval life and literature see Henry L. Harder, "Feasting in the Alliterative *Morte Arthure*," in Benson and Leyerle, eds., *Chivalric Literature XIV*, pp. 49–62. See also B. J. Whiting, "Gawain: His Reputation, His Courtesy, and His Appearance in Chaucer's *Squire's Tale*," *MS* 9(1947):189–234.

he will describe Cambalo's combat in the lists with two kinsmen for Canacee and return to take up where he left off, presumably to tell of Cambalus's success in retrieving the falcon's beloved by means of Canacee's magic ring. This catalogue of events reveals the kaleidoscopic variety of the composite romances. Cambuskan's conquests would appeal to the reader of the Alexander legends. The connoisseur of the tournament would look forward to Cambalo's unequal joust. The promise to speak "of aventures and of batailles, / That nevere yet was herd so grete mervailles" (lines 659–60) hints at a rising interest in the chivalric component of the romance.[19]

I argue that The Squire's Tale is a composite romance left unfinished by design. In practical terms the incompleteness of the tale enables Chaucer to expand the generic variety of The Canterbury Tales without damaging the design of the work as a whole. A full-length composite romance would have rivaled the entire Canterbury Tales in size.[20] As it stands, with the concluding plot summary to mollify the Miltonic reader who demands to be told the end of the story, The Squire's Tale is an elegant compromise. The form of the interrupted tale allows Chaucer to sketch in the distinctive effects, pace, and atmosphere of the composite romance without distending the frame story by requiring it to swallow an entire narrative of this kind at one gulp. The Squire's Tale shows Chaucer, the incorrigibly experimental poet, looking on the romance of his own day "with a freendly ye" (lines 671–72):

> Appollo whirleth up his chaar so hye,
> Til that the god Mercurius hous, the slye —

and so the tale ends. Chaucer, like his own Franklin, middle-aged, can follow the pace of the young man's romance only so far. Then he begins to hop further and further behind, until, slier than Mercury, he lets the car of

---

[19] Giraldi Cinthio's sixteenth-century defense of Ariosto emphasized the importance of variety in the later romance. See Giraldi Cinthio, On Romances, trans. Henry L. Snuggs (Lexington: University Press of Kentucky, 1968), p. 23.

[20] The length of Lane's continuation of The Squire's Tale (note 1 above) suggests the space needed to work out Chaucer's plot summary. On the problem of style and poetic economy see Pearsall, "The Squire as Story-Teller," p. 84.

Apollo fly off without him.[21]

Identifying *The Squire's Tale* as Chaucer's attempt at composite romance demands a radical change in our view of Chaucer's method and intent. The single Oriental source for the tale, sought for so long by so many students of Chaucer, vanishes. Instead, Chaucer joins his contemporaries in selecting details of older narratives to amalgamate in new alloys. Like *The Squire's Tale*, the composite romance deserves greater critical respect for its distinct and distinctive qualities, qualities better understood by the Renaissance than by our own age. Its variety of incident, complex social detail, and broadening geographic scope that makes air travel a necessity are attractive elements shared by the tale and its neglected contemporaries.

In *The Squire's Tale*, Chaucer has assembled the picture of a young man's imaginary world. Both the Squire and his tale are "to be continued," though not on the road to Canterbury (lines 677–80):

> As to my doom, ther is noon that is heere
> Of eloquence that shal be thy peere,
> If that thow lyve; God yeve thee good chaunce,
> And in vertu sende thee continuaunce![22]

Perhaps Chaucer could find or imagine no more perfect mirror of a young man's mind than a new and unfinished romance.

---

[21] Compare *Anelida and Arcite*, lines 47–48, "the slye wey / of that I gan to write."
[22] Compare M. Y. Offord, ed., *The Parlement of the Thre Ages*, EETS, vol. 246 (London, 1959), lines 109–256.

Reviews

JUDSON BOYCE ALLEN, *The Ethical Poetic of the Later Middle Ages: A Decorum of Convenient Distinction*. Toronto: University of Toronto Press, 1982. Pp. xix, 327. $45.00.

Judson Boyce Allen's new book will take its place beside those other metacritical studies of medieval literary commentary designed to keep us from falling into what D. W. Robertson called the "rancid solipsistic pit into which the tendencies of post-romantic thought have thrust us." This is ostensibly a study of the ways in which medieval commentators dealt with texts, both sacred and secular, but is also about the expectations of the medieval audience. *Decorum* is therefore intended as a salve for the misrepresentation of medieval texts through modern eyes; in this sense the book has a good deal to offer. It provides us with additional materials that may be used to reconstruct the "horizon of expectancy" of the medieval reader and may help us to avoid some of the unfortunate consequences of wrenching a text from its place in literary history.

At its best *Decorum* is a sourcebook of hitherto inaccessible literary commentary marshaled under a historical-critical thesis: that literature as moderns define it was unknown in the later Middle Ages and that the body of material that we call literature was in fact classified as ethics. Allen is mainly concerned with demonstrating the ubiquity of this identification through a generous sampling of lengthy excerpts from Latin commentaries (mostly from thirteenth- and fourteenth-century manuscripts, listed in a separate table, pp. 325–27). The selection is actually too generous; the point that at least the commentators read literature in terms of ethics is well taken, but it is made with almost polemical insistence. The dominance of the Latin materials combined with excruciatingly literal English translations renders *Decorum* very heavy going indeed. It should be added that connections between the commentators and the more general audience of medieval poetry are never explicitly handled; such connections must be established for the thesis to have much relevance to medieval audience outside the influence of the academic commentator.

But Allen is not content with providing materials for the study of late-medieval intellectual history; he also details the course of a personal odyssey, a saga of his own conversion from the solipsistic heresies of the New Criticism to the light of Historical Scholarship, a quest for the genuine "textuality" of the medieval poem. Only the intelligence and wit of the first and last chapters and the solid (but dry) historical investigation of the intervening ones redeem these excursions into the mind of a modern trying very hard to think like a medieval. We are led through weighty commentaries, cited to show us, among other things, that we should not expect to find in a medieval poem a "plot in the University of Chicago sense." Allen is painfully aware that his work is commentary that will itself be commented upon. Out of this self-conscious critical posture come such statements as these:

> At this point it would perhaps be prudent to stop.... The historian is by definition under no obligation to pursue the question of value further....
>
> But the historian is also a person. I do believe that these medieval facts— attitudes and definitions of readers and readings of texts— are of absolute as well as historical value....
>
> I said at the very beginning of this book that my chief theoretical presumption was that critics who write about literature betray themselves, in the long run, even more than they inform what they are writing about. Therefore it should be possible to find the medieval definition of literature in what the medieval critics wrote about it. This I hope I have done. But in so doing I have myself written about literature, and in so doing have deposited a document which should fall under my own theoretical presumption, and betray me. This I happily admit, because I know that my mind functions in a post-Cartesian world, and understand my self-betrayal as that of one inevitably interested in point of view, subject-object relations, the phenomenological predicament. Further, I claim that my interest in the medieval critics' self-betrayal is not only an interest which my own epistemological make-up permits me to exercise—further, it is precisely that interest which, when exercised self-consciously, permits me to allow for the predicament of my own point of view. [p. 300]

Such personal asides are not only distractions from what might be a most helpful study — they at times destroy the credibility of the critical approach

138

itself; the pitfalls of "relativism" are never very far from the reader's mind.

The strong points of *Decorum* are of two kinds: first, contributions to our understanding of how the medieval mind accepted and interpreted the material of poetry; second, applications to literary works whose "textuality" has never before been so completely located in the realm of the ethical. In the first category are observations on how a medieval reader (in all cases a commentator) expected to participate in the created fiction through placing himself in the poem and, more important, once in the poem, expected to encounter a truly credible reality. This is accomplished not through Coleridge's "willing suspension of disbelief" but through "ordinary belief," "that feature of the human psyche which responds affirmatively to consideration." In fact, Allen contends, for the medieval mind "the whole Coleridgean distinction" is "irrelevant and meaningless." In one sense, all of *Decorum* is devoted to removing the post-Romantic critical tendencies that would deny the "alterity" of the medieval work. Alastair J. Minnis's recent essay "Chaucer and Comparative Literary Theory" (in Donald M. Rose, ed., *New Perspectives in Chaucer Criticism* [Norman: Pilgrim Books, 1982], pp. 53–70) is a valuable companion to Allen on this point. Minnis's convenient discussion of the technical terms used in literary commentaries (*accessus, forma tractatus, ordinatio libri* — the *forma tractandi* of Allen's discussion) is a useful complement to *Decorum*. In his attempt to reconstruct the historicity of medieval texts, Allen's purpose is to define a functional theory of literary interpretation that was considered important not only by the audience but by an artist who was aware of the ethical importance of every feature of his composition. The second strength of this work is Allen's investigation of the responses of Chaucer and Langland to the idea of poetry as enacted ethics.

In a brief discussion of *The Canterbury Tales*, Allen does little more than abstract the thesis of *A Distinction of Stories: The Medieval Unity of Chaucer's Fair Chain of Narratives for Canterbury* (see the review by Derek Pearsall, *SAC* 4 [1981]) — that nearly all the tales are, in one sense or another, exemplary tales concerning marriage and that the tales compose a "normative array" that describes an ethical pattern. But his reading of *The Legend of Good Women* as "an enactment. . . of the full complexity of the meaning of meaning" opens new possibilities for a reconsideration of the poem. Allen reads the *Legend* as beginning in books and working through a dialectic so that "what is now literal may become meaning and commentary and what is now commentary may exist as letter." Alceste is the "image of remembrance."

Allen observes that Chaucer's interest in revising the *Legend* was related to his concern with the "philosophy of poetic language." It was to Chaucer "a poem about making poems" (see especially pp. 269–75). Allen then turns his attention to *Piers Plowman*, a work more obviously suited to a discussion of the efficacy of language in general and of poetry in particular. The provocative discussion of *Piers* is all too brief, however; Allen suggests that the question the poem asks is, "How may a person become a true person?" In construing a "normative array" as a response, Langland depends upon—in fact, he erects his poem upon—an "array of themes already defined elsewhere as an ordered set," an arrangement of scriptural passages as outlined in biblical concordances.. Using the B text Prologue as a test case, Allen raises some interesting questions about the perplexing narrative form of the poem; *Piers* is an "experiencing text" in which the process and the form (the *forma tractatus* and the *forma tractandi*) are one. Another suggestion for future *Piers* studies occurs in a note (p. 112): that the Will of the poem may be not the human faculty but rather an aspect of God. If this is so, Allen suggests, it "turns the whole notion of the quest for salvation upside down." Unfortunately, the idea is not developed further.

It is regretable that more of this book is not devoted to applications of medieval theory to medieval art—such as there are tend to come as welcome interludes in this collection of lifeless commentators, who (though Allen would not admit it) quite probably provoked as many yawns of indifference in the audiences of their own day as they do in ours.

A. J. COLAIANNE
Virginia Polytechnic Institute
and State University

ANNA BALDWIN, *The Theme of Government in* Piers Plowman. Cambridge: D. S. Brewer, 1981. Pp. vi, 107. £12.00.

MARGARET E. GOLDSMITH, *The Figure of* Piers Plowman. Cambridge: D. S. Brewer, 1981. Pp. viii, 128. £12.00.

These two monographs are harbingers of a new series of Piers Plowman Studies to be published by D. S. Brewer. Both volumes share high standards of production and clarity of style. Likewise, both books are rather old-fashioned but comfortably sane in their literary-critical approaches. There is, then, much to be hoped from succeeding volumes in this series. Nevertheless, despite the technical excellence of both, the unevenness between the books remains striking, with Anna Baldwin's book seeming notably superior to Margaret E. Goldsmith's in at least three important aspects: the value and freshness of the information provided, the coherence of the argument, and the relevance and validity of sources of evidence. Although neither book can lay claim to being that rara avis, the completely convincing, definitive treatment, Baldwin's book will surely provoke even the seasoned *Piers* scholar to some thoughtful reconsideration of settled opinions. More frequently, however, it will succeed in simply informing one of details of medieval English governmental practices and their relevance to *Piers Plowman* about which one could have had, in one's ignorance, no prior opinion at all.

Baldwin's investigation of the theme of government focuses on what she sees as an apparent paradox in Langland's outlook: "How can the absolutist ideal of monarchy embodied in the *Visio* king be made compatible with the more merciful, even democratic ideal practised by Piers, Conscience, and Christ?" As Baldwin sees it, Langland envisions three possible answers to the question of " 'how much power should the king have?' " These alternatives she designates a "theocratic" theory, a theory of "limited monarchy," and an "absolutist" theory. Although the terms seem unhappy in their potentially deceptive connotations, few would quarrel with Baldwin's opinion that, ultimately, Langland favors a king directly administering equity through the counsel of his own reason and conscience (the "absolutist" theory) as opposed to a king creating justice *ex nihilo* by fiat (the "theocratic" theory) or a king fettered by the precedents of common law ("limited monarchy"). Baldwin sees similarities with Wyclif's views (e.g., pp. 10–11, 51) in Langland's advocacy of such "absolutist" monarchy. Although she seems to overinterpret the Goliard's speech in B Prologue 141–42 as one advocating "limited monarchy" (whereas he is commonly understood to be opposing only the admonitions toward mercy offered by the angel and the lunatic), most would accept her contention that Langland's use of the rat fable carries "absolutist" implications. Especially convincing is Baldwin's analysis of changes from B to C toward "a clearer statement of 'absolutism'" (though she sometimes appears to forget, as on p. 3, that C represents not only a *clearer* statement of materials in A and B but also a more conservative stage in the development of the author's ideas and therefore is sometimes *different* in conception as well as expression from the earlier recensions).

Baldwin's second and third chapters (an analysis of the arrest of Meed and the dispute of Peace with Wrong) form essential reading for anyone working with these parts of *Piers Plowman* in the future. So far as I am aware, no one has explicated so thoroughly the satiric ramifications of Meed's allegorical procession toward London insofar as these touch on the specific corruptions of regional and local government. Even more valuable, however, is the discussion of the relationship between these episodes and the evolution and functioning of the royal "prerogative courts." Baldwin considers the point of Meed's arrest and the trial of Wrong as being that "the king had used his absolute power to enforce justice when law had failed."

Assuming that this interpretation has been amply established, Baldwin next pursues the other side of the paradox she has perceived, viz., that Langland depicts several "subject-kings" in his narrative (most notably Piers and Conscience) who, though leading the folk with a kind of charismatic authority, never assert royal authority in their own behalf and act (as does Christ himself) more as "limited monarchs" than as the absolute monarch of the *Visio* whose behavior Langland seemed to endorse. Hence Piers and Conscience are in no position, nor do they wish, to impose their own ideas of justice on the folk. As Baldwin observes, "It is the community, rather than the king or his representatives, who share the responsibility for social justice and harmony here" (p. 55). While Baldwin concludes that the dichotomy she has traced in Langland's attitudes toward kingship and government is not indicative of an inconsistency in the poet's political ideals but only of a change in audience (from "the present king of

England" in passus 2–4 to "the subjects and Christians who are reading the poem" in the case of the later passus), she has not completely persuaded me that the supposed dichotomy exists at all.

For one thing, it is difficult to see the portrait of the king of passus 3–4 as a very flattering one, much less an ideal. In what sense can a king be said to be idealized who is barely saved from enforcing the disastrous union of his own conscience with corruption? An ideal king would not, presumably, require such delicate and indirect reminders as that embodied in the exemplum of Saul and the Amalekites. Also, Baldwin's "dichotomy" seems seriously endangered by a passage at the end of passus 4, where Conscience and Reason both appear to say that even "the *Visio* king" cannot compel obedience to virtue (lines 182–87; italics mine):

> Quod Conscience to þe kyng, "*but þe commune wole assente*
> *It is wel hard, by myn heed, herto to brynge it,*
> And alle youre lige leodes to lede þs euene."
> "By hym þat rauȝte on þe Rode!" quod Reson to þe kynge,
> "But I rule þus youre Reaume rende out my guttes —
> *If ye bidden buxomnesse be of myn assent.*"

The logic of these reservations is, in fact, what provokes the next episode. The sermon of Reason to the folk results from the need to win their agreement so that "buxomnesse [may] be of myn assent." Moreover, many scholars have pointed out that, the king's adverse judgment notwithstanding, nothing is done at his court to impede Meed's activities. She is left with her most loyal retinue of "a Sisour and a Somonour" and "a Sherreues clerk," and, although she seems to disappear from the narrative at this point, her evil influence is amply attested throughout the rest of the poem.

Baldwin's thesis, therefore, seems to me a pardonable distortion resulting from her preoccupation with an area of the poem that, while badly in need of explication for modern readers, is not of primary importance to the poet's outlook, which is ethical and theological. Because Baldwin is interested in Langland's political thought, she is forced to isolate passus 3–4 from the rest of the poem and to ask herself to which of the competing theories of monarchy Langland seems most sympathetic. But proceeding in this way causes her to overlook what appears to be the poet's final opinion on this matter: although some sorts of rule are clearly preferable to others, politics itself is insufficient as a solution to human problems. There is no dichotomy in that message, for it is in harmony with a central theme of the whole poem.

Goldsmith's book represents an attempt to define the nature and role of "the figure of Piers Plowman," an endeavor frequently undertaken in the past but never before the object of a complete monograph. Within very broad limits Goldsmith's discussion of the Plowman's identity proceeds by means of a sequential treatment of the poem's various episodes. However, within individual chapters the discussion sometimes suffers from a special type of incoherence that makes it difficult to understand exactly what is being asserted about Piers or how so many different sorts of assertions can be compatible. The pressure of the incompatible traits that Goldsmith finds in the text concerning the Plowman leads her at times to infer that the figure is one that develops by quantum leaps (i.e., that Piers is a kind of grand-scale equivocation), but the reader will perhaps find it as easy to infer that Goldsmith herself is the source of at least part of the equivocation she sees in the character of Langland's central figure. The heart of the problem seems to lie in Goldsmith's indecision about whether to adopt a basically inductive or deductive approach to the material under discussion. The result is that she repeatedly seems to fall between those two stools.

At several points in early chapters we are offered what appear to be synthetic, static definitions of Piers and his role, but these definitions are then embarrassed by various pieces of evidence examined in Goldsmith's later discussions. For example, in an early chapter, "The Epiphanies of Piers," Goldsmith offers the hypothesis that Piers embodies "that 'pattern of righteousness' [mentioned by Saint Augustine in *De Trinitate* 8.9] which has the power to stir Will to 'a more ardent charity'" (p. 17). Similarly, at the beginning of the next chapter, "Images and Transformations," she speaks of "Piers the Christian's pattern, the *forma justitiae*, which is nothing less than man bearing the Image of God" (p. 20). There is scarcely anything novel or startling about such statements, and most readers will probably agree with them. Still, Goldsmith must retreat when she confronts Piers for the first time in the actual context of the poem, for it seems that what she has told us about the Plowman heretofore is inapplicable. Hence she speaks of "this Piers" (as opposed to others) in conceding that, in the pardon scene of passus 7, "those critics who have associated this Piers with *homo carnalis* are substantially right" (p. 40).

It must be admitted that there is nothing inherently inconsistent in Goldsmith's view of Piers. He may be, as her investigation suggests, a stable vehicle with a rapidly shifting tenor. Yet her presentation of this view is disjointed, with few hints in earlier chapters to warn us of the complexities that lie ahead. Furthermore, it is difficult to determine exactly where in the poem Goldsmith wishes to locate the Piers she has begun by defining as the *forma justitiae*, for her Augustinian theological preconceptions require her to be almost as dissatisfied with the Piers of the Tree of Charity as she was with the Piers of the pardon episode. Paradoxically, she describes Piers at the tree as hitting after the Fiend "in righteous anger" (p. 68) immediately after a discussion in which she characterizes the Plowman's role in shaking down the apples as a sinful one. She asserts that his motive in shaking the apples should be read as paralleling that of Saint Augustine in the famous pear-tree episode of the *Confessions*: "If the teacher that Langland most admired could convict himself of 'evil for the sake of evil,' clearly even Piers himself could not be exempt from that propensity: even the just man, acting wilfully, does sin" (p. 67).

The example cited above is particularly apt in that it returns us to the heart of the problem with this book: Goldsmith's determination to deduce the influence of the four great Latin fathers in *Piers* wherever possible. To be sure, Goldsmith is very forthright (pp. 3–4) in arguing the case for Langland's veneration of the fathers in question (a case with which this reviewer has no quarrel). But she infers falsely from this veneration that they are the *sole* important theological influence on him (forgetting, apparently, that late-medieval custom dictated that one seldom cited one's contemporaries, even when borrowing liberally from them) and that one can, therefore, always find a suitable and sufficient gloss for *Piers* in those fathers — especially Augustine. While the second of these inferences has enough practical truth (if applied with sensitivity) to be tempting, Goldsmith sometimes appears to turn it on its head in application, using *Piers* to gloss Augustine in a manner reminiscent of the reductivism of Robertson and Huppé's *Piers Plowman and Scriptural Tradition*. Indeed, in certain instances (i.e., pp. 15–19 and 40–46) it seems as though the coherence in the discussion owes more to the sequence of patristic texts cited than to passages from the poem itself. Symptomatic of this tendency is Goldsmith's practice of introducing scriptural texts seldom quoted in *Piers Plowman* (e.g., Psalms 4 and 36) and asserting their importance to Langland on the basis of their importance to Augustine or Ambrose in contexts that seem quite distant from those in which they are found in Langland's poem. Conversely, Psalm 14, which is one of Langland's favorites, receives scant attention—presumably because it was not a favorite of Augustine.

It might seem petty to detail such objections if Goldsmith's instincts were better than her methodology, but unfortunately she remains steadfast to her principles far too often. The results are the sort of incoherence I have described and some serious misreadings of tone and content (as with the discussion of Piers and the pardon). It is distasteful to have to register such strong disapproval of a book into which a considerable amount of honest research and thought have gone and to repudiate the efforts of a scholar as diligent and fair-minded as Goldsmith seems to be. Even so, candor requires admitting that the book is one that will only confuse novices and exasperate experts.

ROBERT ADAMS
Sam Houston State University

MARIA WICKERT, *Studies in John Gower*. Translated by Robert J. Meindl. Washington, D.C.: University Press of America, 1982. Pp. xiv, 249. $19.75 hardcover, $9.75 paper.

PETER G. BEIDLER, ed., *John Gower's Literary Transformations in the* Confessio Amantis: *Original Articles and Translations*. Washington, D.C.: University Press of America, 1982. Pp. viii, 141. $19.75 hardcover, $8.25 paper.

Studies in John Gower was the Habilitationsschrift of Maria Wickert (1915–59) at the University of Cologne, and was published by that institution's press under the title *Studien zu John Gower* in 1953. The present volume is a translation into English of this valuable and—in 1953 particularly—ground-breaking book. Wickert's primary subject is the *Vox clamantis*, Gower's major work in Latin. That poem contains 10,265 lines of elegiac verse, modeled for the most part on Ovid. There are seven books, each with subdivisions and prose headings, as is Gower's manner; the first three have individual prologues also. As Wickert amply demonstrates, the poem is an extremely intricate one, allusive, tough, and obscure by turns. Tackling it in 1953, roughly a decade before the first translation was published by Eric Stockton (*The Major Latin Works of John Gower* [Seattle: University of Washington Press, 1962]) and before John H. Fisher's watershed study of Gower's total output (*John Gower: Moral Philosopher and Friend of Chaucer* [New York: New York University Press, 1964]), was no light undertaking. It is hardly insignificant that after thirty years Wickert's study remains the only full-scale attempt to assess Gower's Latin.

In every way this scholarly silence seems a pity, since the *Vox clamantis* is an important poem and one about which we would do well to learn more. Composed, it is thought, in the later 1370s but with subsequent additions and changes reflecting the tumultuous events of 1381 and later, the *Vox* is in Wickert's view a unique heterogeneity of forms skillfully crafted by Gower to advise the young King Richard II, to provide humankind with moral counsel (as is his obligation as a good Christian), to bring to light religious corruption, and — in what Wickert has termed the "Visio" particularly — to vilify the instigators of social unrest. Since this "Visio" was written quite likely while the heat of the Peasants' Revolt was still on him by a Kentishman living in London, the first book of the *Vox clamantis* offers us one of the few accounts by an intimately involved eyewitness. To the chagrin of various historians who have gone to the *Vox* seeking "facts," however, Gower's version of the revolt is emotive, expressionistic, and heavily allegorized. Wat Tyler becomes a jaybird, Simon Sudbury becomes the Trojan priest Hellenus, and other notables are transformed into assorted animals and Trojans in a tortuous dream sequence whose best literary descendant is perhaps the "Nighttown" chapter in James Joyce's *Ulysses*. Wickert's analysis of this nightmare is learned and illuminating. She shows painstakingly that Gower's models for the "Visio" were less beast fable than prophetic poetry such as that of John of Bridlington and, of course, contemporary sermon practices. Wickert is also a reader of subtle sensitivity and no little psychological insight. She is thus able to detect and identify the dream logic in a sequence easily as forceful — and as rambling — as any in *Piers Plowman*, all the while placing it carefully in an appropriate literary and social context.

What she manages for the "Visio" section Wickert carries out as well for the remaining books of the *Vox*. Her two-part third chapter ("The *Vox Clamantis* and the Medieval Sermon") is noteworthy for its investigation of the image of the "homilist as archer," which she traces through the Bible and the works of the fathers. Chapter 4 demonstrates how Gower was influenced by and used the *speculum regis* literature so common in the later Middle Ages. In chapter 5, she draws together points raised earlier about the true nature of Gower's "class critique" (to be carefully distinguished, in her view, from estates satire), showing it to contain elements of a new, sophisticated analysis of social structure based on the realities of multiple occupations in late-fourteenth-century England, in addition to the "already...antiquated" (p. 133) triadic analysis that had been the norm. This she combines with a look at "moral" Gower's world view as poet, Englishman, and internationalist Christian. Throughout, her comments on Gower's poetry, his sources, and his intellectual milieu are penetrating and broadly applicable: her study touches on Gower's Anglo-Norman *Mirour de l'omme*, makes pointed use of Auerbach, and extends the work of G. R. Owst. Of course, she is not accurate in all her conclusions. In her first chapter, and again in the third, she theorizes extensively about what might be meant by the different attitudes expressed in the three recensions of the *Vox* toward the king and commons and their mutual responsibilities within the state. But surely this is to complicate matters unnecessarily. Gower rightly comprehended that a new political theory has emerged with the accession of Henry IV and adjusted his poem to include it. For many readers her most useful chapter will be her last. In it she provides some of the most intelligent and perceptive criticism yet of Gower's poetic theory and skills in the *Confessio amantis*. "Gower's Narrative Technique" is surely on a level with C. S. Lewis's oft-quoted observations on the *Confessio* in *The Allegory of Love*; like that chapter, this of Wickert's represents a benchmark for serious readings of Gower's English poem, and particularly of the tales ("Acteon," "Pygmalion," and "Florent") she singles out for discussion.

Wickert's *Studies in John Gower* is seminal, in short. As the first to explore comprehensively the interconnections of Gower's three major poems, Wickert cleared the way for Fisher, whose own book has in turn enlightened a generation of Gower readers by pursuing these connections even further. That the book is not well known we owe undoubtedly to its focus on a difficult and lengthy Latin poem and to its own composition in Wickert's scholarly, if not unduly knotty, German. Now, thanks to Robert J. Meindl, the latter of these barriers at least has been removed. His translation is excellent—clear, accurate, and relatively free from the unidiomatic (though an occasional "Germanism" slips in, as on p. 74, when he translates "Sein *Mirour de l'omme* handelt zunächst 'de vitiis et virtutibus'" [p. 72] as "His *Mirour de l'omme* first *deals*..."). Moreover, Meindl has made several changes in the style and layout of the volume that, in the main, are helpful in rendering the text more accessible. Thus Wickert's long sentences and paragraphs are often broken up for the benefit of English readers unused to German custom; all the footnotes are translated (a great benefit for many, since Wickert quotes extensively from an array of Latin and medieval French sources); adjustments are made to accommodate current reference form (i.e., Wickert's ubiquitous "Bodleiana" becomes simply "Bodleian," her "*Mod. Phil.*" becomes *MP*). Not all changes are felicitous, however, or brought about with the reader's comfort in view: Meindl would have done better to leave the footnotes at page bottom, or at least to have included them in a separate section in the back, than to print them at the close of each chapter in cramped fashion following the final line of text. One might also point out various typographical errors: "Sophis" for "Sophia," p. 49; "horbor" for "harbor," p. 55; "Baptists's," p. 72; "assoication," p. 79; "quck" for "quick," p. 95; "astonomy," p. 109; "aims" for "alms," p. 151; "fiteen," p. 154; "psychmachia," p. 181; "nympths," p. 220; "Pygaleon," p. 221; and also "Hunterain," p. 18, for the Hunterian manuscript in Glasgow—a slip apparently retained from Wickert (p. 11). Finally, prospective buyers of *Studies in John Gower* ought to note well its unfortunately fragile binding. The paper copy of this reviewer lost a dozen leaves after a single reading, with easily twice that many more attached by but a stitch or two. Blind economy of this sort in the publisher in no way does justice to the merits of the author, the translator, or the book itself, and it would be sad indeed if such parsimony prevented Wickert's fine scholarship from finding its way to a widening circle of study shelves.

John Gower's Literary Transformations in the Confessio amantis: Original Articles and Translations is, as the title implies, a collection of work by different hands. Edited by Peter G. Beidler, of Lehigh University, the volume contains, in the first half, two essays by the editor (on the tales of "Acteon" and "Acis and Galatea") and fourteen by his former graduate students Carolyn Koepke Brown (the tales of "Deianira and Nessus" and

"Pygmalion"), Judith C. G. Moran ("Pyramus and Thisbe" and "Midas"), Natalie Epinger Ruyak ("Phebus and Daphne" and "Neptune and Cornix"), Nicolette Stasko ("Iphis" and "Iphis and Araxarathen"), Karl A. Zipf, Jr. ("Icarus" and "Echo"), John B. Gaston ("Ceyx and Alceone" and "Leucothoe"), and Douglas L. Lepley ("Argus and Mercury" and "Tereus"). The purpose of all sixteen essays is to compare Gower's adaptations of Ovid's *Metamorphoses* to their originals to answer the question, "Did Gower merely retell the classical narratives which were his favorite sources, or did he put his own distinctively medieval and personal stamp on them?" (p. vii). Part 2 of the book offers a longer examination by Beidler of the relationship of Gower's "Tale of Nectanabus" to its probable source (the Anglo-Norman *Roman de toute chevalerie* by Thomas of Kent) and translations of the *Roman* and Julius Valerius's *Res gestae Alexandri Macedonis*, executed by Patricia Innerbichler De Bellis and Edna S. deAngeli, respectively.

In a collaborative volume one necessarily expects to find a certain unevenness among the contributions, and this is the case here. Overall, Beidler comes out best by comparison, in part because of his evident generosity in cutting himself short to leave space for others. His discussion of the "Tale of Acteon," while owing something to Maria Wickert, is nonetheless crisp and to the point. Like Wickert, Beidler treats Gower's emphasis on Acteon's complicity in the sacrilege for which he was punished as both a major modification of Ovid and a justification for its appearance in the *Confessio* as an illustration of the sins of the eye. A similar analysis is directed at "Acis and Galatea," which Beidler shows is thoroughly recast by Gower to remove the complex sympathy that Ovid evokes for Polyphemus through his striking lament and simple, unpremeditated response to finding Galatea in the arms of Acis. In Gower's version Polyphemus has no lament—indeed, he is virtually silent—and he ruminates on his envy of Acis before laying plans to kill him. Again Gower has carefully adjusted his source to fill his need—in this case, a tale exemplifying Envy. Beidler's longest discussion, of the "Tale of Nectanabus" and the *Roman de toute chevalerie*, makes essentially the same point about Gower's skill in altering sources to suit his poem. One of the difficulties facing Beidler here, however, is that Gower doubtless was aware of at least three accounts of the Nectanabus story, and, therefore (as Beidler remarks in his brief introduction, p. 81), precise conclusions about what was modified and what borrowed are impossible to draw. Another problem is that in this essay alone of all the pieces here collected no attempt is made to demonstrate why the tale is appropriate to its function as exemplum in the *Confessio*. Because sorcery was connected with Gluttony as a "sin of the mouth" in the Middle Ages, Gower's choice of this story is apt. Pointing this out would have strengthened Beidler's case. Still, Beidler's is the most thorough treatment of the "Nectanabus" currently in print and has real value as an introduction to the tale and its little-read sources. Moreover, his assertion that in the presentation of details surrounding Alexander's birth Gower may have intended a "kind of rough parallel to the New Testament stories of the Annunciation and of Christ's birth" (p. 88) is suggestive, if not thoroughly substantiated by Beidler's brief essay and ought to be pursued further.

The essays by Beidler's students are surprisingly good — terse, useful, no-nonsense work that lends the volume much potential value as a supplementary reading for undergraduate survey courses including Gower. One or two seem to miss the point a little or fail to drive it home with assurance. There is also a unanimity of opinion about them (all stress Gower's "humanizing" of Ovid's characters, his greater emphasis on "realism," and his rejection of multiple-narrative viewpoints) that doubtless reflects the concerns of the mentor-as-editor. Nonetheless, every essay adds its measure to what we know about Gower's poetic endeavor. Particularly illuminating are Carol Koepke Brown on "Pygmalion," John B. Gaston on "Ceyx and Alceone," Judith C. G. Moran on "Midas," Karl A. Zipf, Jr., on "Echo," Nicolette Stasko on "Iphis and Araxarathen," Douglas L. Lepley on "Tereus," and Natalie Epinger Ruyak on "Neptune and Cornix."

What may make *John Gower's Literary Transformations* most helpful in the long run, however, is the publication in such accessible form of the texts of Thomas of Kent and Julius Valerius. Both accounts of the birth of Alexander, while part of longer works quite well known in the Middle Ages, have been available in more modern times only in hard-to-come-by editions long out of print (Paul Meyer, 1886, and Bernard Kübler, 1888). The translations of Patricia Innerbichler De Bellis and Edna S. deAngeli enhance the suitability of these excerpts for classroom use. Scholars may, of course, quibble variously about translations that, in De Bellis's words, are "neither rigidly literal nor poetic" (her rendering of "Li baron de la vile" as "the village baron," pp. 98–99, is a case in point), but they are readable and not inaccurate. The decision by the editor to include them in his volume was a wise one, certainly.

Formally, *John Gower's Literary Transformations* comes off somewhat better than does *Studies in John Gower*. Perhaps because Beidler's book is glued and not sewed, its pages are solidly affixed (University Press of America take note), and do not annoy the reader by pulling out in handfuls. Typographical errors are present, the most serious being *Journal of English and Germanic Philosophy* for *Philology* on p. 81. Others, however, should be corrected as follows: "unequivocably," p. 14; "gristly" for "grisly," p. 17; "foothaste" for "foolhaste," p. 27; "*Metamorphoses*" and "perservering," p. 33.

On the whole, then, Beidler's collection makes a solid contribution to the field of Gower studies. Coupled with the translation of Wickert's influential volume, it represents a strong advance in our available knowledge of late-medieval poetry in England. Chaucer scholars, as well as those at work in other areas, will stand to benefit directly from the presence of both books on their library shelves.

R. F. YEAGER
Warren Wilson College

PIERO BOITANI, *English Medieval Narrative in the 13th and 14th Centuries*. Translated by Joan Krakover Hall. Cambridge: Cambridge University Press, 1982. Pp. x, 309. $42.50.

With the writings of Northrop Frye, Walter Ong, Wayne Booth, and other recent critics, discussion of the narrative process has taken on a new dimension. Just as the emergence of the concept of transformational grammar has converted linguistic analysis from static to dynamic, the emergence of the concept of narrative transformations has become the starting point for transactional criticism. Major transformations of structure and style occur in the passage from oral to written narrative. These transformations alter radically the relations between author and audience. Piero Boitani's lively study is well versed in both American and European contributions to transactional literary theory. The first half of his book treats pre-Chaucerian and non-Chaucerian narrative; the last half is devoted to Chaucer. In his final essay, on Chaucerian narrative, the theoretical bases of his own criticism are most clearly set forth. When the earlier narratives are considered in the light of this conclusion, their role as precursors to Chaucer's literary achievement becomes clear.

Boitani's first chapter, "The Religious Tradition," explores the didactic narratives of the homiletic and penitential traditions. The commentary is more descriptive than analytical, detailing the variety in the stories and tracing the drift from instruction toward entertainment. We are dealing here more with authorial intent and the preservation of manuscripts than Boitani's treatment allows, because "solas" has no doubt always existed alongside "sentence," but there is no doubt that in extant materials the sermon was the first "seedbed of themes for storytelling," and narrative appears to have developed gradually away from exemplification toward mimesis. The earliest legends, in the "Katherine group," were written more for devotion than for entertainment. Later collections like the *South English Legendary* and the *Golden Legend* introduce drama and fantasy to please the audience. *St. Erkenwald*, *Patience*, and *Cleanness* mark the emergence of a conscious literary art.

The next chapter, "The Comic Tradition," chronicles a further movement from the exemplary toward the entertaining. The characteristics of the religious narratives were determined by the intentions of the clergy; those of the comic tales, by the demands of the laity. Since all we have preserved in this vein (exclusive of Chaucer) are *Dame Sirith*, the *Fox and the Wolf*, and two or three other pieces, the chapter is necessarily short, but Boitani concludes by observing that such narrative was not without its exemplary intention; it simply made its point by ridicule rather than by admonition.

In his third chapter, "The World of Romance," Boitani adjudges the English non-Chaucerian romances on the whole inferior to their French originals. To please their bourgeoise audiences, their makers stripped them of formal requirements, structural complications, and subtleties of *sen*. Commentary on the individual romances is sensitive and informed. Boitani follows Derek Brewer and other recent critics in finding the chief contribution of the non-Chaucerian romances to be their achievement of natural dialogue that made possible the naturalness of the dialogue of Chaucer and Shakespeare. *Gawain and the Green Knight* shows the same psychological depth and conscious artistry compared with the other non-Chaucerian romances that *Patience* and *Cleanness* do compared with other didactic narrative.

Pearl and *Piers Plowman* are treated in the next chapter, "Dream and Vision." These poems are viewed as advancing beyond exemplary instruction and popular entertainment to "teleological narrative," whose interest derives more from the play of ideas than from physical adventure. Boitani denies the separation between poetic and religious impulses in these poems. He finds that narrative and religious instruction reinforce one another, as they do in the *Divine Comedy*. The comparison between the polysemous structures of *Piers Plowman* and the *Divine Comedy* is particularly instructive.

In the chapter "Narrative Collections and Gower," Boitani quotes Viktor Shklovsky to the effect that frame stories can be found only in written literature, and he surveys the various types of collections, from mechanical successions like the *Alphabet of Tales* to dramatically motivated collections like the *Confessio Amantis*. This analysis paves the way for the perspicacious treatment of Chaucer's poems in the next 140 pages. This treatment is divided into three sections: (1) the dream poem, (2) the romance, and (3) the narrative collection, paralleling to a certain extent the structure of the first half of the book. Chaucer's poems are perceived as literary artifacts, embodying different materials, for a different audience, an audience that up until this time had taken its pleasure in reading Latin, French, and even Italian literature. Already in *The Book of the Duchess* reading appears as an authenticating device that enables the narrator to draw upon the whole literary tradition, confronting reality *sub specie aeternitatis*. By addressing a reading public instead of a listening audience, Chaucer created in English a written art form. As Boitani puts it (p. 187):

For Chaucer the book (literature) both causes the dream and exists within it. And Chaucer was in fact the first European writer to use this formula, which was to become a distinctive feature, if not a *topos*, of Western culture. At the beginning of the fourteenth century Dante, in the episode of Paolo and Francesca, had consecrated the book as an occasion for love, sin, murder and eternal damnation; now, in the second half of the century, Chaucer consecrates it as the key and integrating element of the dream experience — one of the fundamental activities of the human psyche — and on the basis of this the book becomes the occasion for the quest of love, nature and poetry. Thus, before Petrarch's humanism, or at least independently of it, literature became one of the driving forces of European civilization.

Boitani follows Deter Mehl in viewing *Troilus* as a poem intended more to be read than to be recited. He points out how closely its structure and narrative technique are modeled on that of the *Filostrato*, indicating how much of Chaucer's literary technique he learned from the Italian poets who for nearly a century had been wrestling with the problem of communicating with a reading audience. However, Boitani cautions against the supposition that Chaucer achieved the transition to modern fiction. He believes that Chaucer could not have imagined the role for the narrator delineated by many of his modern critics. And he believes that Chaucer's characters never attain psychological autonomy; they remain until the end incarnations of models.

In the final section of the book the critical basis for Boitani's criticism becomes most apparent, as he explores the author-reader signals in *The Legend of Good Women* and *The Canterbury Tales*. As with *Troilus*, he denies an essentially mimetic intent in *The General Prologue* and the links between the tales, pointing out how completely the characters of the pilgrims and their interactions are viewed through the eyes of the narrator. The commentary on individual tales is fresh and enlightening — particularly that on the *Pardoner's* and *The Nun's Priest's Tales*. Boitani concludes with a coda on the vast transformations that have occurred between the monolayered narrative of the *Fox and the Wolf* and the multilayered structure of *The Nun's Priest's Tale*.

Every part of this book is rewarding, but its special contribution is the recognition of Chaucer's intellectual, literary narrative mode, in contrast to the monitory, oral mode of so much non-Chaucerian Middle English narrative. Chaucer's achievement provides the foundation upon which all subsequent literature in English has been built. Especial attention should be called to the felicity of the writing in *English Medieval Narrative*. Although it is described as translation, the text reads more smoothly than many books composed originally in English.

JOHN H. FISHER
University of Tennessee

J. D. BURNLEY, *Chaucer's Language and the Philosophers' Tradition*. Chaucer Studies, vol. 2. Cambridge: D. S. Brewer; Totowa, N.J.: Rowman and Littlefield, 1979. Pp. ix, 196. $30.00.

By finding the language of moral philosophy in Chaucer's poetry, J. D. Burnley recovers a domain of affective Christian values (mainly patience, compassion, and pity) resting uneasily between stoical ethics and penitentially focused analyses of vice and virtue. He does this by explicating the tyrant *topos*, giving us its lexicon and its sometimes surprising transformations, along with the lexicon of its antitypes. Here Burnley does all medievalists a service. But, given the title of his study, Burnley, of course, would go further: by showing the presence of that moral vocabulary in Chaucer's poetry, he addresses the Chaucerian critic especially and joins such scholars as Judson Allen (*A Distinction of Stories*, Columbus: Ohio University Press, 1981) in suggesting the moral function of characters and the ethically exemplary function of tales. When Burnley turns to Chaucer, however, he shifts from strength to weakness — this because of a naïve literary insinuation: that the appearance of a moral vocabulary in appropriate poetical contexts becomes prima facie evidence of Chaucer's moral direction. Stated so baldly, that insinuation could hardly appeal to so undogmatic a scholar as Burnley. But it nevertheless is the evil genius in his method — despite his disclaimer that he will not interpret Chaucer, hoping only to trace the presence of a moral-philosophical vocabulary and, perhaps, here and there suggest the direction an interpretation might take.

Of course, Burnley's literary sins diminish or not given one's own sense of Chaucer's poetry. For me, Burnley's pervasive conflation of things narrators say with Chaucer's own, morally unmediated voice; his seeming indifference to immediate literary contexts; and his sublimely flat sense of voice and rhetorical stance — these breed poor readings, as occasionally does Burnley's insistence on the tyrant *topos*. One example, a just one, I hope, will have to suffice. Because the language of saintly prudence includes "pacient," "stable," "ferme," "stedefast," "constant," "sad," "symple," "benygne," and "wys" or "rype," Burnley can explore the ironies generated by the application of that language to a notoriously unstable subject — Criseyde and her "slydynge of corage." Ignoring the immediate narrator context — the curious resort just here to parallel *effictio* — Burnley seizes on "slydynge" in the same spirit that earlier guided his focus on "sodeyn" (though the narrator insisted that Criseyde did *not* love Troilus suddenly). He convicts Criseyde of negating the ideals of moral philosophy, thus becoming "an example of instability" (p. 95). Surely Criseyde is more than this. Insecure, unsure, and eventually disastrously yielding to Diomede, yes, but she is also "sobre," "symple," and "wys" in the very portrait that ends on "slydynge of corage." The irony and the pity here are not simple: perhaps she is too tender of heart. The narrator avoids telling us exactly how Diomede "bereaves" Criseyde of all her pain, and surely her portrait is not that of a tyrant's. To make her a tyrant figure, Burnley must see her as superficial in her virtues and trivial in her actions. Only then can she become something transparent, rather than an enigma—someone whose actions cast doubt on all of our certainties, the moral among them.

The medieval tyrant figure embodies passion, cruelty, injustice, and heartlessness (no room, apparently, for a benign tyrant). Its antitype is first that of the rationally guided moral philosopher (Seneca)—who exercises prudence and temperance. For Boethius, Gower, Chaucer, and others, the Senecan type gives way to the prudential but compassionate man, with the possibility here extended into an affective psychology in which intent is the key to virtue.

The first chapter reconstructs the tyrant *topos*. As a moral symbol, the tyrant indicates a disordered body politic and a king "oppressed by fierce and unrestrained passions" (p. 17). Thus the metaphorical transference of the *topos* to any strong passion becomes possible, Burnley argues, allowing Chaucer to use the *topos* in love, marriage, and parent-child contexts as well as in judicial ones. Burnley's linguistic method—identifying colloca-tions of words that characterize the *topos*—allows him to find aspects of the tyrant figure in unlikely places (mainly by tracing words traditionally associated with the *topos*). Here we find something tyrannical about the *topos*: poets cannot use its vocabulary without implying the entire *topos*. This confuses differences between analogy and metaphor, thus vitiating both as ways of formal argument by implication or as ways of expressing likeness.

In Middle English, the words for the *topos* include "cruel," "irous," and "wood," along with "hard," "dangerous," and "wrathe." *Melibee* centrally offers us a lord counseled out of his tyrannical passion, and, ingeniously, Burnley sees Phebus Apollo in *The Manciple's Tale* as an example of "tyranny, with its reckless impetuosity" (pp. 20-21). The point is that a language of tyranny appears ("trouble wit," "ire," "smyteth gilteles") and that Chaucer thus succumbs to the traditional associations—a dubious claim given the possibilities here of parody and that Phebus kills his *guilty* wife (though perhaps unadvisedly) and then invents her innocence. Against such figures as Phebus, Burnley offers us Theseus—a character who heeds pleas for "pite" and "mercy," thus conforming to a model of the ideal ruler.

From tyrant as lord or king, we move to tyrantlike behavior, especially in Love's service, and especially in relation to the God of Love. In reviewing *The Parliament of Fowls*, *Troilus and Criseyde*, and *The Book of the Duchess*, Burnley offers a decidedly moral reading: from the man in black, to Troilus, and on to the poet-narrator in the *Prologue* to *The Legend of Good Women*, Burnley suggests a "certain rationalistic distaste of the passion [Love]" on Chaucer's behalf, thus placing Chaucer alongside Gower as morally exercised over love's irrationality, its caprice, its "inaccessibility to rational analysis," and its disregard for established order (p. 31). This is to see Chaucer as principally the composer of *Mel*, *The Parson's Tale*, and various moral lyrics—all read as forms of spiritual autobiography.

Mel of course takes us to Prudence and eventually to Patience. Prudence involves preconsideration, which Burnley notes is as essential to true *gentilesse* as is pity, and is a guide first to virtuous action and finally to salvation. It anchors the moral philosopher, participating in Seneca's *tranquillitas* and *firmitas* and in Boethius's *patientia*. Medieval Christianity adds humility, meekness, and hope, thus allowing for a transference of the philosopher image to saints. But when Burnley turns to Chaucer's characters, he practices a double simplification: reducing verbal images to their traditional outlines (thus precluding eccentric authorial nuance) and confining characters to the symbols they most conveniently represent. Here the Wife of Bath exemplifies tyranny for abusing her husbands within a "topsy-turvy" moral framework (p. 85); whereas everything justifies Cecilia because hers is a Saint's Life. Burnley does rightly observe that most of Chaucer's references to tyranny and its antitypes are in passing, usually to set tone or to sketch in the idealism of a stock character. But tone and the rhetorical contexts for a character's idealism (the *NPT*'s widow, for example) are complex affairs not well served by a focus on a particular moral lexicon.

Yet even as I cavil, Burnley's assertions can suddenly moderate themselves. Although offering Griselda as the "philosophical wife" — steadfast, firm, and stable, someone who seeks "no more than to obey the will of her husband [though she *wills* it so in that perverse, paradoxical battle]" — Burnley then, about sixteen pages later, says that Chaucer subscribes to no particular philosophical system, that instead Chaucer prefers traditional teaching that had become thoroughly poeticized. Perhaps this is so, yet Chaucer will do several things at once. He may join Gower over claret and profess the good of love modulated by reason, but such a traditional ideal could give him very little insight into love or the ways of prudence (and insight seems to be what so many of his narrators seek). That ideal could not in itself help him understand what love means in relation to his own experience or to the fictionally expressed experience of others. Chaucer's private moral philosophy would give him no way of seeking truth; rather, its only object would be a way of living, of behaving. Burnley wants Chaucer to work out a moral program that a medieval audience would appreciate, even though for us that program may produce unsatisfying results. What interests me about this is that I see our dissatisfactions reflecting Chaucer's (otherwise why the rhetoric of endings for *TC* or the blatant shift to an empty, formal ending for *PF*?).

The book ends with chapters on feeling and "gentilesse," with the exclusiveness of a courtly "gentil herte" contrasted with the "pietas" and charity all true Christians share. Burnley further cogently notes that "gentilesse," "pitee" and love are "interdependent and imply a union of feeling with one who is perceived to be our similitude" (p. 157). This helps answer undergraduates who wonder why Criseyde should care a fig whether or not Troilus loves her. She would deny both her class and her "gentilesse" not to care, much as the Prioress misplaces her "gentilesse" by caring too much for her dogs (comical similitude).

I wish more had been done with Chaucer's views on the "transcendental, affective, relational ethic implicit in the New Testament" — an ethic that preoccupies Burnley all too briefly in chapter 8, "Beyond Reason." We learn that here "the letter of law is to be renounced for the sake of equity, and sacred texts are to be read in a way that corresponds with the impulse of charity. . . . Even ritual observance must come second to compassion" (p. 148). Sapience gives way to virtuous intention. Surely Chaucer interests himself in intention and in matters of feeling when he seeks to understand love. Lydgate witnesses to part of this in a passage Burnley quotes from "Complaynt of a Loveres Lyfe": *"And whoso that shal writen of distresse / In party nedeth to know felyngly / Cause and rote of al such malady"* (lines 187–89).

To "know feelingly," I suspect, is the heart of Chaucer's inquiry into love, "gentilesse," prudence, saintliness, or whatever interests him. Burnley turns from such a Chaucer to a poet who inquires less than he judges and who plays the moral ironist in a surprisingly low style (surely he would have wanted to move as well as instruct his audience). Feeling enters only in the aridly scholastic context of perceptual psychology: that one must have some softness of heart to perceive anything other than one's own fancies. Yet it is in understanding the subtle relationships between truth telling and feeling that Chaucer proves preeminently a philosopher. If we seek a philosophical Chaucer, we need to go beyond Burnley's focus. We need to leave the prosaic enclosures of moral philosophy and enter the worlds in which Chaucer explores how our subjectivity either enhances or cripples our understanding of truth—thereby affecting the quality of truth telling for narrator after narrator as well as teller after teller.

JOHN M. HILL
U.S. Naval Academy

JANET COLEMAN, *Medieval Readers and Writers, 1350–1400.* New York: Columbia University Press, 1981. Pp. 337. $27.50.

In a personal aside in his translation of Ranuph Higden's *Polychronicon* (ca. 1327), John Trevisa updates Higden's earlier remark concerning the ubiquity of French in the schools, saying, ". . . in alle þe gramere scoles of Engelonde, chilren leueþ Frensche and construeþ and lerneþ an Englische . . . now children of gramer scole conneþ na more Frensche þan can hir lift heele." The change in the tutelage in the classroom mirrors the rapid change elsewhere in this society and marks a first movement away from the basic assumptions of the late Middle Ages concerning the efficacy of Latin for the literate man. This vernacular tuition also underlines the growth of a nascent English middle class, a class that was later to raise its voice against

Richard's absolutist policies and his war against the French. The classroom pedagogy that both Higden and Trevisa thought worthy of comment contributed to the demise of that fundamental assumption of the Middle Ages that authority was not only beneficent but divinely appointed and hence demanded our obedience. Tuition in the native tongue exercised an influence on such disparate phenomena as the Wyclifite challenge to lawful dominion, the growth of an urban mercantile class, the cry for scripture in English, and the increased use of English in all areas of government. The substitution of English for French or Latin in the class-room, although perhaps only a small part of the tumultuous social mosaic of the second half of the fourteenth century, is a potent symbol of the general collapse of traditional authority in the half century between 1350 and 1400, a collapse culminating in Richard's execution.

The literature of this age was, "like the society that it reflected and that patronized it, experiencing transition" (p. 280). With these words Janet Coleman states in a general way her belief that the turmoil of the society gave way to an equally tumultuous literature, a literature characterized by "the unstable genres and the shifting narrative focus of many of the long and didactic poems" (p. 280). It is Coleman's thesis that only by re-establishing the nonliterary context of the age can we adequately grasp the meaning of these poems. To such an end, she traces the social upheaval and the age's literary oeuvre in four major chapters: vernacular literacy and lay education; the literature of social unrest; memory, preaching, and the literature of a society in transition; and theology, nonscholastic literature, and poetry. Her first chapter examines the reading habits of the aristocracy and the "middle classes"; through an inventory of extant wills she is able to discern something of the literary taste of both groups. Her most striking conclusion is that the difference between the aristocratic courtier and the petit bourgeois was no longer one of literacy but rather one of taste. She contends that members of the growing urban mercantile class not only were literate but were patrons for the new literature and were themselves the intended audience for such socially and theologically oriented texts as *Piers Plowman*, *Pierce the Ploughman's Creed*, *Richard the Redeles* and *Mum and the Sothsegger*. The decline in the rigidly-adhered-to legal status of the differing estates in favor of a classification based more on economic and functional importance is well represented both in imagina-tive literature, e.g., *Pierce the Ploughman's Creed*, and in the laws of

Parliament. And as more individuals were able to move between these class distinctions and avail themselves of increased wealth and its privileges, i.e., education, they required an imaginative literature consonant with their recent experience of social mobility. The chivalric values of romance loved by the nobility did not please this new literate and urban middle class.

Coleman argues that it is the poetry of the second half of the fourteenth century that reflects all factors of the social maelstrom; it attacks political, social, and ecclesiastical corruption where it finds it and gives eloquent voice to the demands of an increasingly powerful literate middle class. She divides this literature of social complaint into seven categories and defines the salient features of each. Her method is to illustrate through an examination chiefly of the content of the poetry of the period — that is, in Latin, French, and Middle English — the pressing social, theological, and political issues. She argues that the simultaneity and immediacy offered by such verse justifies our viewing these poems as "documents bristling with contemporary issues" (p. 60). She distinguishes intelligently between the political-complaint poetry of the earlier part of the fourteenth century — poems like "Against the King's Taxes" in MS Harley 2253 — and those of the last two decades by arguing that the poetry of the first half of the century is more balanced, examining both sides of each question in a scholastic fashion, whereas the complaint poetry of the closing years of the fourteenth century is polemical, rather like much of the corpus of MS Digby 102, with little or no interest in the earlier tradition of debate and with an authorial persona who represents himself as arbitrator of what is socially, politically, and religiously correct. The chapter concludes with a sympathetic, but not novel, commentary on Gower's work and its central place in the poetry of complaint.

Coleman's fourth chapter is fascinating and ambitious, covering such subjects as the impact that books of exempla and *distinctiones* had on the memories of fourteenth-century preachers, on the degree and type of Scripture translation, on the function of the *forma praedicandi* in sermons, on the impact of the Wyclifite movement on lay literacy, and on the social and political significance of Lollardy. Her general thesis proposes that the growth in the production of books caused a concomitant increase in social mobility and a diminution in the capacity of memory — a diminution that in turn fostered the need for greater book production. This chapter is stimulating but fraught with problems. For example, her assertion, an interesting one, that allegorization seems to develop only in literate ages is manifestly wrong. Allegory was not uncommon in the Old Testament, e.g., the riddle of Ezekiel (17.3–8) concerning the vine and the two eagles. Coleman underestimates the importance of earlier translations of Scripture into English verse. Those translations did not diminish the importance of Scripture and did confront the congregation "directly with the Word," since in many instances the original text was itself poetic. An examination of the manuscripts of the Northern Homily Cycle (manuscripts dating from the late 1320s through 1425) show that the clergy preached the gospel pericope for the Sunday *translated* from the Vulgate into English verse. Indeed such translation of the Gospel pericope for the Sunday can be illustrated in a great number of thirteenth- and fourteenth-century vernacular sermon codices, many of which remain, unfortunately, unedited. Her careful and illuminating scrutiny of the period between 1350 and 1400 underestimates the contributions — though she is indeed aware of them — made by an earlier age to biblical translation; e.g., the *Surtees Psalter* (ca. 1250–1300) is a good idiomatic translation of the entire Psalter in verse; somewhat later we have Rolle's careful translation of the Psalter with accompanying exegesis; this is followed by the *Midland Prose Psalter* (ca. 1325–50), and of course the Canticles were also translated.

The Psalms have always been a special case in medieval scriptural translation. But if we turn from strict translation to paraphrase — or, more accurately, paraphrase-translation — presented in verse, there was in the thirteenth century solid historical precedent for the translators of the fourteenth century; e.g., *La Estorie del Euangelie* (MS Dulwich College 22, ca. 1250) is a paraphrase of the Gospels with the standard inclusion of homiletic and apocryphal items. A great many lives of Christ were written between the midthirteenth and late fourteenth century that incorporate Gospel material, e.g., *Passion of Our Lord* (MS Jesus College, Oxford, ca. 1300).

Coleman's final chapter concerns the nature of late-fourteenth-century theological dispute and its representation in the literature of the literate laity. Coleman's grasp here is certain, and she deftly illustrates how, for example, the intellectually rigorous theology of Ockham and his followers "filtered" down to find a home in vernacular literature and how the pastoral catechesis that concerned the laity moved from the laity into the schools and there effected a change in the learned debates within the universities on the subject of ethics. Of course, in the greatest compositions of this period such a rigid scheme of "up–down" will not do. The nexus between the bewildering variety of theological, social, and political critique and the poet is a complex one, with the author of *Piers Plowman*, for instance, "thumbing continuously through the handbooks on his desk to help him find an orderly, vernacular path through the thicket of theological and social opinion on the vexed question of Christian salvation and 'rendering what one owes' for it."

Coleman has written a perceptive, ambitious, and sprawling volume. Her grasp of the historical fabric of this complex half century is firm and enlivens her reading of the literature. My most serious reservation is that it attempts too much; we are not given sufficiently sustained investigations in a particular area, with the result that I found myself at times unable to see the sum of the thesis for the parts. The bibliography is valuable, and the breadth of reading it encompasses is encyclopedic. This is a book from which scholars from a number of disciplines will profit. It points to a more nearly complete understanding of the complex relationship between literature and society, and for this Coleman is to be commended.

THOMAS J. HEFFERNAN
University of Tennessee

RICHARD KENNETH EMMERSON, *Antichrist in the Middle Ages: A Study of Medieval Apocalypticism, Art, and Literature*. Seattle: University of Washington Press, 1981. Pp. x, 366. $19.50.

Scholarly works often must make a choice between two audiences: Are they to be written for specialists in a rather narrowly defined field or for generalists whose interest is spread over a somewhat larger territory? A book on Chaucer may, on the one hand, speak only to those who are well within the borders of its scholarly tradition; on the other, if it attempts to address a more general audience, it runs the risk of being received with impatience, at best, by scholars. *Antichrist in the Middle Ages* takes on the difficult task of addressing specialists and nonspecialists alike; that is to say, it is a book addressed both to those whose field is medieval apocalypticism and those whose interest is almost any area of the Middle Ages. This book is an important contribution to medieval studies not least because it successfully engages the interest of both audiences.

To those whose interest is medieval apocalypticism, it presents a warning, perhaps even an implied polemic (though there is nothing polemical about the tone of this work, which is consistently respectful to previous scholarship—and thoroughly acquainted with it as well). The warning is that in the past scholarship has tended to concentrate too narrowly on one side of the Antichrist tradition, emphasizing its radical and millenarial aspects at the expense of a more conservative tradition that is, though less well known to moderns, more pervasive. The first three chapters of the book define this Antichrist tradition, treating it first in terms of its relationship to medieval apocalypticism generally, then in terms of the exegetical interpretations that are its basis, and finally in terms of a vita, that is, in terms of the characteristic features of the life and deeds of Antichrist as these were understood throughout the Middle Ages.

As Emmerson demonstrates in his impressive perusal of an exceedingly wide range of primary sources, well integrated in the body of the text and usefully presented in an extensive bibliography and copious notes, the Antichrist tradition is rich and varied. To the generalist this study therefore provides an invitation to use the Antichrist tradition as a help in understanding those works of art, literature, and theology which have been identified as having apocalyptic content. He himself provides us with a model of such analysis in chapters 4 and 5, which deal with the influence of the Antichrist tradition in art and literature, respectively. Chapter 5 covers didactic literature, drama, allegory, and finally, in the most stimulating analysis—offering as it does the outline of a new reading of the poem—*Piers Plowman*. His examples, effective as they are, are necessarily somewhat schematic and therefore best seen as a summons to the reader both to go more deeply into these texts and to examine others as well, using the insights and resources that the book has brought together.

There is an implied warning in this part of the book as well, however. If the first part provides a corrective against conceiving the Antichrist tradition too narrowly, that is, seeing it only as it relates to radical strains of medieval apocalypticism, the second part implicitly warns against seeing Antichrist too broadly: it warns against a tendency to use the word "Antichrist" as a synonym for anything vaguely apocalyptic. Emmerson convincingly demonstrates throughout the book that the tradition is rich and many-sided. But he is equally convincing in his demonstration that the tradition is specific. Once again without polemical tone, Emmerson warns against those who use Antichrist to mean the devil, or merely someone who has sinister connections.

Instead, as he summarizes for us in the far-from-tautological conclusion of this book, "Antichrist is Antichrist — not Satan, not the pope, but a man with devilish connections who will come for a short time in the future to deceive and persecute the righteous, kill the prophets Enoch and Elias, and finally be destroyed before the Second Advent of Christ" (p. 237). Those who make the acquaintance of this Antichrist through Emmerson's careful scholarship may well find their reading of many medieval texts enriched. Chaucer himself comes to mind as one author who may well have drawn on this tradition in ways that still remain to be discovered in figures such as the Pardoner. Because of such possibilities, this study is not only significant but exciting as well.

RONALD B. HERZMAN
State University of New York

P. L. HEYWORTH, ed., *Medieval Studies for J. A. W. Bennett (Aetatis Suae LXX)*. Oxford: Clarendon Press, 1981. Pp. xi, 425. 12 plates. £27.50.

The death of J. A. W. Bennett on January 29, 1981 has made this book, which was intended as a Festschrift for his seventieth birthday, into a memorial volume. It is, I think, the kind of Festschrift and the kind of "In Memoriam" that Jack Bennett would have wanted. The book is — beautifully — printed in his beloved Oxford, edited by a former pupil and close friend who now teaches in Canada, and packed with fifteen essays representing a fairly wide range of the topics that interested him (the only major lacuna is the seventeenth century, but it would be impossible to cover the whole range of Jack Bennett's interests, and the editor has wisely chosen the Middle Ages). A short, sympathetic biography and a few pages on "The Learned Adviser" (of Oxford University Press) by Dan Davin open the volume. A very useful list of the published writings closes it. We now have a first full portrait of Jack Bennett the man, the teacher and tutor, the scholar and writer—and his picture on the frontispiece aptly completes it.

The fifteen contributions to *Medieval Studies* do not have a common theme—this makes the volume difficult to review, and I shall often limit myself to summing up the core of an argument—but they fall broadly into three major categories: textual and philological, critical, and historical and bibliographical. Needless to say, these continually overlap as befits Jack Bennett's idea of scholarship.

N. F. Blake's "On Editing the *Canterbury Tales*," Derek Brewer's "Observations on the Text of *Troilus*," and P. L. Heyworth's "The Punctuation of Middle English Texts" clearly belong to the first group, though an attentive reading of them would be very healthy for many "pure" literary critics. To study the textual variants of a poem, as Derek Brewer does empirically for *Troilus*, is not, of course, a sterile exercise. Gianfranco Contini has made a science of it. Here some of Brewer's conclusions, however tentative, are of great relevance to the study of the poem; one instance "calls into question much of that theory of revision of Root's which is nowadays accepted as fact" (p. 128). Peter Heyworth's examination of punctuation in Usk's *Testament* and Chaucer's *Book of the Duchess* and *Troilus*, with a final example from *The Merchant's Tale*, makes the convincing point that "if editors of Middle English texts" could "be persuaded to take 'the problem of punctuation' more seriously" we could look "for a much sharpened awareness of an author's language...and a corresponding diminution of confident and misguided editorial assumptions that if a reading is right the sense will take care of itself" (pp. 156–57). Norman Blake's very well argued case in favor of the Hengwrt manuscript (following a line that he has been pursuing for some time) as the one that best represents the only copy-text that was Chaucer's own copy, should make all students of *The Canterbury Tales* pause.

Norman Davis's "Language in Letters from Sir John Fastolf's Household" is an important contribution to the history of fifteenth-century English. His analysis of passages from Thomas Howys, John Russe, William Barker, and John Bokkyng shows "something of the complexity of the process by which regional men of varied experience moved towards a common form of written English" (p. 346). Neil Ker edits, and comments on, the lists of "The Books of Philosophy Distributed at Merton College in

1372 and 1375." This is fascinating work of the historico-bibliographical kind and one that opens up new perspectives on our view of the background of people such as Bradwardine, Reed, and Strode and also of figures hitherto considered as minor who must however be thought of as highly representative of the average Oxford clerk in the fourteenth century.

Douglas Gray, in "A Middle English Illustrated Poem," and John Stevens, in "*Angelus ad virginem*: the History of a Medieval Song," play on the interrelation of the lyric with other forms of art (illumination and music). Both usefully print the texts they examine with the addition of appropriate plates. The Litany in the Beauchamp Hours studied by Gray is an excellent example of an illustrated poem — one in which "the illustrations...have some structural, as well as devotional, purpose, in that they indicate each stage of the Litany, and each group of spiritual beings, saints, etc., to which the reader's prayer is directed" (p. 188). The Latin and English versions of *Angelus ad virginem* — Nicholas's favorite song in *The Miller's Tale* — and the monophonic and polyphonic settings of what must originally have been a chanson, prove "the shifting and (*vis-à-vis* the liturgy) ambiguous status such a song might have" (p. 323).

With the pieces by Meg Twycross and Emrys Jones we enter the field of literary criticism. Two different approaches but a very high degree of subtlety and perceptiveness are to be found in both essays. In "Playing 'The Resurrection,'" Meg Twycross recounts the experience of producing and staging a medieval English mystery play for a twentieth-century audience. Thus the York *Resurrection* becomes a critical experiment. When "actors and audience are very close to each other," the "illusion is not broken." The actors still belong to a different world, and the audience "have no independent hand in the action" (p. 273, 275). But a different kind of "complicity" is created, especially in the comic effects, and there is no private soliloquy any more. Twycross gives very interesting examples, and her analysis of the end of the play, the three Maries' lamentations, the Resurrection and the Magdalen opens up new perspectives on the emotional involvement of the spectators of medieval drama. Emrys Jones, in "Commoners and Kings: Book One of More's *Utopia*," focuses on the literary and even "poetic" nature of More's *Utopia*. He reads the Cardinal Morton episode and Raphael's speeches in book 1 in a strikingly subtle way. The book's thematic structure, the part imagination plays in it, and the interweaving of dramatic and discursive styles in the first and second parts are brought out very convincingly. This is one of the most rewarding essays in the collection.

Of the remaining six articles, five are exclusively devoted to three of the greatest authors of fourteenth-century English literature — Langland, Chaucer, and Gower. Why was the *Gawain* poet left out? Jack Bennett wrote four volumes of *Supplementary Notes on Sir Gawain and the Green Knight*. The fourth article, Peter Dronke's "Arbor Caritatis," begins with Langland to plunge deep into the world of allegory.

M. A. Manzalaoui's " 'Noght in the Registre of Venus': Gower's English Mirror for Princes" is a discussion of book 7 of the *Confessio* and in particular the influence the *Secretum secretorum* had on it. John Burrow's "Langland *Nel Mezzo del Cammin*" is devoted to passus 11 and 12 of the B text of *Piers Plowman*. George Kane's "Music 'Neither Unpleasant nor Monotonous' " is a study of Langland's versification. The two most important contributions here seem to me to be the two latter ones. Kane's claim that "as for Langland, his alliterative long line works, and *its effective operation is explicable in terms of modern criticism*" (p. 62, italics mine) has far-reaching implications, as his own analysis of many lines in *Piers Plowman* proves. I can only quote 15.42–43:

> *Presul* and *Pontifex* and *Metropolitanus*,
> And oþere names an heep, *Episcopus* and *Pastor*

as one of Kane's best examples. Here "Langland's concept of language as *a game of heuene*" and "the abundant wit in his style" are shown in "the contrast between grand Latin and homely English, the modulation in the separateness of alliteration and musical accent in *Episcopus*, and the secondary alliteration of its tonic syllable with *Pastor*." These are indeed "elements in our impression of the Dreamer's misguided elation" (p. 61).

John Burrow's reading of *Piers Plowman* 12.1–11 is based on the medieval tradition of the ages of man and several parallels with Dante. It casts new light on Langland's poem. If, as Burrow convincingly maintains, "the age of forty-five has for Langland the significance attributed to it by Varro, Dante, and Bartholomaeus: it marks the boundary between 'myddel age' and 'olde elde' " (p. 27), and if passus 11–12 of *Piers Plowman* are therefore concerned with the deep significance of man's life, the "Dantean" character of Langland's poem, which many scholars in the past have tried to identify, is finally clear. Burrow points out similarities and differences with great finesse, and indeed the final section of his article is founded on his identifying a basic contrast between Dante and Langland. For whereas "the first canto of the *Inferno* has as its consequence nothing less than the whole action of the *Divine Comedy*, . . . the 'autobiographical' episodes of Passus 11–12 turn out, in fact, to be strangely lacking in consequence" (p. 37). Burrow asks himself why Langland should do this and thinks that "the only satisfactory answer . . . is frankly to take these passages as referring not to a fictional narrator, 'Will,' but to William Langland himself" (p. 38). It is a very plausible solution and one that would agree with the lack of precision that distinguishes *Piers Plowman*. On the other hand, I am reluctant to accept it as conclusive evidence. The argument could be turned upside down: if one assumes the general lack of tight consequentiality in the poem (and there is more than one instance of this — indeed it seems to me to be almost a "method" of the author), one is left with yet another suspended thread, a superimposition of references and meanings. Both Wills, just like both Dantes at the beginning of the *Comedy*, will be found "nel mezzo del cammin."

Helen Cooper's "The Girl with Two Lovers: Four Canterbury Tales" is an excellent example of pragmatic criticism applied to questions of genre, plot, imagery, and ideas. The four tales under consideration are the Knight's, the Miller's, the Merchant's, and the Franklin's, and they are continually cross-read so as to bring forward "the similarities and differences in Chaucer's handling of the same motifs and images" (p. 66). The love "triangles" of the title are the point of departure, but that basic pattern varies depending on the genre of the tales. The action of the gods, the significance of gardens, the seasonal setting, the marriage theme, "the way in which the characters have to face the consequences of chance, of interruptions to the normal ordering of the world" (p. 74) are the main points on which the author concentrates. I found the exposition clear and illuminating and would recommend it to all students of Chaucer.

John Norton-Smith's "Chaucer's *Anelida and Arcite*" is full of insights on many particular points. The poem's sources, for instance, are examined with great clarity, and some are identified conclusively for the first time. *L'Intelligenza*, the *Teseida*, Dante, Statius, and Ovid (I found the tracing of Corynne as inspiration and personal reality in the *Amores* and the *Tristia* particularly interesting) take their proper places. I am not so sure that at least two of the four hypotheses suggested in this piece — however stimulating and provocative — can be ultimately considered more than hypotheses. Norton-Smith argues, out of manuscript evidence, that the *Anelida* is "a complete, finished poem" (p. 82, first hypothesis). But is *Anelida* an "unfinished" poem simply because there is, at the end of the text as it is normally printed, "a single stanza of rhyme royal which follows the end of Anelida's complaint" (p. 83)? My impression is that the whole poem testifies to Chaucer's uncertainty about its final nature and purpose. *Anelida* begins in a distinctively epic manner and then turns into a complaint, a lyrical piece ("Stace," precisely, "and after him Corynne"). It is not just a matter of "invocations," which could, of course, preface both epic and lyric (though the latter mainly in Latin — there is no invocation to the Muses at the beginning of any of the pieces in Petrarch's *Canzoniere*). The main problem is the mixture in the poem of a narrative and a nonnarrative genre. Were the two moods reconcilable in 350 lines? *The Complaint of Mars*, for instance, is much more coherent. If the last stanza of *Anelida* was added by someone else, does not this indicate that Chaucer's contemporaries themselves felt that the poem is "unfinished"? I agree wholeheartedly with Norton-Smith's third and fourth hypotheses, that "the author" of *Anelida* "evolves a positive attitude toward the function of poetry as an 'art' which operates along the lines which classical poets and Renaissance writers had imagined for it" and that "the most convincing affiliation with Chaucer's writings for *Anelida and Arcite* lies with the poet's Italian concerns" (pp. 82–83). These two points are brilliantly expounded in the essay. Yet why should *Anelida* not be "paired" (not automatically, but reasonably) with *The House of Fame*? What is the ultimate message of *The House of Fame* (another "unfinished" poem) but that "poetry, closely allied to the function of the faculty of memory both preserves what otherwise would be lost, and confers a memorable record in terms of causes and effects in the area of human history both public and private" (p. 82)? At this stage it will be clear that I do not find Norton-Smith's second hypothesis ("the poem . . . was written between the completion of *Troilus* and the evolution of *The Legend of Good Women*," p. 82) completely convincing. I agree that it is not an early composition, but I still think that it was written before *Troilus*. In the *Anelida*, Chaucer is indeed "inscribing his own memorial and farewell to the elaborate, highly intricate *musique artificielle* of the French school" (p. 98), and the poem does indeed belong "to the poetic memorials of the pagan Old World" (p. 98). So does *Troilus*, which only passes from the Old to the New World in its last twelve stanzas. So, I think, does the *Legend*, where Dante, Boccaccio, and contemporary "fiction" dominate the *Prologue* but Virgil and above all Ovid dictate the choice and the themes of the legends.

Peter Dronke's "Arbor Caritatis" has so far been left out of my discussion. It is the kind of *pièce de resistance* that we would expect from Dronke, and one in which his control of both the general frame and the vast amount of detailed material is superb. The *ouverture* and the conclusion are inspired by Huizinga, Goethe, and Benjamin, and the whole article is dominated by Benjamin's concept of the "disorder of allegorical scenery." Although Benjamin elaborated this to interpret Baroque art and maintained that "modern allegory, born in the sixteenth century, is distinct from medieval allegory" (but the two are for him "precisely and essentially linked"), Dronke's application of this concept to the story of the image of the tree of charity is extremely fruitful (and a justification for the application is supplied by Bernard Silvestris and indeed by Dronke's own *Fabula*). The point of departure of this long and fascinating journey is— appropriately for a book dedicated to Jack Bennett—*Piers Plowman* 16, where the "shifts and fluctuations" of the image and its meaning prove that "the 'disordered scenery' was Langland's poetic choice" (p. 213). The successive stages of this journey—both backward and forward through time—do indeed indicate that "the most memorable allegoric trees had always been presented with the help of disordered scenery" (p. 213). There is only room here to mention the authors and works that mark the growth of this exuberant plant and that Dronke analyzes with his usual subtlety and breadth of approach. Augustine, the *Speculum virginum*, the *Roman du Vergier et de l'arbre d'amors*, the *Arbor amoris*, Joachim of Fiore's *Liber figurarum* and *Concordia novi ac Veteris Testamenti*, Guillaume le Clerc's *Bestiaire*, Jacopone da Todi, Mechthild of Magdeburg, the *Pastor Hermas*, a tenth-century sequence, Lambert of Saint-Omer's *Liber Floridus*, Hildegard of Bingen's *Scivias*, Ramon Lull's *Arbre de filosofia d'amor*, Flavius Mithridates' translation of the *Bahir* for Pico della Mirandola (excerpts from Hildegard and Flavius are printed in the appendix)—these are the various branches of Dronke's tree. That J. A. W. Bennett would have especially liked them within this volume is, I think, beyond question. That

students and scholars will find this an excellent, stimulating, and rewarding book I have no doubt.

PIERO BOITANI
University of Perugia

ALICE R. KAMINSKY, Chaucer's "Troilus and Criseyde" and the Critics.
Athens: Ohio University Press, 1980. Pp. xiv, 245. $15.00.

In his Prologue to the Confessio Amantis, Gower writes, "Bot it is seid and
evere schal, / Between two stoles lyth the fal." Just so it may be said again
about Alice R. Kaminsky's Chaucer's "Troilus and Criseyde" and the
Critics. Kaminsky avers that she has "read exhaustively in the areas of
Chaucer scholarship and criticism" and that she presents the "most relevant
and most representative [instances] of certain crucial positions" (p. xiii).
Moreover, her study "attempts to identify and assess the methodology
employed by critics" so that the volume "should have paradigmatic value
that extends beyond the field of medieval literature" (p. xiii). The dust
jacket labels the book an "essay in metacriticism," though Kaminsky never
herself applies this term to her work. She does indeed discuss the work of
Hirsch, Hartman, Frye, and others in her introduction, but she indicates
that in this book "the most crucial issue [is], 'What is Truth in Criticism?'"
(p. 4). In the quest for Truth, she seems to endorse an analogy with
scientific inquiry, and she finally declares that "I will attempt to determine
the extent to which the hypotheses of each critical approach yield plausible, or correct, or objective interpretations" (p. 12). Throughout the book
she judges criticism according to what has been "proved" or on whether its
method is "objective, verifiable" (p. 38) or whether an approach can
"supply us with a 'correct' or 'objective'...interpretation" (p. 71). The
peculiar demands of such an inquiry ensure that the book falls between two
stools, into a critical or scholarly vacuum.

Kaminsky divides the criticism that she has read into historical, philosophical, formalist, and psychological approaches. Each section is satu-
rated with the terms not of criticism but of philosophy. Critics are
overruled or dismissed on grounds of "exclusive disjunction" (p. 9),

"genetic fallacy" (p. 17), "a very obvious *petitio principii*" (p. 24), "priv- ileged hypothesis" (p. 37), "*post hoc* reasoning" (p. 60), "a model tautol- ogy" (p. 83), and so on. Even characters can be refuted: "Troilus is guilty of the either-or fallacy" (p. 62). Such logic chopping does not identify the best insights or the most useful commentaries on the poem. Judgments of this sort require more general criteria and common sense, and Kaminsky often overlooks these in her discriminations. For example, in her discussion of historical criticism she gives more attention to the work of John Gardner, Edward Wagenknecht, and George Williams than to D. W. Robertson, though in grouping them together she seems to consider all equally valuable (or flawed). Likewise, in the philosophical section she names B. L. Jefferson "the foremost exponent of this view" (p. 43). She takes time to consider seriously, or refute, critics such as Cummings, Dodd, Denomy, and Slaughter, while she neglects or passes quickly over the writings of Bloomfield, Howard, Muscatine (whose *French Tradition* is not men- tioned under formalistic criticism), and Spearing, omitting entirely the latter's short book of 1977. Her refutation of critics' positions and argu- ments appears at times to reflect a mismanagement of what the critics themselves have to say, as in her report of Bloomfield and Donaldson on the narrator of the *Troilus*. Partly as a result of her concern with logical consistency, Kaminsky almost always prefers explications and arguments that deal with a single passage or point to systematic readings, historical expositions, or overviews. Book-length studies (including those by McAlpine and Rowe) consequently receive short shrift, apparently because they admit exceptions or are tied to matter outside the poem; in the same way the most influential critics are slighted because of their reliance on cultural background and complex argument.

Although at some points one feels uncertain whether Kaminsky is offering an interpretation of a critic or her own opinion, she does several times state her own views. She claims, for example, that Chaucer did not produce an "original poem": "I believe that *Troilus* is essentially 'a great adaptation'" (p. 26). The definition and usefulness of such terms, both within and outside her arguments, remain unclear. In evaluating the intellectual density of the poem, she asserts, "There is no evidence in *Troilus* of a philosophical mind analytically probing the complex issues of existence," and she responds to Hoccleve's comparison of Chaucer to Aristotle by declaring, "What this statement reveals is that Hoccleve did not really know his Aristotle" (p. 69). In her consideration of critics' "insatiable preoccupation" with Boethius, she offers a précis of the *Consolation*, to which she appends the conclusion: "Even this cursory summary of Boethian thought should explain why a modern theological student would prefer the more profound Thomas Aquinas" (p. 44). For the most part Kaminsky opposes the authority that historical critics of any shade implicitly claim for their method; she clearly prefers a more direct, impressionistic approach to the *Troilus*, one that acknowledges that Chaucer "used more than books to write his poetry; he was certainly influenced by his experiences as a member of the human race" (p. 179). This outlook leads her to value a number of vivid if eccentric essays, and among the critics she seems most to favor are Helen Corsa, Ian Robinson, Meredith Thompson, and Mark van Doren.

The most original contribution of the book is not, then, its bibliographical or historical information but Kaminsky's reading of Criseyde. She characteristically admires close readings of this protagonist, particularly those involving her sexuality, and through a series of considerations gradually builds to an interpretation. She argues for a sexual pun on *queynt* (4.313) and more generally that Chaucer "would quite appropriately use the obscenity when necessary" (p. 117). Kaminsky goes on to argue that such meaning is indeed necessary, for "close scrutiny of Criseyde's behavior makes Boccaccio's heroine seem like an innocent sensualist. Criseyde's sexual responses are more complicated, more illicit, and more puzzling" (p. 153). Among such responses, as an instance of Criseyde's "fickle sexuality," her "capricious nature, generous to a fault in bestowing heart and body" (p. 154), Kaminsky would include intercourse with Pandarus on the morning following the night with Troilus (arguing for a sexual pun on "hoolly," 3.1502). Criseyde is a sexual survivor: "She likes men and reacts with pleasure to their desires" (p. 159); "Chaucer has provided us with signposts that she will use her sexuality to guarantee not only her pleasure but her security. Unlike Troilus, she has learned to dissociate sex and love" (p. 162); "even if. . .she and Troilus have a clandestine marriage, she can still take a lover without being castigated as evil. The modern world accepts as a fact of life the transitory nature of human relationships" (p. 159); "We believe in her because we recognize that she resembles certain kinds of Criseydes alive and well and living in Paris. Note that other kinds of women are also alive and well, but these Nanas and Bovaries do not have as high a survival rate. . . . For the real Criseyde who stands up for me today, a sensual woman with a strong will to survive, is a composite of my view of human sexuality as I see it dramatized in *Troilus*" (p. 163). Kaminsky further tries to rehabilitate "sodeyn Diomede" through sexuality: "If we start with the premise that there is nothing inherently evil about trying to 'make it' with an unmarried woman, it is easy to take a more affirmative position on Diomede. . . . The preference for a slow or fast lover is, after all, a matter of taste, and some modern women might well prefer Diomede; perhaps medieval women did as well" (p. 167). Alongside this one must note that Kaminsky dismisses feminist interpretations, such as those by Arlyn Diamond or Maureen Fries, as "an essentially modern reading of [Criseyde's] role which reflects the shift in attitude towards women" (p. 165)—apparently, that is, too clearly intellectual or consistently ideological.

In her conclusion Kaminsky remarks, with some pique, the appearance of a study of the *Troilus* that "illustrates how any novel discussion can be published regardless of the level of substantiation in the analysis" (p. 173). *Troilus. . .and the Critics* certainly contains novelty, and none of the dull or methodical surveying one might expect to find in a book of this title. But it is unclear precisely for whom this book is intended or to whom it will appeal. Such uncertainty may merely reflect the features of traditional criticism that Kaminsky disposes of as riddled with contradictions. Yet for whom does one write such a survey, if not for those who read the poem carefully and who read—and write—the criticism? To ignore, or dismiss out of hand, traditional views is surely no way of reshaping opinion. If critical issues were so simple, conclusions so obvious, the poem so straightforward and unprepossessing as Kaminsky claims, there might be justification for refusing to engage the arguments of earlier readers. But none of these things is so, and thus Kaminsky's book offers little to those who take Chaucer's writing, and writing about him, seriously.

The book contains several typographical errors: p. 11, line 41, for *fautous* read *fatuous*; p. 45, lines 20–21, delete one *also*; p. 126, line 34, for *Boccacio* read *Boccaccio*; p. 171, line 24, for *Reiss"* read Reiss.'

THOMAS HAHN
University of Rochester

FRANCES MCNEELY LEONARD, *Laughter in the Courts of Love: Comedy in Allegory from Chaucer to Spenser*. Norman, Okla.: Pilgrim Books, 1981. Pp. x, 192. $18.95.

Frances Leonard writes spiritedly about comic scenes in poems of the late-medieval "allegory of love" tradition in English. Her thesis, that comedy need not undermine the decorum of allegory and can even make it more effective, is one that few will want to contradict. For underlying the argument (and providing its impetus) is a dubious assumption that most readers feel that allegory is serious business and ought never be funny. For the average critic (it appears she has the patristic critic especially in mind) comedy and allegory "must be inimical." But is it so? The principle seems to have been formulated too much in the abstract. All readers of the *Roman de la Rose*, here acknowledged as seminal, know that love allegory can be comic. And religious allegories (*Piers Plowman*, *The Castle of Perseverance*) have hilarities of the letter that do not detract from but enhance spiritual meaning. It is puzzling why the author supposes her audience needs to be convinced otherwise.

I find the main issue, which is what comedy does to or for allegory, is never quite brought to a hard, sharp focus. It is adumbrated in phrases like "Chaucer's mature efforts to make comedy and allegory serve the same end," but Leonard does not seem to face the central question of whether comedy and allegory in dynamic linkage create an effect that is somehow more than the sum of the effects that each would achieve in isolation. General statements like "The combination of comedy and allegory is designed to increase the complexity of [poets'] vision and expression" leave the reader suspended, yearning for solider ground and a stabler foundation in theory.

In regard to the nature of comedy, for example, Leonard enlists the aid of potent authorities (Frye, Langer, Bergson) but exploits their thought rather less than she could have; the result is that comedy is never pinned down long enough for positive identification (by her own admission comedy "is protean and will not be wrestled to the ground"). And so it is in her analysis, which often bewilders the reader with a wealth of definition. Comedy is at once a form of drama and a narrative mode, a way of seeing and a style of writing, an aspect of authorial tone and a category of reader reception, something distinct from satire and yet in several cases apparently its equivalent. A reluctance to distill comedy down to its essence is accompanied by a reliance on metaphorical rather than univocal statement: comedy is "a child of reality," the comic vision a "celebration of human existence," "a rapid movement of the mental eye." On the more practical level of determining simply what is funny, Leonard sometimes goes overboard: "Any event that recurs without significant variation ...provoke[s] laughter," or, "Devotion to detail for the love of detail is comic."

The analysis of allegory is similarly lenient. The author rejects as too narrow C. S. Lewis's restriction of allegory to personification allegory whose *significatio* is an inner action (yet seems to adhere to it where the concept proves convenient, as in *The Faerie Queene*), and she rules out exegetical allegory as irrelevant to the tradition of love, perhaps properly so. But what is left is a latitudinarian view that makes practically all figurative statement allegorical. If Lewis says that none of Chaucer's important poems is a true allegory, Leonard notwithstanding calls him allegorist. Comedy is duly found essential to the meaning of his comic poems, but that meaning having been defined as allegorical, there is, ipso facto, no conflict between comedy and allegory, rather (and not surprisingly) an effective conjunction. So with Chaucer's dream visions: *The Book of the Duchess* is "an allegory about human feeling and understanding" and deserves the designation because Blanche is not named directly but is spoken of in figurative terms. The author can thus raise as the main critical issue the presence of comedy in allegory (and put it satisfactorily to rest), whereas most readers will continue to see the problem as one of comic elements in an elegy.

With other poets her task is the reverse. Allegory is abundantly evident in *The Golden Targe*, *The Palice of Honor*, or *The Pastime of Pleasure*, but here true comedy is in such short supply that the concept must perforce be broadened to accommodate Dunbar's high burlesque, Douglas's low mockery, and the rare interlude in Hawes that functions merely as comic relief. While her comments on how these poets employ humor are consistently illuminating, they are just as consistently ad hoc and do not contribute much to a general theory of the relationship of comedy to allegory.

Perhaps the fundamental point is whether allegory as a semiotic mode (and not a literary genre) can admit of humor. If humor results from the perception of incongruity in a relation, the only way allegory itself could be comic were if incongruity were perceived in the relation of *figura* to *significatio*, as when a fox were to be depicted as Sloth (in what might be termed "vertical" incongruity). But for Leonard what determines whether an allegory is comic is its tone, which is controlled by the letter. Thus humor arises if an element on the literal level is found sufficiently incongruent with another on the same plane — "horizontal" incongruity — as when Sir Guyon inadvertently beheads his opponent's horse. But this action will be funny (or not) depending on its congruency with other elements in its literal context, and irrespective of whether we acknowledge an ulterior significance to the literal event. Surely this means that the humor of the action in an allegorical poem is fundamentally nonrelevant to allegory as a mode of referentiality (except in the case of "vertical" incongruity, as above). Comedy reinforces the relation of *figura* to *significatio*, to be sure, but does so by making the literal action perspicuous, not by rendering the relation itself incongruous. Seen this way, the problem of whether comedy and allegory can coexist and cooperate seems less of an issue than this book makes of it, and what we learn about comedy in allegory finally comes from the author's sensitive close readings of individual poems rather than from a successful theoretical synthesis of the two.

JOHN BUGGE
Emory University

GEORGE B. PACE and ALFRED DAVID, eds., *The Minor Poems, Part One. A Variorum Edition of the Works of Geoffrey Chaucer*, vol. 5. Norman: University of Oklahoma Press, 1982. Pp. xxviii, 223. $38.50.

The *Variorum Chaucer*, a collaborative project of some forty-two Chaucerians, was originally planned as commentary upon the entire canon of Chaucer's works. In 1979 it was expanded to include a series of facsimiles with the publication of the inaugural volume of the Variorum, *The Canterbury Tales: A Facsimile and Transcription of the Hengwrt Manuscript with Variants from the Ellesmere Manuscript*, edited by Paul G. Ruggiers. The facsimile series is designed to represent the tradition upon which subsequent editors have based their texts. The commentary series is designed to provide newly established texts, collations of the manuscripts and of the printed editions, explanatory and textual notes, critical and textual introductions, and bibliography. Its purpose is to provide a summary of 600 years of the textual and critical commentary.

The Minor Poems, Part One, is the second volume to be published in the Variorum Edition. The texts and collations, textual essays, and textual notes for this edition are the lifework of George B. Pace, who prepared and submitted them in 1978, before his untimely death. The critical introductions and general explanatory notes to the poems are the work of Alfred David, who also saw the volume through press. The year 1975, when George Pace had essentially completed his research on the text of the poems, is the formal "cutoff" date for references to recent publications. In citing references and abbreviations for the titles of Chaucer's writings, the editors follow the guidelines for the *Variorum Chaucer*. Instead of using the sigils for the manuscripts in Robinson's edition, the editors of this volume have assigned each manuscript a unique sigil. This sigillation of the manuscripts is reasonable but may at first cause some confusion.

References to other works cite the last name of the author, the date of the work, and line, volume or page numbers. Full references are given in the Bibliographical Index, from which there are a few omissions. For the Bible, Dante, Ovid, and Virgil no editions are cited.

Although Chaucer's twenty-one minor poems have generally been considered together, Pace and David have divided them, mainly for reasons of economy, into two distinct groups. *Part One* presents fourteen poems: *Truth, Gentilesse, Lak of Stedfastnesse, The Former Age, Fortune, The Complaint of Chaucer to His Purse, Adam Scriveyn, The Envoy to Bukton, The Envoy to Scogan, To Rosemounde, Merciless Beaute, Womanly Noblesse, Against Women Unconstant*, and *Proverbs*. This heterogeneous group includes five moral and didactic poems often designated the Boethian Group, four somewhat humorous poems addressed to individuals, four short love poems, and the gnomic verses called *Proverbs*. The poems are arranged not chronologically but according to form and subject. There is no category of "doubtful" poems, and *A Balade of Complaint* has been rejected. The Introduction includes (1) a critical essay on the poems as a group and their place in Chaucer's life and works, (2) an account of the establishment and presentation of the texts and apparatus, (3) a list of fifty-five manuscripts containing *The Minor Poems*, (4) a chronological list of the printed editions, with commentary on individual editions and the treatment of *The Minor Poems*, (5) a discussion of the rules for the collations, and (6) an explanation of the practice followed in the notes. Separate introductions to each poem survey previous critical commentary, address particular problems, and treat authenticity, date, genre, source, style, and topical allusions.

The "Textual Essay" briefly describes the manuscripts (of the Text), lists textual authorities, provides bibliographical information, and discusses the textual aspects of authenticity if the authenticity of a poem is in question. The Text of each poem, printed with a corpus of substantive variants, is a "near-transcript (clear errors adjusted) of the manuscript thought to be the best." The Text is an instrument of collation against which is read a large number of manuscripts and editions. For half of the poems of *Part One*, there is agreement on the best manuscript (for several of the poems there is only one extant manuscript). For the other seven poems there is minor disagreement on *Fortune*, *Proverbs*, *Purse*, and *Against Women Unconstant* and distinct disagreement on *Gentilesse*, *Lak of Stedfastnesse*, and *Truth*. For the best manuscript of these seven poems Pace has sought compromises and has placed weight on majority choice. The Text is not an exact transcript of the chosen manuscript (copy-text) but it is the "manuscript with any obvious errors removed." For emending the copy-text, Pace and David have followed Klaeber's procedure (*Beowulf* 1950:cxc) of using italics to indicate alteration of words and square brackets for the addition of letters or words. The copy-text for *Adam*, *Truth*, and *Women Unconstant* are unemended. In the other poems emendation has been kept to a minimum.

Part One of *The Minor Poems* is the "first attempt to give complete collations for all known manuscripts." Ninety manuscripts are identified, transcribed, collated, and recorded. All printed copies of *The Minor Poems* from Caxton (1477) through the 1721 edition of Urry were collated, but only certain ones are recorded. The very early editions are considered with the manuscripts to show the connection of early printed texts to various manuscripts. The variants for all printed copies from Caxton (1477) through Thynne (1532) are recorded with the manuscripts. The collations for the later (edited) editions are in the Textual Notes and have as a core Skeat's Oxford Chaucer (1894), the Globe edition (1898), Koch's *Geoffrey Chaucers Kleinere Dichtungen* (1928), and Robinson's second edition (1957). The four core editions were regularly collated, but not regularly recorded, with the Urry edition of 1721 and Richard Morris's revision of 1870 of the Aldine Chaucer, as well as Baugh's edition (1963) and Donaldson's second edition (1975). Fisher's edition, which appeared after the notes were completed, is included for some poems.

Pace's transcription of *The Minor Poems*, begun in 1949–50 in England, covers approximately 80 percent of the manuscripts. For the remainder he has relied upon Chaucer Society prints, photocopies, and photostats. "For all the copy-texts of my original assignment I had transcripts from the manuscripts." The Textual Notes, which are blended with the Explanatory Notes, record the collations of the later editions and comment upon the readings but do not argue for a particular reading. All the manuscripts have been assigned approximate dates taken from printed sources, and no attempt has been made to correct or revise them.

The critical commentary is concerned with the literary, social, and political milieu of Chaucer as a court poet. Although the "stylized complaints tell us only very indirectly about the actual world Chaucer inhabited," David suggests that the envoys, didactic poems, and love lyrics do reveal a good deal about daily life as Chaucer knew it: his relations with royalty, friends, and Adam Scriveyn. Since many of the poems are short and informal, David finds that they sometimes strike a personal note and represent Chaucer's urbane manner. David suggests that a lyric poem in Chaucer's time was a "poetic statement on some matter of passing interest, intended for private reading, not necessarily for public performance." On page 6 he notes that a lyric poem in Chaucer's time "is not a means of self-expression in the Romantic sense, but it has become a way of communication among members of a social and literary circle. With Chaucer and his contemporaries the Middle English lyric arrives at its Augustan period." Yet on page 8 he concludes that "most of the poems presented in *Part One* of this edition give every indication that they were composed freely and spontaneously." It is not clear what David means by the Augustan period of the Middle English lyric.

The problem of dating individual poems has become, according to David, less certain since the nineteenth century. The date of the Envoy to *The Complaint of Chaucer to His Purse*, once fixed between September 30 and October 13, 1399, is no longer considered so definite. The Boethian group of poems have naturally been assigned to the 1380s, the period of *Boece* and *Troilus*, but scholars disagree on the dates of individual poems

and argue for later dates for some. David summarizes that it is hazardous to
see historical events mirrored in lines that are later taken to be common-
places. Regarding sources, David claims that the increase of knowledge has
created doubts regarding attributions. He admits that the moral poems
echo phrases and longer passages but notes that "some of the lines for
which specific sources have been proposed turn out to be common topics,
the stock-in-trade of ancient and medieval authors." "Chaucer's mind,"
according to David, "is stocked with the words of other poets and with
rhetorical phrases, but in these works [*The Minor Poems*] he does not seem
to be consulting his library or following a source."

This edition is handsomely produced by the University of Oklahoma
Press in the same beautiful design as the inaugural volume of the *Variorum
Chaucer*, which was the winner of the 1979 Southern Books Award for
design. The paper used for the printing of *The Minor Poems, Part One*, is
seventy-pound Warren's 1854 and has an effective life of at least three
hundred years. Scholars and serious students will find this well-researched
and carefully edited volume *cum notis variorum* most useful for future
research upon Chaucer's somewhat neglected lyrics.

PAUL M. CLOGAN
North Texas State University

J. J. N. PALMER, ed., *Froissart: Historian*. Woodbridge, Suffolk: Boydell &
Brewer; Totowa, N.J.: Rowman and Littlefield, 1981. Pp. xi, 203.
Maps and tables. £20; $47.50.

The *Chronicles* of Jean Froissart (ca. 1333–1410) are the most ambitious
and colorful of later-medieval chronicles, and through the translations of
Lord Berners (1523–25) and Thomas Johnes (1803–10), which have often
been reprinted in whole or part, they have long been popular in English.
For Chaucerians they have the particular interest of recording Chaucer's
presence in an embassy to France in 1377 (see *Chaucer Life-Records*,
pp. 49–51), the only time Chaucer is mentioned in a contemporary
chronicle. But although Berners and Johnes give us good translations, the
texts they used are sometimes faulty or deficient, each represents only a

single version of a much revised work, and there is no amply annotated edition of these or any other English translation. Even the two principal editions in French, that of Kervyn de Lettenhove (1867–77) and that of the Société de l'histoire de France (initiated in 1869 by Siméon Luce and still in progress), chiefly present a single version apiece, and Froissart scholarship has made many recent discoveries that they do not incorporate. *Froissart: Historian* is the first book devoted to the *Chronicles* as a whole. The work of ten able English, French, Dutch, and American scholars, it should be consulted not only by historians but by anyone who cites or even reads Froissart.

J. J. N. Palmer's introduction traces Froissart's enormous influence: until Kervyn de Lettenhove and the SHF edition, Froissart's accounts of the fourteenth century went largely unquestioned, in outline and detail, by British and Continental historians alike. But since then "attacks on [his] accuracy and veracity have become legion and are scattered in scores of periodicals and hundreds of books on dozens of different subjects" (p. 5). Froissart's account of the political conflict in England between Richard II and the Appellants in 1386–88, for example, is vivid and exciting but entirely unreliable, owing in large measure to his use of the literary device of interlacing. And Manly showed the confusions and inaccuracies of the account of Chaucer's embassy. But Froissart's mistakes continue to be perpetuated by the unwary. Recently both Barbara Tuchman (in *A Distant Mirror*) and, quite gleefully, John Gardner (in *The Life and Times of Chaucer*) follow that version of the *Chronicles* that tells how, in 1370, the Black Prince ruthlessly slaughtered the inhabitants of Limoges. They overlook another version in which the slaughter is considerably less, and, as previous historians have demonstrated and as Richard Barber also does in the present volume (pp. 33–34), it is probable that few civilians were in fact killed. We are almost in the paradoxical situation of having to distrust Froissart unless he is corroborated by independent testimony—in which case his testimony would not really be necessary.

Palmer says that "it is hoped that these essays will...do something to redeem Froissart's reputation," will counteract the recent tendency to "diminish the apparent value of the *Chronicles* to an unacceptable degree," and will demonstrate the worth of Froissart to the historian "in his efforts to recreate the mental and social dimensions" of the period (p. 5). It may appear that the first two of these ends are hardly achieved, for

Froissart: Historian abounds with statements to the effect that Froissart "was quite capable on occasion of inventing facts in order to enhance the verisimilitude of his narrative, or of manipulating both facts and text to achieve a dramatic purpose" (p. 51), that "like most chroniclers (and their modern successors, the tabloid newspapers), he reported what he thought would interest his intended audience" (p. 37), or simply that he can be a "treacherous guide" (p. 80). The contributors suggest a number of reasons for his unreliability. Froissart came late to writing the *Chronicles*: Chandos Herald's *Life of the Black Prince*, one of his earliest sources, was apparently not written before 1385 or so. The eyewitnesses whom Froissart liked to consult often had inaccurate, incomplete, or tendentious memories and in some cases may even have been pulling his leg (Pierre Tuccoo-Chala, pp. 128–29; P. E. Russell, p. 95). He failed to use all the documents, such as newsletters and chronicles, that were available to him, and he did not have access to the diplomatic and administrative documents from which history is chiefly written nowadays. He apparently never witnessed a battle, and, for all his travels, his frequent geographic howlers show that he did not visit many of the regions about which he wrote with assurance.

Nevertheless, these essays recognize how valuable Froissart is. For example, John Bell Henneman defends him against Perroy's accusation of blindly adulating the aristocracy. J. van Herwaarden demonstrates Froissart's importance for the history of the Low Countries. J. W. Sherborne shows when he can be trusted, and when he cannot be, about Richard II. Philippe Contamine surveys Froissart's knowledge of military matters and shows how well he understood strategy, tactics, logistics, finance, and the rapidly changing technology. Even P. E. Russell, whose classic study, *English Intervention in Spain and Portugal in the Time of Edward III and Richard II*, was severe on Froissart, has some compliments to bestow. And the contributors are unanimous in acclaiming how well and how subtly Froissart achieves his oft-stated goal of depicting the chivalric ideal (Henneman is particularly good on this). Thankfully, medievalists no longer take the fourteenth century to be an age of debased chivalry or Froissart to be a somewhat unwitting historian of that debasement—an attitude that seriously weakens, for example, G. G. Coulton's book on Froissart, *The Chronicler of European Chivalry*.

Two essays in *Froissart: Historian* will be of special interest to literary scholars, Palmer's "Book 1 (1325–78) and Its Sources" and George T.

Diller's "Froissart: Patrons and Texts." Briefly, there are four principal versions of book 1: the A version in a number of manuscripts (not the basis of any published edition), the B version also in a number (the basis of the SHF edition), the Amiens version in a single manuscript (the basis of Kervyn de Lettenhove's edition), and the Rome version in a single manuscript (published by Diller in 1972). The consensus has long been that this order represents the successive versions of book 1, leisurely composed and revised during Froissart's long life. But Palmer analyzes the versions and arrives at a number of equally sound but mutually contradictory conclusions about their order of composition. He argues that they were all composed simultaneously in the years following 1390 and that Froissart "did not see his revisions as superseding his earlier efforts but simply as alternative — and equaly valid — versions of events" (p. 24). Without studying the versions with Palmer's thoroughness, I cannot support or refute his conclusions, but his evidence is mighty persuasive, and he is no mean philologist (it will be recalled that Palmer redated the death of Blanche of Lancaster and therefore of *The Book of the Duchess*; his demonstration of the historical worthlessness of the *Chronicque de la traison et mort de Richart II* in the *Bulletin of the John Rylands Library* for 1978 is brilliant). With equal audacity Diller analyzes some aspects of the style of the *Chronicles*, particularly the verbs and their tenses, and concludes that Froissart did not himself indite his history but, for all its length, dictated it, in all its versions, to a scribe. Both Palmer's and Diller's arguments are so novel and so contrary to modern assumptions about the act of literary composition that they must be entertained with great sympathy and seriousness.

Only a few excepton will be taken to this fine volume. Palmer concedes that *Froissart: Historian*, like all other collaborative efforts, did not assume the final form originally planned for it. Perhaps for that reason, in the book's only serious omission, there is no separate essay on Froissart's treatment of England and the English conduct of war under Edward III. Froissart may not have been mistaken about John of Gaunt's political ambitions in 1376–77, as one contributor says he was (pp. 52, 57), but historians have long denied as malicious slander numerous sources, English and Continental, that clearly reveal those ambitions. This is a carefully produced and proofread volume, with an excellent index and bibliography. But "Simon Luce" (p. 10) should of course be "Siméon Luce"; the editor speaks (p. 5) of a contributor's alluding to "'blanket condemnation'" of Froissart on p. 82 below, but the passage in question mentions "blanket disapproval," which is not quite the same thing, on p. 83: "résumé" lacks its first accent (p. 63); and several contributors call John of Gaunt "Gaunt" as though this were a surname or title. Berners's translation and Diller's edition of the Rome manuscript are in the list of abbreviations (p. ix) but not the bibliography.

SUMNER FERRIS
California State College (Pennsylvania)

ANNE F. PAYNE, *Chaucer and Menippean Satire*. Madison: University of Wisconsin Press, 1981. Pp. xii, 290. $22.50.

Chaucer and Menippean Satire is an important book. Its principal value lies in its thoughtful placement of Boethius and Chaucer within the context of the ancient tradition of Menippean satire, a tradition about which very little has been written but which is valuable in the understanding of Chaucer's mixed style and ironic postures. Moreover, it brings us close the heart of certain philosophical concerns of both Boethius and Chaucer.

Menippean dialogue differs from the Socratic in several ways. Characterized by great freedom of invention and fantastic situations (whether on earth, in the nether regions, or in the heavens), the Menippean genre tests philosophical systems and rigid conclusions through irreverent mockery, ironic juxtaposition, mixed style, and agile tonal shifts. Although similar in some ways to Socratic dialogue, especially in its wariness of prejudiced positions, Menippean dialogue more frequently employs stereotyped characters who converse from distinctly different levels of perception—one a "know-it-all who is free of the restrictions and responsibilities faced by ordinary human beings" (p. 9) and the other a more ordinary person who questions but is persuaded to listen, like it or not. The latter, with whom the audience is more likely to identify, tends to be comic in his naïveté and often seems engaged in an endless, perhaps utopian, quest. But despite his limited ability to understand or obtain a secure position or perspective, and despite the virtual certainty that the concoctions of his brain will be claptrap, he embodies an unquenchable hope, a titanic enthusiasm, and an irrepressible freedom to think that is "his most elating gift and his most terrifying burden" (p. 16). Although the know-it-all *deus* figure is undercut through many-leveled irony, the truth of uncertainty is better than the comfort of false security.

In defining Menippean satire, Payne ranges from Lucian's *Philosophers for Sale*, *Menippus*, *Zeus Catechized*, *The Downward Journey*, and *Dialogues of the Dead*, where the desacralization of myth is a constant feature, to Petronius's *Satyricon*, Apuleius's *Golden Ass*, Martianus Capella's *Marriage of Philology and Mercury*, and Nigel Longchamps's *Mirror of Fools*, along with nods toward influence of the genre on later works as diverse as *Hamlet* and Roth's *The Breast*. The chapter on Lucian's dialogues explores techniques of ironic counterpoise with which the author undermines absolutes. Lucian posits "a clueless but many-faceted universe" (p. 52) wherein man with amazing energy busies himself with insoluble problems in whatever corner he chooses, enjoying a freedom that always hovers at the edge of laughter and the ludicrous. Payne is shrewd and witty in her presentation of Lucianic modes of cynical debunking.

The chapter on Boethius grows out of Payne's analysis of Lucian, and it is indeed instructive to view *The Consolation of Philosophy* from that perspective. Payne is quite right, it seems to me, in arguing that more attention should be paid to the "reduced laughter" of the piece and to insist that Philosophy does not have the last word. But her argument fails to acknowledge adequately, it seems to me, how uncynical and essentially neo-Platonic the tone of the *Consolation* is. Boethius celebrates the power of reason in the *Consolation*; it is a magnificent gift, and although Philosophy may be limited in her perceptions and language, her voice has no kinship with "claptrap."

If Payne's book has a fault, it is in the tendency to impose a Lucianic cynicism on Boethius and Chaucer, and, for that matter, upon the reader, who, once ideas have been debunked and the idiocy of philosophical concoctions exposed, is apparently to be saddened with thoughts of bleakness. I do not find this to be the effect of the *Consolation*, or of Chaucer. Boethius is in no way a cynic, despite the evidence that Payne so carefully musters that he writes within a Menippean tradition. Although he may well be playing with Lady Philosophy, who in turn plays with the narrator of the piece, that playfulness does not impinge upon the author's earnest belief in the *summum bonum*. That Boethius recognizes that the *summum bonum* surpasses his power of understanding or Philosophy's ability to explain is a logical necessity rather than a matter of wit. If the good did not surpass his powers of understanding, it would not be the *summum bonum* or worth his belief.

I had the same problem with some of Payne's readings of tonal effects in Chaucer, as we shall see. She thrills a bit too much at ideas of bleakness, emptiness, and idiocy, as if seeking goblins to frighten herself with. At the same time she places too much value on freedom, without fully savoring the importance of conditional necessity to which Boethius and Chaucer resonate so subtly. Although human schemes, including religious schemes, are frequently reduced to rubble in Chaucer, we are not left on some barren plain filled with angst and an overpowering weight of futility. Chaucer, especially, is a poet who appreciates the ambiguity of walls and cages. It may be, in fact, that the Menippean tradition is not in its inner reaches as negative as Payne implies.

But I do not wish to overstate this reservation, which mainly is directed toward the tone of scattered moments in Payne's argument — moments that are essentially rhetorical rather than substantive. Payne is quite aware of the optimistic resilience of Boethius and Chaucer and in several instances counterbalances the cynical tendency of her position with eloquent testimonies on the energies of the imagination and its power to create and re-create and to entertain itself. Her chapter on Boethius is very well done. After identifying the *topoi* and techniques of Lucian that are found in the *Consolation*, she divides the treatise into five sections: an opening section, which introduces the *topoi*, then a sequence of philosophical juxtapositions, which characterize diverse attitudes — the Cynic (books 2–3, pr. 9), the Platonic (book 3, no. 9–4, pr. 5), the Aristotelian (book 4, pr. 6–5, m. 1), and the Augustinian (book 5, pr. 2–6).

One wonders, in view of these traditional philosophical positions, what effect upon her argument some acknowledgment of the *Protrepticus* tradition would have, that tradition which views Boethius as a great teacher, which Usener and, more recently, Bommarito (*DAI* 40 [1979]; 3336A) have seen as the germinal background to the *Consolation*. That is, to what extent is the work intended to be didactic, and what precisely is being taught? Is it simply the limitations of reason and the resilience of the desire to know? Payne emphasizes the originality of Boethius's treatise. The source materials are not there as instruction in their derived content per se; rather, they stand as representatives of the games the mind plays with itself. Payne's point is that the subtle ironies generated by the multiple perspectives heighten one's "awareness that all theories and systems should remain inferior and subordinate to the principle of the free, exploring mind" (p. 77). If Payne is right, what seems on the surface to be didactic and derivative gives way through the Menippean qualities of the work to a deep-set originality that surpasses in subtlety the instructional value of traditional *Protrepticus* literature.

Payne views the *Consolation* as a work in the tragic mode:

> The tragic sense embedded in the *Consolation* arises in Boethius' perception of man's perpetual failure. The failure that matters is not his inability to stay at the top of Fortune's wheel but his inability to translate his experience of whatever cast into something intelligible and complete. In a very broad sense, the tragic sense that pervades the book is that common to the Menippean dialogue, the knowledge that man is not provided with images or words that are adequate to contain his electrifying inklings of reality. [P. 80]

It is here, it seems to me, that Payne's insight becomes most useful to Chaucer students. What she has done is place what some have seen as nominalistic tendencies within both Boethius and Chaucer in a well-established literary tradition that is both philosophical and mock-philosophical. She juxtaposes the befuddled "I" in the *Consolation* with the *deus* figure Lady Philosophy, but not exclusively to the former's disadvantage. The "I" embodies an "awareness of the inescapability of chaos" (p. 85) and thus deserves our pity. Philosophy is gently mocked as well, in large part by virtue of the fact that she exists on an abstract plain within man's mind rather than within experience.

But although the circumstance of the *Consolation* is tragic, Payne acknowledges that the world as the author Boethius sees it is basically congenial to man. The *Consolation* differs from the Lucianic dialogues in that

> instead of an uninhibited attack from a detached point of view on human constructs, myths, morals, laws, customs, and theories . . . we have a portrayal of man's dialectical necessity to accept these constructs, to organize, to order, to insist that

the universe can be understood as a graspable entity. The circus arena is as comprehensive as in Lucian, but there is only one ring, the act a single one, and it is rather more apparent in the end that this is the place where man will exist as long as he thinks. [Pp. 82–83]

It is the *thinking* that is man's strength and weakness. The *Consolation* is "an archetypal image of the mind's struggle to come to terms with chaos and certainty, freedom and limitation" as it fights "to forge its meanings. In Boethian terms, man does not face a dead God, or a cosmic indifference, but a continual stream of friendly information and concern from all sources able to advise him" (p. 84). Payne suggests, quite rightly it seems to me, that it is this congenial attitude rather than the bleak one she also portrays that has drawn so many readers to him.

The last six chapters, two each on Boethian topics and Menippean treatments in *Troilus and Criseyde*, *The Nun's Priest's Tale*, and *The Knight's Tale*, are intricately argued. Payne is a master at explaining logical inconsistencies in which characters trap themselves. She is an unusually sensitive reader of irony, always alert to linguistic subtleties and misprisions as she explores Chaucer's treatment of fortune, happiness, love, freedom, foreknowledge, free will, fragmentation, the power of language, and beauty. I found her analysis of the potentialities of double death in *NPT* to be impressive, where the hungry fox, intent upon destroying Chauntecler's body, first numbs his mind through clever language, thus robbing the cock of his freedom twice over. I also found her treatment of Criseyde to be perceptive. Criseyde, in her disenchantment, lends herself well to a Lucianic perspective. Payne's treatment of Troilus's determined exercising of his free choice is likewise excellent. I have difficulty, however, with Payne's reading of the Epilogue of *TC*, where she sees the narrator, his story having failed him absolutely, switching frantically to a Christian vision through "random outbursts on a variety of inconsistent subjects" that belie any attempt to believe that he here represents for the author a definitive alternative. "All the characters [the narrator included] have struggled with varying degrees of energy to project into the meaningless nothingness of habits, conventions, and uninterpretable events, a pattern of coherence through which they can achieve happiness.... Willy-nilly, they defeat themselves" (p. 154).

It is with readings such as this that I part company with Payne and return to my earlier reservations about her approach. Although she opens up with sure access a number of profound features of the Chaucerian vision, her failure to acknowledge or allow for real religious issues in the poetry (not just foolishly imagined ones) seems to me to be a peculiarly modern handicap. There are deep-felt religious positions in both Chaucer and Boethius that cannot be resolved through aesthetics or an affirmation of beauty or human invention (cf. her treatment of *KnT*), but rather through faith, or, if it sounds less offensive to modern ears, trust. Certainly trust governs the tone of those passages in the *Consolation* in which the "I" attunes himself to the "continual stream of friendly information" about which Payne speaks and labels "congenial." From that perspective the *Consolation* is not tragic, but rather comic—a celebration. That kind of trust seems to me to be pervasive in Chaucer's writings as well; it accounts for the heartiness and healthiness of his vision. Nor does it diminish his appreciation of beauty or artistry or human wit or folly. Perhaps *The House of Fame* serves to make the point. This dream vision embodies all the Menippean elements that Payne speaks of—the mockery, the oppositions, and the frustrated search for authority that always gets undermined in the poem with laughter and irony. By the end we are amusingly aware that, even if the "man of gret auctorite" were to speak his mind and be identified, the dreamer's dilemma would not be solved, simply because he—despite his celebrated brain—would have to interpret what he apprehends and would be as constrained by habits, passions, predilections, and his persistent inability to concentrate, as he was when dealing with the story of Aeneas that he found engraved before his very eyes. His recurrent frustrated appeals—"God turne us every drem to goode!" and (more futilely) "but God, thou wost!"—however ludicrous and absurd, resonate throughout the poem and seem to be his only consolation. Perhaps that circumstance is tragic. And so it seems, if man is an end in himself. But the witty point is that man is neither beginning nor end, and when he assumes so the effect is risible. Chaucer and Boethius really believe that, and whether we do or not is irrelevant. They are not Voltaire, despite the fact that all three delight in Menippean satire.

RUSSELL A. PECK
University of Rochester

WOLFGANG RIEHLE, *The Middle English Mystics*. Translated by Bernard
Standring. London and Boston: Routledge & Kegan Paul, 1981. Pp.
xvi, 244. $32.50.

This volume is a translation of the revised work originally published in
1977 as *Studien zur englischen Mystik des Mittelalters unter besonderer
Berücksichtigung ihrer Metaphorik*. It is a balanced and perceptive contribution to the subject of Middle English mysticism with its development of
a vernacular idiom. While not ignoring earlier homiletic treatises and
manuals of asceticism, Riehle concentrates upon the use of metaphor in the
Cloud group and in the works of Walter Hilton, Julian of Norwich,
Richard Rolle, and Margery Kemp. Riehle's conservative linguistic comparisons of these English mystics with their German contemporaries is a
welcome addition to recent scholarship. Continuing the method of Hope
Emily Allen, Riehle's comparative approach focuses upon John Tauler,
Meister Eckhart, Mechthild of Magdeburg, Henry Suso, and Rudolf of
Biberach. While drawing linguistic parallels, the author is careful to
indicate likely areas of German influence while observing the more likely
possibility of common Latin sources. Indeed, the English are seen to be
much more biblical than their theoretical German counterparts. Much of
their language, when not purely biblical, is Augustinian, Victorine, Bernardine, and Franciscan.

While not intended as a theological study, Riehle's discussion is theological in just the right way. In his thorough treatment of mystical metaphor Riehle hints at the appropriateness of this figure of speech to its
didactic purpose. Certainly, throughout mystical literature a close analogy
operates between the transformation of the individual from carnality to
spirituality, and the metaphoric movement of language from concrete to
abstract. Metaphor contains within its own nature the transforming of
experience from the sensual to the sublime. The value of the "word"
correctly interpreted is its reflection of the conjoining of natures in the
"Word Incarnate." As John Fleming has shown (*An Introduction to the
Franciscan Literature of the Middle Ages*), the parallel was of particular
importance to Franciscan thought since it links the nature of language with
Christ's childhood and Passion—the two foci of the order's effective response to Christ's life and the two foci of late Latin and vernacular
mysticism.

Chaucerians have been known, for good or ill, to dip into the volumes of Migne for their understanding of theology and for insight into the signs and symbols of "secular" texts. Of significance for the student of Middle English literature in general are Riehle's occasional mentions of a relationship between the diction of English mysticism and the vocabulary of Chaucer, Langland, and others. Several times the author takes issue with the *MED*'s omission of interpretations of words introduced by mystics into the vocabulary of English prose. That a writer such as Chaucer might have employed such meanings in his poetry could add considerably to our understanding of medieval irony — or of a particular text. Indeed, Riehle discusses mystical prose as if it were poetry (for Rolle it often is) and consistently demonstrates the German tendency to coin new words and the English tendency to give new meanings to old words and Latin borrowings. This metaphoric "incarnation" of words has as its basis a pseudo-Dionysian sense of the ineffability of the Divine. Riehle's study of mysticism as popular theology directed to a lay audience indirectly indicates that the mystics might well give the modern reader a more immediate and linguistically valid insight into the fourteenth-century "secular" use of theology than can be provided by patristic texts and the language of the schools. To see mysticism in this light is to illuminate our concepts of pilgrimage, the operation of grace, apocalyptic images, and the Exemplarism of Christ.

Riehle's first chapter discusses the public for mystical literature in England and reminds the reader of the feminine audience and the many wills attesting to both noble and middle-class audiences. Beyond this prologue to the study proper, Riehle (contrary to Evelyn Underhill) suggests the possibility that there were organized lay groups in England with affinities to the Beguines, the Brethren of the Common Life, and the Friends of God. If these groups were in England, the author considers the likelihood of German influence upon English mysticism to be greater than perhaps others have assumed. The probability of influence is the subject of chapter 2. Riehle believes that the author of the *Cloud* could have known Rudolf of Biberach's *De septem itineribus aeternitatis* and that Suso could have influenced Rolle. While of the four only Rudolf is known to have been Franciscan, it seems safer to assume that the affective piety and the devotion to the Holy Name point to a "Franciscan" strain common to both German and English mysticism.

Chapters 3 to 5 discuss the metaphors of love derived from the Song of

Songs, the mystical language of preparation for the *unio*, and the metaphorical language of the soul's pilgrimage to God. In these chapters the author gives us the language of purgation. The soul is the "bed" of God, the locus of "love longing" between two lovers. Riehle mentions the interrelationship between the courtly and religious use of "love potion," "love arrows," "love letters," and the "love knot," but a full discussion of implications is clearly a matter for other studies. One particularly interesting observation is the mystical reference to the Passion of Christ as a "ring dance" in both Rolle and Mechthild of Hackeborn. Riehle dismisses Rosemary Woolf's contention that Rolle knew the caroling God of Love in the *Roman de la Rose*. On the purely theological level, it seems that Rolle and Mechthild view Christ's voluntarism as the "dance of love," or gift of grace, enabling the soul to "gather herself inward" to self-knowledge, become an "empty vessel," and seek God with a "naked intent." Riehle sees the basis of this language of preparation in Saint Paul's injunction to put off the old man and put on the new. Now empty, the soul "climbs" to God with the "foot of love," along the "path of desire." The soul "runs," "leaps," and "flies."

The language of illumination and union is the focus of the rest of the volume. In chapter 6 God is seen as "light," "healing wound," "circle and center," "abyss," "wilderness," and (*pace* Tillich) "ground." This section emphasizes the affective devotion of Franciscan and Bernardine Christocentrism which lies at the root of English mysticism. Technical terms for the *unio* itself center on "onyng" and its offspring: "binden," "fastnen," "knitten," "couplen," and "joinen"—and on the *raptus* or "ravishing," so much a part of Rolle's, Julian's, and Margery Kemp's ecstatic visionary emphasis. Of special interest, however, are Riehle's related discussions in chapter 7 on the *familiaritas cum Deo* and the *commercium cum Deo*. Riehle sees Gregory the Great as the probable source of this sense of familiarity with God—a familiarity or "homliness" that allows the ascetic to experience God in the Beatific Vision. This *familiaritas* allows man a glimpse into the "derne" or "secree" knowledge of God. In this "homliness" there is an exchange or communion between the soul and God. Interestingly, Riehle cites Richard Misyn's translation of Rolle's *commercium* as "daliaunce." Perhaps the mystics could add much to our perceptions of exchange and dalliance supervised by a host at Hautdesert or on the road to Canterbury.

195

Chapters 8 and 9 deal with the five spiritual senses as modes of experiencing God and with the soul's desire to "have" God or to become the "city" or "castle" in which God dwells. This experience of God dwelling in the soul leads to the consideration in chapter 10 of God as "rest," "sleep," "death," and "complete absorption of self." Linguistically, these considerations lead Riehle to discuss the mystical use of "death" as "rebirth" in the mystical *unio* where the individual "drowns," "dissolves," or "melts" into the divine *commercium*, or "daliaunce."

Riehle's final chapter treats the problem of defining the image of God in the soul. The Rational Soul as the setting of the *unio mystica* is based on the two ternaries of Saint Augustine: *memoria, intelligentia, voluntas* and *memoria, intelligentia, amor*. This Augustinian identification of *voluntas* and *amor* provides a foundation for the mystic's emphasis on a reformation of the soul begun by grace and continued by a conformation to the Exemplar's voluntarism and love. In these final pages of his book, Riehle indicates aspects of late-medieval mysticism that explain the attractiveness this literature of inward *reformatio* had for later advocates of outward ecclesiastical reform.

This volume is logically organized according to the threefold mystical journey and provides the reader with an index of 558 Middle English words carefully cross-referenced to the text. There are forty-eight pages of notes often suggestive of further application of linguistic analysis within and outside the scope of this study. A fourteen-page bibliography is conveniently divided according to topic and author and by primary and secondary sources. While readers will find matters of emphasis with which to disagree—I would identify the English and German mystics more fully with "Franciscan" themes—medievalists will learn much about the mysticism of the period while making their own comparisons with the "secular" poetry of the fourteenth century.

WILLIAM F. POLLARD
Maryville College

PHILIP ROLLINSON, *Classical Theories of Allegory and Christian Culture*.
Appendix on primary Greek sources by Patricia Matsen. Duquesne
Studies in Language and Literature Series, vol. 3. Pittsburgh, Pa.:
Duquesne University Press; Brighton: Harvester Press, 1981. Pp. xx,
175. $17.50.

In Philip Rollinson's study of the theory of allegory in classical antiquity
and its continuation and modification in medieval Christianity, the broadest yet most apposite of his conclusions appear in the following pair of
statements.

All of this would seem to confirm one of Robertson's major hypotheses, that all
worthwhile creative writing in the Middle Ages should be or was thought to be
devoted to the presentation or representation of some truth. . . . However, whether
this truth should be narrowly limited to the boundaries, even at their broadest, of
Augustinian *caritas*, as [D. W.] Robertson suggests, is extremely dubious. [p. 85]

At first sight it may well seem to many readers of this review that these
statements describe precisely the convictions that inform their own practice
as interpreters of medieval poetry. Whatever the paths that got them to
this position (and there must be more than one or two), neither those that
are in accord with it nor, for that matter, those that disagree can afford to
ignore or pass over casually Rollinson's work. For the path he has followed is
one that he has largely cleared for himself and now, somewhat optimisti-
cally but justifiably, invites others to take: "The empirical survey of
allegorical theories I am attempting here is intended to provide a common
basis or starting point for future critics and criticism of allegorical poetry"
(p. xiii).

The survey is indeed notable for its emphasis on the practical analysis
and objective description of its subject. It is also clear that its prominent
references to the work of D. W. Robertson, Jr., have been motivated by a
respectful recognition of its contribution to medieval studies rather than by
a desire to contradict or limit it. The author pursues his chief aim, to trace
the career of allegory and related rhetorical terms in the surviving theoretical works of Greek and Latin antiquity in his first chapter and to ascertain
and assess their impact on the development of allegorical theory in Christian culture in his second chapter, without becoming involved with inter-

pretative questions pertaining to specific allegorical poems of the Middle Ages and the Renaissance. Consistent with this effort to avoid partisanship in the approach of the two main chapters are the short introduction, which contains a useful list of relevant works, authors, and terms and a chronological chart by centuries (from the fourth B.C. to the fourteenth A.D.) of important writers from Aristotle to Nicholas of Lyre, and the two appendices. The first, a translation by Rollinson of the late-fourth-century A.D. grammarian Diomedes' treatment of tropes in his *Ars grammatica*, is rich in examples from the poems of Virgil. The second, much longer appendix is an assemblage of translations with introductory commentaries by Patricia Matsen of the definitions and theories of types of "other-speaking" and "other-meaning" (hitherto unavailable in English) from authors in Spengel's *Rhetores Graeci*.

This concentration on classical rhetorical theory counteracts the perfunctory acknowledgment that it had something to do with the development of allegory, as students, old and new, of the subject so readily aver in their attempts to extrapolate a theory of allegory primarily, if not exclusively, from literary sources. As if in response to the observation that classical rhetoric was as important as philosophy to early Christianity by the now rather unfashionable Werner Jaeger (*Early Christianity and Greek Paideia* [Cambridge, Mass.: Harvard University Press, 1961], pp. 77–78), Rollinson's work raises his subject's stock by raising our consciousness of its complexity and significance. His treatment of elements related to allegory in ancient thought in works by Cicero, Plutarch, Demetrius, Philo, Macrobius, Diomedes, and Quintillian leads to a reiteration and highly informative consideration of the long-standing question for allegorical interpretation of application. The author's sophisticated account of the ramifications of this question, especially in light of his double focus on the development of cues and indicators of the likely presence of abstract meaning that result from the gradual connection between fable and myth with personification and allegory and on the fact that satisfactory literal passages often receive the same kind of interpretation as that to which texts with literal impossibilities or obscurities are subjected, should help us understand why it has no easy or simple answers. Even though we sometimes enjoy a writer's explicit identification of his reference or confidently apply iconographic tradition to the solution of obscure or incomplete reference, there is no one way to conduct our efforts, and every text must be individually considered:

"The interpretive answer is not in the words alone or what their normal literal and figurative implications convey, but in the combination or conjunction of verbal expression and the intended application of that expression" (p. 28).

The second chapter, entitled "The Christian Response," is divided into four parts: the Bible, Saint Augustine (fourth to fifth centuries A.D.), before and after Augustine, and six pages of conclusions that present a multitude of lucidly stated observations and insights. The longest and most important of these is the discussion of Augustine's positions on allegorical interpretation, which is more comprehensive and revealing than any other available. Among its many valuable and discerning features, whose implications pervade this part of the book, is the explanation of Augustine's endorsement of the usefulness of fiction and fable in the service of truth and the consequent effect on our appreciation and perception of his influence on both the reading and the writing of allegory in the later Middle Ages.

Because its writing is densely packed with complex information and adheres to the principles of succinctness and strict continuity, *Classical Theories of Allegory and Christian Culture* is not susceptible of easy summarization. But these very qualities make it a pleasure to read and reflect on, though a number of undetected typographical errors are distracting (p. 18: "subordinted"; p. 51: "*hisotriam*"; p. 72 n. 40: missing quotation marks; p. 76: "be eagles"; p. 79: "communiction"). In addition to providing an analytical survey of the two basic kinds of allegory in the classical theory, the author shows how "the allegory of implied application and the allegory of partial or concealed reference" (p. xix) are modified in the Middle Ages into two-meaning allegory, containing a satisfactory literal sense plus some other additional meaning, and one-meaning allegory, "conceived as involving only one level of hidden meaning, which is to be inferred from the obscure or literally impossible text" (p. xx). Rollinson and Matsen have provided us with an important reference source for the rhetorical terms that played a role in this chapter of literary history. To cite but two examples, I expect that many readers will find the treatment of terms and concepts relating to allegory in the Septuagint, the Greek New Testament, and the Vulgate intriguing and illuminating and that those readers with an interest in the career of fable will find the section on it in Matsen's appendix of special interest.

The few times that Rollinson comes close to going beyond a general statement and making a direct application of his work to the interpretation of specific medieval or renaissance poems, he stops short. In light of his purpose and plan this restraint is quite appropriate. It is also appropriate, as he suggests, to strive for an understanding and appreciation of European allegorical literature on the basis of his work, for until that is done, the story is not complete. As for the first part of the story, it has been well worth the telling.

GEORGE D. ECONOMOU
Long Island University

GREGORY H. ROSCOW, *Syntax and Style in Chaucer's Poetry*. Chaucer Studies, vol. 6. Cambridge: D. S. Brewer, 1981; Totowa, N.J.: Rowman and Littlefield. Pp. x, 158. $40.00.

A title such as "Notes on Syntax and Style in Chaucer's Poetry" would better prepare the reader for what is to be found in the sixth of the *Chaucer Studies* series issued by D. S. Brewer in Cambridge. In his introductory chapter Gregory Roscow sets up a nice middle ground between "two rather different approaches to loose syntax," one, which he erroneously assigns to Margaret Schlauch, "assuming a close correspondence between medieval and modern usage," the other, represented by Norman Blake, "emphasizing their remoteness." He plans to show in subsequent chapters the ways in which "Chaucer's syntax gains an effect of immediacy," emphasizing such features of Middle English usage as a "fondness for discontinuous patterns of word-order and for negative forms of emphatic expression." He promises to set Chaucer's usage in its linguistic and literary context, giving special attention to the popular romances, the models in Roscow's view for important elements of Chaucer's vigorous poetic syntax.

The second chapter, on word order, starts effectively with a discussion of the famous description of tournament combat from *The Knight's Tale*, in which Roscow quotes, and then deferentially corrects and extends a comment on the passage by A. C. Spearing. The front shifting of lexical verbs, taken up next, yields two apparently interesting patterns in the scene of

200

Arcite's death in *The Knight's Tale* and Deiphebus's dinner party in book 2 of *Troilus and Criseyde*. Reference to the text, however, shows how inadequate Roscow's description of the passages is. The two close lines in *The Knight's Tale* that supposedly contribute to the emotional impact of the scene surround the discussion of where Arcite's soul went; the second one follows "Now wol I speken forth of Emilye." And the point about the dinner party in *Troilus and Criseyde* is not that "the pace of the narrative quickens" but quite the reverse. What happens is that the narrative stands still while we experience the social amenities, the partial awareness of most of the participants, Pandarus's skill, and the delight he takes in orchestrating the occasion. The pattern pointed out by Roscow is in any event only one of a multiplicity that contributes to the richness of Chaucer's style in that scene. The comment on the line from *The Nun's Priest's Tale*, "Ran Colle our dogge..." (line 3383) is similarly inadequate for this liveliest of Chaucer's crowd scenes; it unaccountably fails to take note of line 3385, "Ran cow and calfe and ek the verray hogges."

The rest of the chapter on word order continues to list out of context the examples for each variation from normal word order to be found in Middle English usage, usually coming to the conclusion that the lines contribute variety and emphasis to Chaucer's style. Subsequent chapters on idiomatic usage, pleonasm, ellipsis, relative clauses, and coordination and parataxis employ the same technique and suggest the absence of system throughout this disappointing book. The examples from popular romance and from Chaucer's contemporaries imply two things: that Chaucer drew from the same native speech as his fellow poets and that the language for poetry in the fourteenth century was closer to colloquial English than it had been in Anglo-Saxon times. Whether they also show the influence of popular romances on Chaucer's style remains a moot question.

A total absence of footnotes matches the absence of explanation of what the examples reflect. At times the comment indicates that a complete survey has been carried out, as in possessive postmodification, which "is not attested elsewhere in Chaucer's works" (p. 69), and relative clauses presenting a consequence of the action in the principal clause which "have no exact parallels in Chaucer's poetry" (p. 104). Far more usual are such phrases as "seldom extend beyond seven lines" (p. 71), "sometimes intervene" (p. 36), "is also quite common" (p. 20), and "Although they are less frequently met with in Chaucer's poetry..." (p. 108). Roscow gives no account of the procedures he carried out, and, except for the implications of his commentary, the reader has no way of knowing whether the examples given are complete, representative in their numbers, the most striking instances, or a mere random selection. This absence of scholarly rigor will make it difficult for others to use the frequently interesting material that Roscow assembles. What we have in the book is a set of observations on a number of syntactical features, some of which contribute to Chaucer's style. We also have a series of critical comments on Margaret Schlauch's exemplary *PMLA* article published in 1952, "Chaucer's Colloquial English: Its Structural Traits." At one point (p. 47) Roscow quotes half of Schlauch's discussion of a syntactic feature as if it were the whole. At no point does he do justice to the balance, sensitivity, and scholarly control of her presentation.

The book includes a general index and a useful "Index of Chaucer Quotations." The bibliography, confined to references in the book, shows some surprising imbalances and omissions. Spearing appears five times; J. A. Burrow and J. A. W. Bennett, twice each. The Tatlock-Kennedy *Concordance* and Muscatine do not appear. Medieval poetics and modern stylistics have each a single item.

CHARLES A. OWEN, JR.
University of Connecticut

DONALD M. ROSE, ed., *New Perspectives in Chaucer Criticism*. Norman, Okla.: Pilgrim Books, 1982. Pp. x, 248. $21.95.

This volume comprises a collection of revised papers, originally read at the conference of the New Chaucer Society in New Orleans in April, 1980, and here organized into three broad thematic sections. But first, George Kane, in an opening paper ("Langland and Chaucer: An Obligatory Comparison"), compares aspects of Chaucer and Langland and modern reactions to them, justly remarking on the extent to which critics of either poet, by ignoring the existence of the other, miss some illuminating comparisons. Kane points out some shared elements in the two poets' education: "rigorous inculcation of Christian doctrine," some experience of the "allegorizing activities of the classicizing friars," and some knowledge of that "old system of moral categorizing, estates satire," together with the common basis of their education in Latin grammar. Kane speculates on Langland's knowledge of profane rhetoric or of courtly and Arthurian literature, as well as on Chaucer's knowledge of French religious allegories or of antifraternal literature. An interesting comparison follows on the two poets' conception of themselves as artists. Along with a self-consciousness about their art and a common tendency to invoke modesty *topoi*, there is also a self-confidence approaching arrogance discernible in both poets, and that this emerges in two poets in comparable degrees at this period "bespeaks a new condition of poetry in post-conquest England." Both poets also register in their poems their personal problems of art and morality, and Kane compares the implications of Chaucer's *Retractions* with Langland's allusions within his poetry to doubts about his own poetic activity ("The poet sees, if only momentarily, the act of composition as self-gratifying and therefore, to the extent that it fails in charity, sinful notwithstanding its ostensible pious objectives of spiritual understanding and moral reform. Here is the real abjectness.... By contrast Chaucer's 'retracciouns' seem serene, almost confident.").

Part 2 of the book consists of five essays on various aspects of literary theory, modern and medieval, as applied to Chaucer. In his essay "Contemporary Literary Theory and Chaucer," Morton W. Bloomfield discusses "what aspects of modern disciplines are...useful in interpreting and evaluating literature," and he reviews the claims of semantics, semiology, literature and philosophy, the concept of speech acts, psychology, and sociology. On the study of social aspects of literature Bloomfield comments that "audience and reader are not to be limited to the 'real' author and reader, but may include the internal audience and reader who are both presupposed in and even brought into Chaucer's poetry." Little has yet been said on that internal audience to whom the so-much-discussed author-persona is presumably speaking. And in an interesting comparison of *MLT* and the tale of Alatiel in *Decameron*, Bloomfield himself anticipates those advances in the study of narratology and literary structuralism he predicts in Chaucer criticism. His concluding comment that our goal is still "to recreate and undistance the past" is the preface to much in the ensuing essays on the relative claims of "alterity" or "modernity" in our responses to medieval literature.

In her "Response" to Bloomfield's paper, Florence Ridley highlights "the preoccupation thinkers of today share with those of the Middle Ages in linguistics and psychology: with the limitations of language, its tendency to falsify experience; with behavior; and with the interrelation between the two." For Ridley it is impossible for us now to rediscover one completely appropriate or "central" approach to Chaucer. However, the study of rhetoric, and of analysis in terms of signs, is in the nature of Chaucer's writing an especially promising avenue of approach. Psychology and sociology are seen as vital analytical tools, for through them are discoverable "equivalencies or correspondences between then and now by means of which we can locate and measure differences and similarities, and thus open the way for understanding and adaptation of modern aesthetic to make possible reception of the medieval artefact."

In contrast to modern theories, Alastair J. Minnis, in "Chaucer and Comparative Literary Theory," offers the example of medieval literary theory, presenting in summary form the teaching of medieval academic prologues and thus providing some contemporary correlative to whatever we may deduce were Chaucer's own ideas on literary creation, for "while we cannot reexperience the past, we can recognize the integrity of past experience." Minnis argues sensibly that we cannot assess Chaucer's distinctiveness and his "'defamiliarization' (notably of literary convention and of genre)" until we know rather better what was familiar to him. And insofar as he suggests that knowledge of such late-medieval literary theory will furnish "criteria for the definition and adaptation of those modern literary concepts and terms that are relevant to Chaucer's writings," Minnis proposes a critical approach to Chaucer that differs from those of his companions in this volume by implying that modern approaches should be chastened by a stricter sense of the historical evidence for contemporary literary attitudes.

It is such inventive modern criticism of medieval literature as that of Zumthor, Jauss, Poirion, and their English-speaking followers that forms the background to Winthrop Wetherbee's "Convention and Authority: A Comment on Some Recent Critical Approaches to Chaucer." Wetherbee notes how application of modern literary theory has exposed "the radically traditional nature of this poetry and its preoccupation with closed systems of literary convention. . . . The programmatic operation of literary convention as Zumthor defines it becomes only a particularly powerful effect of the dislocated and dislocating activity of language itself." And Vance's work on *Troilus*—where such literary convention is seen not as the expression but as the determinant of the operation of the characters' consciousness—is cited here, as elsewhere in this book. Wetherbee very pertinently points out some ways in which these approaches may prove reductive and monotonous and suggests how Chaucer's points of reference in Dante and in classical tradition enable him to break out of any such circularity of reference.

Indeed, it is this question of "just how language 'refers' " that forms the keynote of R. Allen Shoaf's "Dante's *Commedia* and Chaucer's Theory of Mediation: A Preliminary Sketch." Shoaf aims to suggest—by means of an extended discussion of imagery of coinage, falsification, and narcissism in *Troilus* and in Dante—that "Chaucer's position on the problem of referentiality is very much like Dante's."

Part 3 comprises three essays on aspects of Chaucer and the visual arts. Henry Ansgar Kelly's "Chaucer's Arts and Our Arts" sets out with relish to demolish any exaggerated view of Chaucer's interestedness in matters visual. Noting how rarely the visual arts are referred to as arts in Chaucer's times and how Chaucer does not refer to historical artists as Dante and Petrarch do, Kelly suggests that the visual arts were not very important in English literate consciousness at that period. The lack of artistic and architectural detail noted in tales (like *ClT* and *MerT*) set in that Lombardy which Chaucer visited and the lack of painterly verisimilitude in descriptions in *BD*, *HF*, or *KnT* suggest to Kelly "the bookishness of Chaucer's brushes with the fine and applied arts" and that his visual imagery was neither inspired directly nor significantly mediated by a response to paintings, statues, or buildings.

After this zestful challenge John V. Fleming's paper can focus all the more realistically on his subject, "Chaucer and the Visual Arts of His Time." He establishes four aspects of Chaucer's relation to the visual arts: (1) Chaucer's various references to the visual arts in his work, often probably "owing more to the poet's powers of empirical description than to those of his imaginative fancy"; (2) the nature and effect of contemporary visual inspiration available to the poet; (3) ways in which analysis of literary style is to be illuminated by stylistic analysis in the visual arts ("the major features of the Gothic style as they appear in Chaucer's narrative poems"); and (4) ways in which Chaucer's actual mode of writing reflects visual influence by itself exhibiting the techniques, expectations, and iconography of the contemporary arts. Fleming, after noting the iconographic imagination of Chaucer and how visual ideas may have "structural dominance" in some *CT*, ends with the intriguing suggestion that Chaucer also writes the literary equivalent of the artistic "grotesque" in such descriptions as that of the Summoner's "gerland" and "bokeleer."

These ideas make an appropriate preface to V. A. Kolve's "Chaucer's *Second Nun's Tale* and the Iconography of Saint Cecilia," which — together with iconographical scholarship specifically illuminating the background to *SNT* in a way that expands the reader's sympathetic understanding of that tale's form and the way it presents Cecilia's ordeal — contains as well some comments pertinent to Chaucer's larger relationship to the visual arts in a world where his audience had "a shared vocabulary of *signs* — of signifying visual images." For while Kolve agrees with Kelly that Chaucer is not a "painterly" poet, seldom seeking descriptive effects more characteristic of painting than writing, he nonetheless claims him as an iconographic poet who "drew upon the language of sign and symbol in shaping the images his poems make in the mind" and convincingly makes this case in discussion of the Cecilia legend.

Part 4 includes three essays with a common interest in Chaucer's French background, and all are variously concerned with lexical matters. As Fleming comments, "France was *the* cultural fact," and in his "Chaucer and the French Influence," John H. Fisher valuably makes plain the facts about the metrical models provided for Chaucer by poetry in French and explores the modes of French influence to be discerned in Chaucer's writing. Following on from this, with a characteristically arresting argument, E. Talbot Donaldson, in "Gallic Flies in Chaucer's English Word Web," points out that Chaucer sometimes seems to use French constructions in his English (though the relative rarity of this supports the idea that he was wholly bilingual) and that such occurrences are not the confusions of a French speaker but rather the exploitation of French syntax and diction within English for the purposes that Donaldson wittily suggests in the various cases he discusses.

Continuing the theme of the Francophone Chaucer, Barbara Nolan examines "The Art of Expropriation: Chaucer's Narrator in *The Book of the Duchess*," particularly Chaucer's divergences from Froissart and Machaut, by which he is seen to define his own poetic in the opening section of *BD*. Divergence is here held to reveal ironic intent: Chaucer's customary selectivity in borrowing is "parodic expropriation" by which Chaucer "distances himself from, and thereby calls into serious question, the rich tradition of narrative authority" in his French sources. A thoughtful differentiation follows between the characteristics of Chaucer's dreamer and his models in Froissart and Machaut, and this scholarly contribution is valuale whether or not one accepts Nolan's larger concern to see the difference as a conscious critique of the effectiveness of traditional courtly French poetry to handle the serious issues of life and death.

In "Chaucer's Text and the Web of Words," Norman Blake discusses some cruces where modern editors of *CT* follow Ellesmere rather than Hengwrt (wrongly, as he thinks). One result is an unrepresentative tidying up of Chaucer's meter by comparison with what Blake takes as the more authentic evidence of Hengwrt that Chaucer's approaches to meter may well have been more adventurous, even more careless or cavalier, than hitherto assumed. There is an interesting discussion of incorporation of glosses into the text and of editorial impulses to edit Chaucer's text into a more *specific* one in its details than is always suggested by the manuscripts. There are also informative accounts of scribal extension of authentic "Northernisms" in *RvT* and of the "problem" of the teller of *ShT*, seen in the context of scribal responses generally to dialect features and to personal pronouns. One does not have to agree with Blake's every point to find very stimulating, nonetheless, his resolve to try to think through some problems of authenticity in Chaucer's text that have been left undisturbed through that modern lack of initiative in moving beyond Victorian ideas on editing which Blake with much justice castigates.

The collection is most appropriately dedicated to the memory of Elizabeth Salter, for in its concern with the mutual illumination of literary and artistic studies; with Chaucer's cultural background in France, England, and Italy; and with the transmission of literary culture, it matches the range of her interests and offers a fitting tribute to the spirit of her own work in its concern to understand a medieval poet through the fullest application of all that both a historical and a modern sense can provide.

BARRY WINDEATT
Emmanuel College, Cambridge

The Winchester Anthology: A Facsimile of British Library Additional Manuscript 60577. Introduction and list of contents by Edward Wilson and an account of the music by Iain Fenlon. Cambridge: D. S. Brewer, 1981. Pp. x, 47, 225 leaves. $220.00.

The advent of this volume recalls the excitement all students of Middle English manuscripts shared with the appearance of Sotheby's sale catalogue of June 19, 1979. Lot 57 ("The Property of a Gentleman") was one of the most startling discoveries of recent years. The catalogue described it as an "anthology of Middle English Verse and Prose... with nearly 1,800 lines of unpublished verse." The figure is perhaps a little on the high side. But this was clearly a manuscript that merited sustained and authoritative examination. It is fortunate that it should have received it so soon after its acquisition by the British Library (where it is now Additional 60577) in the form of a facsimile published with characteristic enterprise by D. S. Brewer, with excellent introductions by Edward Wilson and Iain Fenlon.

The manuscript is a large one (226 leaves of vellum and paper), containing 229 separate items, a great many obviously very brief. Very few previously known texts of any length appear in it. The most substantial are an imperfect copy of Lydgate and Burgh's translation of the *Secret secretorum* and various prose texts including a fragment of Earl Rivers's *Dictes and Sayings of the Philosophers*, extracts from *The Mirror of St. Edmund* and from Hilton. Apart from the Lydgate and Burgh poem fourteen other recorded poems are represented here (nos. 906, 1825, 1872, 2547.5, 2627, 2676, 2683, 3436, 3168.4, 3297.5, 3985, 4111, 4184, 4215 in the *Index of Middle English Verse*).

The chief interest of the manuscript lies in the number of hitherto unrecorded verse texts that appear (there is only one seemingly unique prose literary text of any length, a translation from the French of some "demaundes of loue"). Some of these are very brief, merely a stanza or a couplet (e.g., nos. 150–52), but others are of greater interest. The most remarkable is a translation of the proem and book 1 of Petrarch's *Secretum* (no. 72) into nearly 900 lines. This is closely followed by a poem (no. 74) in sixteen eight-line stanzas on William Waynflete, bishop of Winchester. Later poems include a translation of the *Cur mundus militat* (no. 120, 40 lines), a verse sermon (no. 121, 158 lines), and two didactic poems (nos. 130–31, 40 and 68 lines, respectively). Also apparently unique are the texts of a number of early Tudor songs (nos. 170–73, 175) and a number of additions made by various sixteenth-century hands.

Clearly the amount of new verse it contains must provide the immediate case for the publication of this facsimile. But there are other reasons of almost equal importance. Chief among these is the manuscript's provenance. Wilson convincingly identifies the manuscript as produced at Winchester by a monk of Saint Swithun's Priory toward the end of the fifteenth century. It was later owned by the noted sixteenth-century book collector Thomas Dackomb and by William Way, a lay singing man at Winchester Cathedral.

Such localized connections, together with the William Waynflete poem, justify the manuscript's designation as the "Winchester Anthology." And such a localization increases the manuscript's interest. For its contents reflect an extensive range of materials for a monastic milieu, not limited to the devotional, pedagogic, and practical but including scientific writings, songs, and secular writings in verse and prose in Middle English, French, and Latin. The manuscript may reflect traces of Waynflete's own humanistic interests as well as affording insight into the nature of late-medieval taste within a localized milieu.

The marshaling of evidence and descriptive accuracy of Wilson and Fenlon place all students of Middle English codicology in their debt. My only querulous complaint is about Wilson's restraint in his discussion of the nature of the apparently unique verse texts. One would welcome fuller accounts of these, or at least the reassurance that Wilson is going to deal with them elsewhere, instead of having them largely passed over in silence generally without even any statement that they *are* apparently unique. Even for some previously recorded texts a little more discussion might have been helpful. For example, no. 111 is a poem by Lydgate. As Wilson notes, it has only fifteen stanzas, where the standard edition has twenty-four. But it might be worth noting both the sequence of stanzas and that three of the fifteen appear otherwise unrecorded (the stanza sequence in Winchester is 1–3, 5, 7–10, X, 11–12, X, X, 14–15). It might have been helpful to have notes on such textual idiosyncrasy.

The decision to print footnotes to the introduction in the outer margins of each page is not an altogether happy one; at a number of points (notably pp. 13–17) they have to be carried over to subsequent pages.

One can only reiterate one's gratitude to the authors of the introduction and to the publishers for making this facsimile available in such an exemplary form.

A. S. G. EDWARDS
University of Victoria

BARRY A. WINDEATT, *Chaucer's Dream Poetry: Sources and Analogues.* Chaucer Studies, vol. 7. Cambridge: D. S. Brewer; Totowa, N.J.: Rowman and Littlefield, 1982. Pp. xviii, 168. $42.50.

With this important collection of translations Barry Windeatt aims "to draw together conveniently in one place the more important narrative sources and analogues for Chaucer's dream poetry which are otherwise difficult of access" and "to enable the reader to gain an impression for himself of the intricate nature of the works. . . and thus to enable assessment of what Chaucer has achieved creatively in his absorption of the French influences upon him" (p. xviii). This book fulfills both purposes well, and while it lacks original texts, it makes a worthy companion to William F. Bryan and Germaine Dempster's *Sources and Analogues of Chaucer's Canterbury Tales.* As with that standard reference work, there are improvements that one might suggest, but the chief needs are filled. Until now students of Chaucer have had to ferret out and translate for themselves most of the French sources, whether they wished to know the background of individual passages or to determine the general nature of the materials with which he was working.

Windeatt appropriately omits Chaucer's materials for the dream poems that are readily available in translation, notably the *Aeneid,* the *Divine Comedy,* the *Romance of the Rose,* and Ovid's poems. He also leaves out sources for minor passages. Most of the works that he includes, then, are French *dits amoureux,* the long love poems that filled the air that young Chaucer breathed but were forgotten even by the Renaissance. As one who has read more than once most of these works that are extant, I was particularly pleased to find the proof drawn together in one place of Chaucer's good taste in his choice of French models. In my view he drew on the best of Machaut's *dits* in making use of the *Jugement dou Roy de*

Behaingne, *Remede de Fortune*, the *Dit de la Fonteinne Amoureuse*, and the *Dit dou Lyon*. Of these poems Windeatt presents *Behaingne* complete, most of the *Fonteinne amoureuse*, the substantial portions of the *Remede* and the *Lyon*, all in the section on *The Book of the Duchess*. Also in that section is my favorite among Froissart's long poems, the *Paradys d'amours* complete. Parts of two other fine *dits* that are major sources for Chaucer and important in the history of Middle French love poetry, Nicole de Margival's *Dit de la panthère d'amours* and Machaut's *Jugement dou Roy de Navarre*, appear in the parts devoted to *The House of Fame* and *The Legend of Good Women* respectively.

All the works named clearly are sources for Chaucer. In his section on *The Parliament of Fowls*, for which the French background is uncertain, Windeatt provides a large set of analogues, some to the *demande d'amour* of the poem and others to the assemblage of birds. He gives complete translations of *Li fablel dou Dieu d'Amors*, of great interest for its early date, and Jean de Condé's *La Messe des oisiaus et li plais de chanonesses et des grises nonains*, a lively work that shows how apparent irreverence is transformed into edification in a medieval poet's allegorization. Although these works can hardly be called near analogues to the *Parliament*, they are happily included. Making less of a contribution to the book are the three debates argued by birds on the question of who is the superior lover, clerk or knight. One of these poems would have sufficed.

Only three non-French works are included, all in the *Parliament* section. It is good to find there *The Dream of Scipio* complete, and also the passage of the *Teseida* which Chaucer draws on in the garden section. The small piece of Alanus de Insulis's *De planctu naturae*, however, is disappointing; it is not even from the part that Chaucer refers to. We are given only the passage about the advent of Nature, and nothing of her dress and visage, the matters for which Chaucer sends us to Alanus's poem (lines 316–18):

> And ryght as Aleyn, in the Pleynt of Kynde,
> Devyseth Nature of aray and face,
> In swich aray men myghte hire there fynde.

To appreciate Chaucer's picture, one really needs to know the impressive portrait alluded to.

Except insofar as all translations are open to quibbles, Windeatt's appeal to me serviceable and felicitous. They are appropriately literal while avoiding word-for-word renditions when they would result in clumsiness. The ten-page preface strikes a good balance in talking about Chaucer's use of particular sources and his imaginative transformation of them. The main disappointment of the book is its failure to provide indications of how each work fits into Chaucer's poems, information such as Bryan and Dempster supply—though sometimes scantily—in their headnotes. In this respect Windeatt gives *The Book of the Duchess* the most satisfactory treatment. In the section on the *Duchess* footnotes to the translations document the parallel passages in Chaucer's poem, and at the end of the book an "Index of Parallels" conveniently summarizes the borrowings. Even with this poem, though, one is left on his own to figure out that while the *Fonteinne amoureuse* is not an important verbal source of the *Duchess*, its central situation provides the main model for that of Chaucer's elegy and that there are major complex parallels in situation between Machaut's *Remede* and *Behaingne* and Chaucer's poem.

Windeatt perhaps consciously rejected such discussion as either readily available elsewhere or too controversial. If that is understandable with the *Duchess*, it is less so with the other works. Exactly how the French convocations of birds relate to each other and to the *Parliament* would assist any reader. Some mention of how Chaucer abridges *The Dream of Scipio*, the relevance of the *Panthère d'amours* to *The House of Fame*, and like information would also be generally helpful. Some of the headnotes, such as the one for the *Jugement dou Roy de Navarre*, do deal with certain aspects of the larger relationships and show that there was no consistent policy of omitting this material.

Notwithstanding, the book is well conceived and well produced. It will make a convenient reference work for students of Chaucer at all levels, and it may well act as an important influence in opening up the whole Middle French tradition of love poetry to their appreciation. No body of work is more relevant to his art and at the same time more undervalued.

JAMES I. WIMSATT
University of Texas at Austin

Books Received

LARRY D. BENSON and JOHN LEYERLE, eds. *Chivalric Literature: Essays on Relations Between Literature and Life in the Later Middle Ages*. Studies in Medieval Culture, vol. 14. Kalamazoo, Mich.: Medieval Institute Publications, 1980. Pp. xii, 176. $9.95.

LARRY D. BENSON and SIEGFRIED WENZEL, eds. *The Wisdom of Poetry: Essays in Early English Literature in Honor of Morton W. Bloomfield*. Kalamazoo, Mich.: Medieval Institute Publications, 1982. Pp. 314. $13.95.

BERNARD BERANKE, ed. *Annuale Mediaevale*, vol. 21 (1981). Atlantic Highlands, N.J.: Humanities Press, 1982. Pp. 138.

IAN BISHOP. *Chaucer's Troilus and Criseyde: A Critical Study*. Bristol: University of Bristol, 1981. Pp. 116. £4.95.

PIERRE BOGLIONI, ed. *La culture populaire au moyen âge*. Montreal: Les Editions Univers, 1979. Pp. 257. $14.95.

PIERO BOITANI, ed. *J. A. W. Bennett: The Humane Medievalist and Other Essays in English Literature and Learning, from Chaucer to Eliot*. Rome: Edizioni di storia e letteratura, 1982. Pp. 411.

DEREK BREWER. *Symbolic Stories: Traditional Narratives of the Family Drama in English Literature*. Totowa, N.J.: Rowman and Littlefield, 1980. Pp. ix, 190. $31.50.

DEREK BREWER. *Tradition and Innovation in Chaucer*. Atlantic Highlands, N.J.: Humanities Press; London and Basingstoke: Macmillan Press, Ltd., 1982. Pp. 181. $42.00.

J. A. BURROWS, ed. *Sir Gawain and the Green Knight*. New Haven, Conn., and London: Yale University Press, 1982. Pp. 176. $15.00.

JANET COLEMAN. *Piers Plowman and the Moderni*. Rome: Edizioni di storia e letteratura, 1981. Pp. 247.

JAMES E. CROSS and THOMAS D. HILL, eds. *The Prose Solomon and Saturn and Adrian and Ritheus*. McMaster Old English Studies and Text, vol. 1. Toronto: University of Toronto Press, 1982. Pp. xi, 185. $35.00.

CLIFFORD DAVIDSON. *A Middle English Treatise on the Playing of Miracles*. Washington, D.C.: University Press of America, 1981. Pp. vi, 87. $14.75.

R. H. C. DAVIS and J. M. WALLACE-HADRILL, eds. *The Writing of History in the Middle Ages: Essays Presented to Richard William Southern*. New York: Clarendon Press, 1981. Pp. xiii, 517.

JOERG O. FICHTE, ed. *Chaucer's "Art Poetical": A Study in Chaucerian Poetics*. Studies and Text in English, vol. 1. Tübingen: Gunter Narr Verlag Tübingen, 1980. Pp. 137.

LINDA GEORGIANNA. *The Solitary Self: Individuality in the Ancrene Wisse*. London and Cambridge, Mass.: Harvard University Press, 1981. Pp. xii, 169. $16.50.

JOHN P. HERMANN and JOHN J. BURKE, JR., eds. *Signs and Symbols in Chaucer's Poetry*. University: University of Alabama Press, 1981. Pp. 257. $19.75.

ANDREW HUGHES. *Medieval Manuscripts for Mass and Office: A Guide to Their Organization and Terminology*. Toronto and Buffalo, N.Y.: University of Toronto Press, 1982. Pp. xxxiv, 470. $47.50.

S. S. HUSSEY. *Chaucer: An Introduction*, 2d ed. London and New York: Methuen, 1982. Pp. 245. $20.00.

DAVID G. KENNEDY. *Incarnational Element in Hilton's Spirituality*. Salzburg Studies in English Literature under the direction of Professor Erwin A. Sturzl. Atlantic Highlands, N.J.: Humanities Press; Salzburg: Institut für Anglistik und Amerikanistik Universität, 1982. Pp. x, 312. $25.00.

PEGGY A. KNAPP and MICHAEL A. STURGIN, eds. *Assays: Critical Approaches to Medieval and Renaissance Texts*. Pittsburgh: University of Pittsburgh Press, 1981. Pp. viii, 149. $12.95.

214

TRAUGOTT LAWLER. *The One and the Many in the Canterbury Tales.* Hamden, Conn.: Shoe String Press, 1980. Pp. 209. $17.50.

BERNARD S. LEVY and PAUL E. SZARMACH, eds. *The Alliterative Tradition in the Fourteenth Century.* Kent, Ohio: Kent State University Press, 1981. Pp. xiii, 213. $19.50.

ROBERT E. LEWIS and ANGUS MCINTOSH. *A Descriptive Guide to the Manuscripts of the Prick of Conscience.* Medium Aevum Monographs, New Series, vol. 12. Oxford: Society for the Study of Mediaeval Languages and Literature, 1982. Pp. xvi, 173. £6.00.

RAOUL MANSELLI, ed. *La religion populaire au moyen âge: problèmes de méthode et d'histoire.* Montreal: Institut d'études médiévales, 1975. Pp. 234. $12.00.

BRUCE MITCHELL and FRED C. ROBINSON. *A Guide to Old English: Revised with Texts and Glossary.* Toronto: University of Toronto Press, 1982. Pp. xiv, 271. $35.00.

A. C. PARTRIDGE. *A Companion to Old and Middle English Studies.* Totowa, N.J.: Barnes and Noble Books, 1982. Pp. x, 462. $30.00.

DALE PETERSON, ed. *A Mad People's History of Madness.* Pittsburgh: University of Pittsburgh Press, 1982. Pp. xiv, 368. $19.95.

JOHN F. PLUMMER, ed. *Vox Feminae: Studies in Medieval Woman's Song.* Studies in Medieval Culture, vol. 15. Kalamazoo, Mich.: Medieval Institute Publications, 1981. Pp. viii, 223. $10.95.

NIGEL SAUL. *Knights and Esquires: The Gloucestershire Gentry in the Fourteenth Century.* New York: Clarendon Press, 1981. Pp. xiii, 316. $44.00.

A. V. C. SCHMIDT, ed. *William Langland, The Vision of Piers Plowman: A Complete Edition of the B-Text.* Totowa, N.J.: Littlefield, Adams and Co., 1978. Pp. xlvii, 364. $8.95.

DAVID M. SMITH. *Guide to Bishops' Registers of England and Wales: A Survey from the Middle Ages to the Abolition of Episcopacy in 1646.* Guides and Handbooks Series, no. 11. Woodbridge: Boydell and Brewer, 1981. Pp. xvi, 286. £15.00.

BENEDICTA WARD. *Miracles and the Medieval Mind: Theory, Record, and Event.* Philadelphia: University of Pennsylvania Press, 1982. Pp. x, 321. $25.00.

JOHN WARDEN, ed. *Orpheus: The Metamorphoses of a Myth.* Toronto and Buffalo, N.Y.: University of Toronto Press, 1982. Pp. xiii, 238. $35.00.

G. A. WILKES and A. P. RIEMER, eds. *Studies in Chaucer.* Sydney Studies in English. Sydney: University of Sydney, 1981. Pp. 120.

NIGEL WILKINS, ed. *Chaucer Songs.* Woodbridge: Boydell and Brewer Ltd.; Totowa, N.J.: Rowman and Littlefield, 1980. Pp. 29. $25.00.

NIGEL WILKINS, ed. *Music in the Age of Chaucer.* Woodbridge: Boydell and Brewer; Totowa, N.J.: Rowman and Littlefield, 1980. Pp. xiv, 174. $35.00.

An Annotated Chaucer Bibliography
1981

By
Lorrayne Y. Baird
Editor and Compiler

With the assistance of:

Claire Clements Morton, *Auburn University*; Virginia E. Leland, *Bowling Green State University*; Martha S. Waller, *Butler University*; Sumner Ferris, *California State College, Pennsylvania*; Robert apRoberts, *California State University, Northridge*; Virginia Scott Zelk, *Central Missouri State University*; Pat T. Overbeck, *Cincinnati, Ohio*; Thomas W. Ross, *Colorado Springs, Colo.*; Shinsuke Ando, Toshiyuki Takamiya, and Keiko Kawachi, *Keio University, Japan*; Charles Long, *Memphis State University*; Nancy Rushmore Hooper, *University of Nevada*; David W. Hiscoe, *University of North Carolina at Greensboro*; Robert R. Raymo, *New York University*; Nan Arbuckle, J. Lane Goodall, and Lynne Hunt Levy, *University of Oklahoma*; Piero Boitani, *Università de Perugia, Italy*; Rebecca Beal and Larry Langford, *Rice University*; Russell Peck and Thomas Hahn, *University of Rochester*; N. F. Blake, *University of Sheffield, England*; Tim D. P. Lally, *University of South Alabama*; Stanley R. Hauer, *University of Southern Mississippi*; Bernard S. Levy, Catherine Cavanaugh, and Virginia Darrow Oggins, *SUNY, Binghamton*; John H. Fisher, Michael Atkins, and Charles Rees, *University of Tennessee*; James I. Wimsatt, *University of Texas at Austin*; Tony Colaianne, *Virginia Polytechnic Institute*; Robert L. Kindrick, *Western Illinois University*; Thomas H. Seiler, *Western Michigan University*; Donald Chapin and Constance Heiatt, *University of Western Ontario*; Hildegard Schnuttgen, Cynthia Ann Dobrich, Jim Villani, Rosemarie Barbour, Dianne Snyder MacMurray, and Ted Pawcio, *Youngstown State University*. In addition to the regular bibliographic staff, the following made ad hoc contributions: Judson Boyce Allen, *Oxford*; David Anderson, *University of Pennsylvania*; Larry D. Benson, *Harvard University*; Ian Bishop, *University of Bristol*; Derek Brewer, *Emmanuel College, Cambridge*; John Bugge, *Emory University*; Robert E. Chisnell, *University of South Florida*; Paul Clogan, *North Texas*

State University; David G. Collins, *Westminster College, Missouri*; P. Dinzelbacher, *Universität Stuttgart*; George P. Economou, *Long Island University*; Joerg Fichte, *Universität Tübingen*; Richard Gill, *Pace University*; Renate Haas, *Universität Duisburg*; John M. Hill, *U.S. Naval Academy*; Linda Tarte Holley, *North Carolina State University*; Traugott Lawler, *Yale University*; Raymond McGowan, *Loyola University*; Glending Olson, *Cleveland State University*; Charles Owen, *University of Connecticut*; Derek Pearsall, *University of York*; Walter S. Phelan, *Rollins College*; Donald M. Rose, *University of Oklahoma*; Bruce A. Rosenberg, *Brown University*; Beryl Rowland, *York University, Toronto*; Norito Sato, *Japan*; Henrik Specht, *University of Copenhagen*; Eugene Vance, *Université de Montréal*; Alexander Wiess, *Radford University*; Nigel Wilkins, *Corpus Christi College, Cambridge*; Toshio Yamanaka, *Japan*.

The compiler acknowledges with gratitude grants for travel and clerical assistance from the Research Council and English Department of Youngstown State University. Special mention must be made of Hildegard Schnuttgen, Reference Librarian in Youngstown State University, for her tireless persistence in procuring hard-to-get items through interlibrary loan.

This bibliography continues those published since 1975 in previous volumes of *Studies in the Age of Chaucer*. Bibliographical information up to 1975 can be found in Eleanor P. Hammond, *Chaucer: A Bibliographical Manual* (1908; reprint, New York: Peter Smith, 1933); D. D. Griffith, *Bibliography of Chaucer, 1908–1953* (Seattle: University of Washington Press, 1955); W. R. Crawford, *Bibliography of Chaucer, 1954–63* (Seattle: University of Washington Press, 1967); Lorrayne Y. Baird, *Bibliography of Chaucer, 1964–73* (Boston: G. K. Hall, 1977); J. H. Fisher, ed., selected bibliography to 1974, full, 1975–79, in *The Complete Poetry and Prose of Geoffrey Chaucer* (New York: Holt, Rinehart and Winston, 1982); and John Leyerle and Anne Quick, eds., *Chaucer: A Selected Bibliography* (Toronto: University Press, 1981).

The annotations are based upon listings in the 1981 *MLA International Bibliography*, with additions. Additions and corrections should be sent to Lorrayne Y. Baird, Department of English, Youngstown State University, Youngstown, Ohio 44555. Authors' own annotations are invited (75 words for articles; 150 words for books). Preferably they should be sent on 5 × 8 cards and should comply with the form of *SAC*'s published entries. For a list of abbreviations for Chaucer's works, see p. 000 in this issue of *SAC*. We search major journals for articles and reviews published in any given year; authors are urged, however, to send citations to reviews and articles that might otherwise be overlooked.

218

Classifications

Periodical Abbreviations

ABR	*American Benedictine Review*
ACB, SAC	Annotated Chaucer Bibliography, *Studies in the Age of Chaucer*
Acta	*Acta* (Binghamton, N.Y.)
AN&Q	*American Notes and Queries*
BSUF	*Ball State University Forum*
CahiersE	*Cahiers Elisabéthains*
ChauR	*Chaucer Review*
CL	*Comparative Literature*
CritQ	*Critical Quarterly*
CRCL	*Canadian Review of Comparative Literature*
DAI	*Dissertation Abstracts International*
DQR	*Dutch Quarterly Review of Anglo-American Letters*
DVLG	*Deutsche Vierteljahrsschrift für Literaturwissenschaft und Geistesgeschichte*
EAS	*Essays in Arts and Sciences*
ECW	*Essays on Canadian Writing*
ELH	*Journal of English Literary History*
ELN	*English Language Notes*
ES	*English Studies*
ESC	*English Studies in Canada* (Toronto)
FForum	*Folklore Forum*
HSELL	*Hiroshima Studies in English Language and Literature*
JEGP	*Journal of English and Germanic Philology*
JMRS	*Journal of Medieval and Renaissance Studies*
KN	*Kwartalnik Neofilologiczny* (Warsaw)
M&H	*Medievalia et Humanistica*
MÆ	*Medium Ævum*
MichA	*Michigan Academician*
MissFR	*Mississippi Folklore Register*
MLQ	*Modern Language Quarterly*
MLR	*Modern Language Review*
MP	*Modern Philology*
MS	*Mediaeval Studies*

NLH	*New Literary History*
NM	*Neuphilologische Mitteilungen*
N&Q	*Notes and Queries*
OL	*Orbis Litterarum*
PAPA	*Publications of the Arkansas Philological Association*
PBSA	*Papers of the Bibliographical Society of America*
PLL	*Papers on Language and Literature*
PQ	*Philological Quarterly*
Rev	*Review*
RES	*Review of English Studies*
RUO	*Revue de l'Université d'Ottawa*
SAC	*Studies in the Age of Chaucer*
SAR	*South Atlantic Review*
SN	*Studia Neophilologica*
SoRA	*Southern Review: An Australian Journal of Literary Studies*
SP	*Studies in Philology*
SSF	*Studies in Short Fiction*
SSL	*Studies in Scottish Literature*
TLS	*London Times Literary Supplement*
YES	*Yearbook of English Studies*
YWES	*Year's Work in English Studies*
ZAA	*Zeitschrift für Anglistik und Amerikanistik*

Bibliographical Citations
and Annotations

Bibliographies and Reports

1. Bazire, Joyce, and David Mills, comps. "Middle English: Chaucer." *YWES* 59(1978):105–21. A bibliographical essay surveying Chaucer criticism for the previous year.

2. Fisher, John H., et al. "An Annotated Chaucer Bibliography, 1979." *SAC* 3(1981):189–259.

3. Kirby, Thomas A. "Chaucer Research, 1980: Report No. 41." *ChauR* 15(1981):356–79. A listing of current research, completed research, desiderata, and publications.

4. Leyerle, John, and Anne Quick, eds. *Chaucer: A Selected Bibliography*. Toronto Medieval Bibliographies. Toronto: University of Toronto Press, 1981. 224 pp.

See also no. 264.

Life

5. Clogan, Paul M. "Literary Criticism in William Godwin's *Life of Chaucer*." *M&H*, n.s. 6(1975):189–98. Godwin's literary criticism of Chaucer's poetry contributed to the Romantic conception of Chaucer the man. His *Life* gives insight into the idea of the Middle Ages in early-nineteenth-century England.

6. Leland, Virginia E., with John L. Leland. "'According to the Law of the Marsh and of Our Realm of England': Chaucer as Commissioner of Dikes and Ditches, 1390." *MichA* 14(1981):71–79. Chaucer's work as commissioner in the marshes between Greenwich and Woolwich may have suggested images for *RvT*. Fellow commissioners may have influenced *GP* portraits.

See also nos. 53, 95.

223

Facsimiles and Editions

7. *MS Bodley 638*. Introduction by Pamela Robinson. The Variorum Chaucer Facsimile Series. Norman, Okla.: Pilgrim Books, 1981; Suffolk: Boydell Brewer, 1982. xliv, 480 pp. Written by various hands in the 15th century, Bodley 638, the latest of the so-called Oxford Group, contains *HF* and *BD*, found in only two other manuscripts, as well as *Anel*, *LGW*, *PF*, *Pity*, *ABC*, *For*, and *Compl d'Am*. Includes a bibliography.

8. *Cambridge Library MS GG.4.27*. Introduction by Malcolm Parkes and Richard Beadle. The Variorum Chaucer Facsimile Series. Norman, Okla.: Pilgrim Books; Suffolk: Boydell-Brewer, 1980–. 3 vols. 1034 pp. Color plates. Among the earliest of the Chaucer manuscripts, the Cambridge Library MS GG.4.27, once lavishly illuminated but now mutilated, is nevertheless the most nearly complete and one of the most reliable of Chaucer manuscripts. Vol. 1 contains *The Minor Poems*, *TC*, and a large part of *CT*; vol. 2, the remainder of *CT*; and vol. 3, *LGW*, *PF*, Lydgate's *Temple of Glass*, color plates, and studies by Parkes and Beadle on the manuscript and illuminations.

9. *Corpus Christi College Cambridge MS 61*. Introduction by M. B. Parkes and Elizabeth Salter. Cambridge: D. S. Brewer, 1978. 368 pp. Written in the early fifteenth century, the Corpus Christi *Troilus*, one of sixteen manuscripts of the poem, is probably the earliest extant text of *TC*. Parkes gives a paleographical description of the manuscript; Salter, an iconographical study of the famous full-color illustration contained in the manuscript. Includes bibliographical references.

10. *Bodleian Library MS Fairfax 16*. Introduction by John Norton-Smith. London: Scolar Press, 1979. 688 pp. 2 plates. The fifteenth-century MS Fairfax 16, considered the finest of the Oxford Group of Chaucer manuscripts, contains *BD*, *HF*, *Anel*, *Mars*, and *PF*. Regarding the frontispiece, a mythological illumination for Mars, Norton-Smith advances a new theory of artistic composition. See also no. 301.

11. *The Canterbury Tales: A Facsimile and Transcription of the Hengwrt Manuscript, with Variants from the Ellesmere Manuscript*. Introduction by Donald C. Baker, A. I. Doyle, and M. B. Parkes. The Variorum Edition of the Works of Geoffrey Chaucer, vol. 1, ed. Paul G. Ruggiers and Donald C. Baker. Norman, Okla.: University of Oklahoma Press, 1979. liii, 1024 pp. Designed as the basic text of *CT* for the *Variorum Chaucer*, the Hengwrt, which may have been produced in Chaucer's lifetime, is one of the earliest and most reliable of the manuscripts of *CT*. Transcriptions of the Hengwrt text, Ellesmere variants included, face each page of the Hengwrt facsimile. Introductions provide historical, biographical, literary, and textual information. See also no. 308.

12. *MS Tanner 346: A Facsimile, Bodleian Library Oxford University*. Intro-

duction by Pamela Robinson. The Variorum Chaucer Facsimile Series. Norman, Okla.: Pilgrim Books; Suffolk: Boydell-Brewer, 1980. 290 pp. Written by various hands in the fifteenth century, the Bodleian MS Tanner 346, the earliest of the Oxford Group, is indispensable in establishing the canon of the minor poems, especially *Anel*, *Mars*, *Ven*, *Pity*. In addition, it contains *BD*, *PF*, and *LGW*, as well as poems by Lydgate and Hoccleve. Includes bibliography. See also no. 295.

13. Thynne, William, ed. *Geoffrey Chaucer: The Workes, 1532* (facsimile). Introduction by D. S. Brewer. London: Scolar Press, 1969. 1040 pp. Thynne's edition was the first substantial effort at a complete edition of the *Works*. Facsimile is accompanied by appendices containing material from the later editions of 1542, 1561, 1598, and 1602.

Editions

14. Blake, N. F., ed. *Geoffrey Chaucer: The Canterbury Tales, Edited from the Hengwrt Manuscript*. London: Arnold, 1980. vi, 707 pp. Following Manly and Rickert, Blake sees Hg as the most reliable early manuscript, but omits links for E–F, which Blake believes were added by someone other than Chaucer—i.e., those links joining *SqT* to *MerT* and *MerT* to *FranT*. Blake contends that the Ellesmere order is a later attempt to modify the Hg order on more logical principles. *CYT* is omitted because Blake feels that it is a non-Chaucerian addition. See also no. 267.

15. Morgan, Gerald, ed. *Geoffrey Chaucer: The Franklin's Tale from The Canterbury Tales*. London Medieval and Renaissance Series. London: Holmes & Meier, 1981. See also no. 300.

16. Pace, George B., and Alfred Davis, eds. *Geoffrey Chaucer: The Minor Poems: Part One. The Variorum Edition of the Works of Geoffrey Chaucer*, vol. 5. Ed. Paul G. Ruggiers and Donald C. Baker. Norman: University of Oklahoma Press, 1982. xlviii, 223 pp. *Part One* contains five moral, or "Boethian," poems, four humorous poems addressed to individuals, four love lyrics, and one gnomic poem: *Truth*, *Gent*, *Sted*, *Form Age*, *For*; *Purse*, *Adam*, *Buk*, *Scog*; *Ros*, *MercB*, *Wom Nob*, *Wom Unc*; and *Prov*. Texts and collations are by Pace; critical introductions and notes, by David. Introductions for each poem survey scholarship and identify important lines of inquiry; prefatory essays deal with dates, allusions, versification, sources, and relevance to Chaucer's life and other works. Includes index and bibliography.

See also nos. 13, 26, 232, 262, 274, 279.

Manuscript and Textual Studies

17. Benson, C. David, and David Rollman. "Wynkyn de Worde and the Ending of Chaucer's 'Troilus and Criseyde.'" *MP* 78(1981):275–77. The three anonymous stanzas that Wynkyn printed at the end of his 1517 edition of the poem suggest that neither the sympathy for Criseyde felt by moderns nor the poet's view of *TC* as a religious work would have been found in an early reader. Wynkyn gives the antifeminist moral that Chaucer's narrator avoided.

18. Blake, N. F. "Chaucer's Text and the Web of Words." In *New Perspectives* (ACB, *SAC* 5[1983], no. 103), pp. 223–40. Studies based uncritically upon the Robinson text may have produced questionable readings in *CT: KnT*, *ParsT* and *Prol*, *ClT*, *ShT*, *GP*, *RvT*, *MilT*, *NPT*. The Hengwrt MS, currently being used for the *Variorum Chaucer* and by Blake, is the earliest manuscript and the best text.

19. ———. "On Editing the *Canterbury Tales*." In *Medieval Studies for J. A. W. Bennett*. (ACB, *SAC* 5[1983], no. 74), pp. 101–19. Most if not all early scribes used Hg, which avoided editorial tampering—introduction of new tales and links, revision of order of tales, "corrections" of lines, words, spellings. "The best an editor can do is follow Hg closely."

20. ———. "The Textual Tradition of *The Book of the Duchess*." *ES* 62(1981):237–48. Nothing in the textual tradition of the three MSS of *BD* supports a thesis of differing exemplars. The lines of *BD* that are found in Thynne's edition but not in the MSS—lines 31–96, 288, 480, 886—should be considered spurious until convincingly authenticated.

21. Brewer, Derek. "Observations on the Text of Troilus." In *Medieval Studies for J. A. W. Bennett*. (ACB, *SAC* 5[1983], no. 74), pp. 121–38. Emends three Corpus readings (1.502, 1.458, 1.89) and notes that evidence does not support the theory of extensive authorial revisions.

22. Caie, Graham D. "The Significance of the Glosses in the Earliest Manuscripts of *The Canterbury Tales*." In *Papers from the First Nordic Conference for English Studies, Oslo, 17–19 September, 1980*, ed. Stig Johansson and Bjørn Tysdahl. Oslo: University of Oslo, Institute of English Studies, 1981, pp. 25–34. *CT* glosses often act as commentary and provide source of quotation; they are not mere insertions by scribes or mere source references.

23. Cowen, Janet M. "Eighteenth-Century Ownership of Two Chaucer Manuscripts." *N&Q* 28(1981):392–93. British Library MS Additional 12524 was owned successively by Samul Smith, Ralph Thoresby, and Horace Walpole. British Library MS Additional 9832, owned by Morell Thurston and then by Joseph Haselwood, was used by Urry for his edition. Both contain lines from *LGW*.

24. Driver, Martha Wescott. "The Early Editions of Chaucer's *Troilus*." *DAI* 41(1981):4391A. Previous investigators of the sixteen extant *TC* MSS assumed three "parent" forms, presumed to represent Chaucer's rescensions. Two MSS

before 1400 may be the work of Chaucer's scribe.

25. Heyworth, P. L. "The Punctuation of Middle English Texts." In *Medieval Studies for J. A. W. Bennett* (ACB, *SAC* 5[1983], no. 74), pp. 140–57. The punctuation of medieval texts, including Chaucer's, imperfectly shows relationships between parts of the sentence. Standardized punctuation adopted in early Chaucer reprints often confuses meaning.

26. Owings, Frank N., Jr. "Keats, Lamb, and a Black-Letter Chaucer." *PBSA* 75(1981):147–55. *The Works*, edited by Speght (1598), sold in 1848 as part of Charles Lamb's library may be the same volume to which Keats refers in his letter of May 3[!], 1818. The copy at Lily Library of the University of Indiana is likely the one owned by Keats and Lamb.

27. Petti, Anthony G. *English Literary Hands from Chaucer to Dryden*. London: Edward Arnold, 1977. Provides samples of handwriting, sections on alphabets, abbreviations, scripts.

See also nos. 7–11, 18, 30, 237, 258, 304.

Sources, Analogues, and Literary Relations

28. Havely, N. R., ed. *Boccaccio — Sources of "Troilus" and the Knight's and Franklin's Tales*. Chaucer Studies, vol. 5. Cambridge: D. S. Brewer; Totowa, N.J.: Rowman and Littlefield, 1980. 225 pp. An edition and translation of *Filostrato*, *Teseida* (excerpts), and *Filocolo* 4.31–34 (excerpts). Includes introduction, bibliography, notes, index of personal names, and three appendices: *The Fortunes of Troilus*; Benoit de Sainte-Maure, *Roman de Troie* (excerpts); and Guido de Columnis, *Historia Destructionis Troiae* (excerpts). See also no. 286.

29. Windeatt, Barry A. *Chaucer's Dream Poetry: Sources and Analogues*. Chaucer Studies, vol. 7. Cambridge: D. S. Brewer; Totowa, N.J.: Rowman and Littlefield, 1982. xviii, 168 pp. The chief French sources and analogues of Chaucer's four dream poems, presented here in translation, are brought together for the first time. Included are Machaut's *Jugement dou Roy de Behaingne*, Froissart's *Paradys d'amours*, Jean de Condé's *Messe des oisiaus*, and the *Fablel dou dieu d'amors*. All or part of fourteen other French poems appear, along with Cicero's *Dream of Scipio* and bits of Boccaccio's *Teseida* and the *Complaint of Nature* of Alanus de Insulis. Footnotes and an "Index of Parallels" document parallel passages to the *BD*.

See also nos. 65, 85, 95, 112, 113, 120, 134, 135, 140, 152, 153, 163, 168, 169, 171, 176, 182, 189, 192, 195, 196, 200, 202, 209, 215, 219, 220, 222, 241, 252–57, 277, 294.

Chaucer's Influence and Later Allusion

30. Bennett, J. A. W. "Those Scotch Copies of Chaucer." *RES* 32(1981): 294–96. *The Meroure of Wisdom* (1490), by John of Ireland, contains a previously overlooked allusion to *TC* and *ParsT*. This work is followed in the manuscript by *Oracio Galfridi Chaucer*, written by Hoccleve but possibly attributed to Chaucer because of similarities to *ABC* and *MLT*.

31. Clogan, Paul M. "Chaucer and Leigh Hunt." *M&H*, n.s. 9(1979):163–74. Hunt's literary criticism of Chaucer contributed to the Romantic conception of Chaucer the poet and offers insight into the history of medievalism in the nineteenth century.

32. Doederlin, Sue Warrick. "*Ut Pictura Poesis*: Dryden's *Aeneïs* and *Palamon and Arcite*." *CL* 33(1981):156–66. In his translation of *KnT*, Dryden imposed a number of pictorial effects — colors, emblems, icons, static scenes, and landscapes — to transform Chaucer into a seventeenth-century gentleman.

See also nos. 5, 26, 77, 207.

Rhetoric, Style, and Versification

33. Bloomfield, Morton W. "Personification-Metaphors." *ChauR* 14(1980): 287–97. This stylistic device occurs when a noun is given personification by the poet's use of a verb (or occasionally a verb phrase, adjective, or adverb). Chaucer uses few of them: the lyrics have more than do the longer narratives.

34. Diekstra, Frans. "The Language of Equivocation: Some Chaucerian Techniques." *DQR* 11(1981):267–77. Chaucer developed a poetic idiom of ubiquitous equivocal effects and prevarication both in the comments of his persona and in the voices of his speakers. Poems touched on include *TC*, *PardT*, *NPT*, *MerT*, and *LGW*.

35. Easthope, Antony. "Problematizing the Pentameter." *NLH* 12(1981): 475–92. "Chaucer's ME pentameter (if that is what it was) had become lost by the beginning of the 16th century and had to be reinvented."

36. Roscow, Gregory. *Syntax and Style in Chaucer's Poetry*. Chaucer Studies, vol. 6. Cambridge: D. S. Brewer, 1981. x, 158 pp. Concentrates on "colloquialism" in Chaucer's syntax in the context of popular romance and poetry, including some examples from Old English, finding that "discontinuous patterns of word-order" and "negative forms of emphatic expression" contribute to vigorous poetic syntax. Includes chapters on word order, idiomatic usage, pleonasm, ellipsis, relative clauses, and coordination and parataxis. Includes bibliography, general index, and an index of Chaucer quotations. No footnotes.

37. Rowland, Beryl. "Earle Birney and Chaucer." *ECW* 21(1981):73–84. Reviews the work of Earle Birney (1930s, 1940s) on Chaucerian irony: dramatic, verbal, structural.

See also nos. 65, 131, 132.

Language and Word Studies

38. Barney, Stephen A. "Suddenness and Process in Chaucer." *ChauR* 16(1981):18–37. The words *sodeyn(ly)* and *proces* are keys to Chaucer's narrative skill. In both his serious and his comical narratives there are sudden changes in events, sudden shifts in emotions. He usually makes the sudden seem humorous, ridiculous, or contemptible.

39. Donaldson, E. Talbot. "Gallic Flies in Chaucer's English Word Web." In *New Perspectives* (ACB, *SAC* 5[1983], no. 103), pp. 193–202. Chaucer at times uses French constructions in his English, as is shown by examples in *RvT*, *KnT*, *TC*, *PardT*, and *GP* (portrait of the Prioress).

40. Holley, Linda Tarte. "The Function of Language in Three Canterbury Churchmen." *Parergon* 28(1980):36–44. The abuse of language, which perverts man's reason and his link to the divine, is seen in the Pardoner, the Friar's summoner and the Summoner's friar.

41. Kerling, Johan. *Chaucer in Early English Dictionaries: The Old-World Tradition in English Lexicography Down to 1721 and Speght's Chaucer Glossaries.* Germanic and Anglistic Studies of the University of Leiden, vol. 18. Netherlands: Leiden University Press; Boston: Kluwer, 1980. 360 pp. A study of Middle English, specifically Chaucer's English; lexicography; and obsolete words. Includes bibliography and indexes, as well as an appendix, "Chaucer, *The Plowman's Tale*, and Henry VIII."

42. Phelan, Walter S. "From Morpheme to Motif in Chaucer's *Canterbury Tales*." In *Proceedings of the International Conference on Literary and Linguistic Computing, Israel*. Ed. Zvi Malachi. Tel Aviv: Katz Research Institute, 1980, pp. 291–316. The lexical morphemes of Chaucer's poetic tales have been marked in the data base as narrative "verbs" or "adjectives" (Todorov: dynamic v. static predicate formulas). The character and percentage of formula *per lexical unit* provide a more reliable measure of formulaic expression than the procedures of Duggan or Wittig.

43. Sasagawa, Hisaaki. "The Historical Present and Perfect in Chaucer's *Knight's Tale*." *Journal of the General Education Department, Niigata University* 12(1981):179–91. In Japanese. The historical present and perfect tenses in *KnT* could be said to function mainly to express vividness, which is closely related to the nature of orally delivered poetry.

44. Shimogasa, Tokuji. "Middle English Adverbs of Affirming." *HSELL* 25(1980):13–28. Several Middle English adverbs of affirmation ("ywis," "wytterly," "sikerly," and "verayment") found in many medieval romances and in many of Chaucer's works function primarily as words of elaboration.

See also nos. 55, 65, 95, 146, 149, 150, 154, 161, 203, 217, 239, 276.

Background and General Criticism

45. Allen, Judson Boyce. *The Ethical Poetic of the Later Middle Ages: A Decorum of Convenient Distinction*. Toronto: University of Toronto Press, 1982. Medieval literary commentators uniformly assigned "literary works" to the category of ethics: poetry served as a kind of "enacted ethics" for the medieval audience. The commentators define and describe this material in terms of the *forma tractandi* (usually a "normative array" of socially accepted ethical principles) and the *forma tractatus* (the ways in which a text might be divided). *CT* have as their central ordering principle a normative array of tales that mainly deal with the theme of marriage. Chaucer's interest in revising *LGW* was related to his concern with the "philosophy of poetic language." It is a "poem about making poems." *MilT* is briefly described in terms of *consideratio* in comedy — the laughter acts as an assent to the normative. In *PardT*, Chaucer fully "exploits the power of the folktale atmosphere."

46. Allinson, Jane Frank. "The Fabliau in Medieval England." *DAI* 42(1981): 1140A. The nine surviving Anglo-Norman fabliaux (three translated from manuscripts are appended) differ from their seven English counterparts (five in *CT*) in depicting higher social ranks, incorporating less violence, and introducing less antifeminism. From 1350 to 1400 French fabliaux influenced both Anglo-Norman and English traditions.

47. Ames, Ruth. "Prototype and Parody in Chaucerian Exegesis." *Acta* 4(1977):87–105. Chaucer accepts such clear-cut moral models as Judith, but satirizes Solomon and Noah, and he is committed to the moral teaching of the Old Testament but amused by popular vulgarization and clerical allegorization. His basic piety is firm.

48. Ando, Shinsuke. "The Ideal of Feminine Beauty: A Comparative Note." *Poetica* 12(Tokyo, 1981):3–9 (in English). A comparison of the medieval descriptions of idealized feminine beauty with depictions of women in medieval and modern Japanese literature points up characteristic Japanese aesthetics and philosophy of beauty.

49. Benson, Robert G. *Medieval Body Language: A Study of Use of Gesture in*

Chaucer's Poetry. Anglistica, vol. 21. Copenhagen: Rosenkilde and Bagger, 1980. 170 pp. Treats Chaucer's use of and experimentation with conventional gesture as modified by generic considerations in *CT, TC, PF, HF, Anel, LGW, BD, Rom,* and minor poems. Includes an appendix of relevant passages. See also no. 266.

50. Blamires, Alcuin. "Chaucer's Revaluation of Chivalric Honor." *Mediaevalia* 5(1979):245–69. Although the prevailing code of honor was belligerent, Chaucer's dissatisfaction with this aggressive style is subtly indicated in *Truth, Mars, Th,* and *KnT* by presentation of "heroic" actions and martial "worshippe" as slightly ridiculous. In *Mel,* Prudence demonstrates that true "honour" lies in man's control over himself.

51. Bloomfield, Morton W. "Contemporary Literary Theory and Chaucer." In *New Perspectives* (ACB, *SAC* 5[1983], no. 103), pp. 23–36. We need an "over-all metaphysics" such as the fourteenth-century "Aristotelian ontology and psychology," or such modern systems as "phenomenology, Marxism, Heideggerian ontology, positivism, . . . existentialism, and Chomskyean rationalism" as approaches to literature of the past, including Chaucer. See Ridley's response, no. 99, and no. 87.

52. Boitani, Piero. *La Narrativa del Medioeve Inglese.* Biblioteca di Studi Inglesi, vol. 36. Bari: Adriatica Editrice, 1980. Trans. Joan Krakover Hall as *English Medieval Narrative in the 13th and 14th Centuries.* Cambridge: Cambridge University Press, 1982. The earliest Middle English narratives, e.g., exempla in sermons, served practical purposes. More deliberately artistic ends can be seen in later collections of legends, exempla, and comic tales; Chaucer and Gower are even more aesthetically sophisticated. Most non-Chaucerian Middle English narratives were intended for recitation (here critical concepts of Auerbach, Bakhtin, Contini, Curtius, Frye, Genette, and the Russian formalists are applied to religious tradition, romance, dream poems, etc.), but Chaucer was the first English author to write consciously for a reading public. *BD, HF, PF, TC, LGW,* and *CT* draw innovatively upon written tradition.

53. Brewer, Derek. *Chaucer and His World.* London: Eyre Methuen, 1978. 224 pp. Treats Chaucer's life and times, beginning with an introductory essay — "an impressionistic description of Chaucer's England" — followed by thirteen chapters on Chaucer's life and works, illuminated at times by Brewer's own experience. Source references are at a minimum. See also no. 269.

54. ———. *Symbolic Stories: Traditional Narratives of the Family Drama in English Literature.* Cambridge: D. S. Brewer; Totowa, N.J.: Rowman and Littlefield, 1980. 190 pp. Underlying many traditional stories is the basic structure of the individual emerging into adulthood and establishing his or her identity by destroying parent-images and finding a beloved equal. A chapter on Chaucer establishes his equivocal and somewhat negative attitude toward this theme. See also no. 271.

55. Burnley, J. D. *Chaucer's Language and the Philosophers' Tradition*. Chaucer Studies, vol. 2. Cambridge: D. S. Brewer; Totowa, N.J.: Rowman and Littlefield, 1979. 196 pp. The medieval tyrant *topos*, with its lexicon and its various transformations, provides the means of studying Chaucer's moral vocabulary. The tyrant figure embodies passion, cruelty, injustice, and heartlessness. Its antitype is first that of the rationally guided moral philosopher (Seneca)—who exercises prudence and temperance. In this tradition Chaucer shows a rationalistic distaste for love (passion), with his moral position becoming most clear in *Mel* and *ParsT*. Criseyde and the Wife of Bath are tyrantlike in their behavior; Theseus and Griselda, along with Cecilia and Prudence, are antitypes. See also no. 273.

56. Burrow, J. A. "The Poet as Petitioner." *SAC* 3(1981):61–75. Although Chaucer frequently uses petitionary devices, he seldom seems comfortable in the humble role (cf. *For*, *Purse*, *Scog*). Usually he distorts the pattern in fictive and outrageous fashion (*HF*, *LGW*) to make jest of humility.

57. Chamberlain, David. "Musical Signs and Symbols in Chaucer: Convention and Originality." In *Signs and Symbols* (ACB, *SAC* 5[1983], no. 73). Chaucer uses both conventional and original musical signs, some *in bono*, some *in malo*. His originality manifests itself in five main areas: "single signs, elaborate combinations, vivid contrasts, recurring symbolism, and overall structure," as noted in *CT*, *PF*, *BD*, *HF*, *TC*, *Boece*, *LGW*, *Mars*.

58. Chisnell, Robert E. "Chaucer's Neglected Prose." In *Literary and Historical Perspectives of the Middle Ages*. Ed. Patricia W. Cummins, Patrick W. Conner, and Charles W. Connell. Morgantown: West Virginia University Press, 1982. pp. 156–73. Neglected through modern predilections that ignore the intellectual milieu of the fourteenth century, Chaucer's prose works deserve more enlightened attention.

59. Clogan, Paul M. "Literary Genres in a Medieval Textbook." *M&H*, n.s. 11(1982):199–209. The pedagogic techniques in *Liber Catonianus*, a standard textbook used by Chaucer, show the combination of grammar and morality, the study of the *artes* as a study of ethics, and the integration of the ethica in the *Septennium* of the liberal arts in the thirteenth and fourteenth centuries.

60. Cooper, Helen. "The Girl with Two Lovers: Four Canterbury Tales." *Medieval Studies for J. A. W. Bennett* (ACB, *SAC* 5[1983], no. 74), pp. 65–80. *KnT*, *MilT*, *MerT*, and *FranT* share the same plot—the story of the girl with two lovers—and show striking interrelations and variations of episodes, conventions, images, and ideas.

61. Diekstra, F. "Chaucer's Way with His Sources: Accident into Substance and Substance into Accident." *ES* 62(1981):215–36. In most of his poems Chaucer exploits the traditional material to create a double view, one inherent in the material and the other produced by his handling of them. He inherited this

technique from Jean de Meun; in *BD* and the *Roman*, for example, the Reason figures likewise fail ironically to communicate their wisdom. *NPT* and *PardT* provide other prominent examples of the double view.

62. Fichte, Joerg O. *Chaucer's "Art Poetical": A Study of Chaucerian Poetics.* Studies and Texts in English, vol 1. Tübingen: Narr, 1980. A pattern of Chaucerian poetics emerges through four themes—courtly love, morality, order, and poetry—found in his early poetry (*BD*, *HF*, and *KnT*). Starting as a poet of courtly love, Chaucer overcame limitations of this theme by analyzing its philosophical, moral, and artistic implications; assessing ethical values; searching for a principle of order; and determining the function of poetry. His quest leads from a limited awareness of the power of poetry to the recognition that the poetic act creates order in a confused world—the essence of Chaucerian poetics as seen in *BD*, *PF*, *HF*, and *KnT*. See also no. 278.

63. Finlayson, John. "Definitions of Middle English Romance: Part I." *ChauR* 15(1980):44–62. Confused in definition, "romance" designates both a value system and a method of treatment. The presence of the marvelous, courtly love, and chivalric adventure is not enough to form a definition. A parody like *Th* helps, since it indicates what is expected and can therefore be successfully ridiculed.

64. ———. "Definitions of Middle English Romance: Part II." *ChauR* 15(1980):168–81. Romances are distinguished not by the presence of certain features—the erotic, the fabulous, etc.—but by attitudes toward those elements. *WBT* is "deliberately" not a romance.

65. Fisher, John H. "Chaucer and the French Influence." In *New Perspectives* (ACB, *SAC* 5[1983], no. 103), pp. 177–91. In his early poetry Chaucer tried to use a purely native English vocabulary; his later works show a more comfortable use of the cultural vocabulary with which he and his bilingual audience were familiar.

66. Fleming, John V. "Chaucer and the Visual Arts of His Time." In *New Perspectives* (ACB, *SAC* 5[1983], no. 103), pp. 121–36. Further enquiry can illuminate Chaucer's references and response to the visual arts, the artistic materials actually available to him, the applicability of artistic principles to his literary style, and the extent to and manner in which he appropriates the techniques and iconography of contemporary visual arts. Applications to *RvT*, *GP* portrait of the Summoner, and *FrT*.

67. Friedman, John Block. "Another Look at Chaucer and the Physiognomists." *SP* 78(1981):138–52. As contrasted to W. C. Curry's "humoral physiognomy," another type, "affective physiognomy," involving such details as movement of eyes or eyebrows and color of cheeks, is restricted in use to aristocratic or courtly characters, not those of the fabliau world.

68. Fries, Maureen. "The 'Other' Voice: Woman's Song, Its Satire and Its Transcendence in Late Medieval British Literature." In *Vox Feminae: Studies in*

Medieval Woman's Songs. Ed. John F. Plummer. Studies in Medieval Culture, vol. 15. Kalamazoo: Medieval Institute, Western Michigan University, 1981, pp. 155–78. The vernacular "woman's song" focuses on the beloved (not the speaker's feelings) passively, powerless to control the beloved—features that serve as a context to analyze the "comic sex- and/or class-role reversal" in *RvT*, *MerT*, and Antigone's Song and Criseyde's "aube" in *TC*.

69. Gardner, John. "Signs, Symbols, and Cancellations." In *Signs and Symbols* (ACB, *SAC* 5[1983], no. 73), pp. 195–207. While "Robertsonianism" has produced scholastically defensible but totally lunatic readings, such as *MilT* as a "Christian meditation," it has also brilliantly illuminated *BD*. Its chief failure is tone deafness toward *WBT*, *HF*, etc. *PF*, *LGW*, *TC*, *Anel*, *MkT*, *MilT* have been shown much richer than we knew. *CYT* cancels *SNT*.

70. Green, Richard Firth. *Poets and Princepleasers: Literature and the English Court in the Late Middle Ages*. Toronto: University of Toronto Press, 1980. Treats the modus vivendi of medieval poet in the context of the king's intimate circle, the literate court, the court of love, the writer as adviser or court apologist. See also no. 284.

71. Haas, Renate. *Die mittelenglische Totenklage: Realitätsbezug, abendländische Tradition und individuelle Gestaltung*. Regensburger Arbeiten zur Anglistik und Amerikanistik, vol. 16. Frankfurt: Lang, 1980. The lament for the dead is a literary form that critics have found difficult to appreciate, even in Chaucer. The book sketches the sociocultural background in medieval England in connection with older traditions, native, biblical, Greco-Roman, medieval Latin, and French, thus providing a context for Chaucer's laments for the dead (*Pity*, *BD*, *LGW*, *PhyT*, *ManT*, *NPT*) and his influence in this genre on Skelton, Spenser, and Dryden. See also no. 285.

72. Hendrickson, Rhoda Miller Martin. "Chaucer's Proverbs: Of Medicyne and of Compleynte." *DAI* 42(1981):1140–41A. Proverbs appear conventionally in most of Chaucer's early works, usually to lament changes in fortune. In the short poems *For*, *Buk*, and *Scog*, however, Chaucer's proverbs become personal. In *TC* and *CT* proverbs spoken by characters (especially Melibee and Prudence) signal need for action to impose order and acquire wisdom.

73. Hermann, John P., and John J. Burke, Jr., eds. *Signs and Symbols in Chaucer's Poetry*. University: University of Alabama Press, 1981. Essays by various hands. See nos. 57, 69, 97, 101, 187, 194, 216, 224, 245.

74. Heyworth, P. L., ed. *Medieval Studies for J. A. W. Bennett*. Oxford: Clarendon Press, 1981. The festschrift includes fifteen essays on medieval topics: Langland, medieval music, Gower, poetry and art, drama, punctuation, the "arbor caritatis," Thomas More, Sir John Fastolf, and articles on Chaucer and related matters. See nos. 19, 21, 25, 147, 205, 237.

75. Hussey, S. S. *Chaucer: An Introduction*. 2d ed. London and New York: Methuen, 1981. 245 pp. Essentially a reprint of the first edition with additional notes and an expanded bibliography.

76. Kane, George. "Langland and Chaucer: An Obligatory Conjunction." In *New Perspectives* (ACB, *SAC* 5[1983], no. 103), pp. 5–19. Comparisons of Chaucer and Langland may rescue *CT* from the Bradleian fallacy (i.e., treatment of Chaucer's literary characters as historically actual).

77. ———. "Outstanding Problems of Middle English Scholarship." *ACTA* 4(1977):1–17. Chaucer scholarship provides an example of the need for the correction and reassessment of texts, authorship, chronology, and influences on Middle English literature.

78. Kelly, Henry Ansgar. "Chaucer's Arts and Our Arts." In *New Perspectives* (ACB, *SAC* 5[1983], no. 103), pp. 107–20. In the Middle Ages the term "art" meant the liberal arts or almost any serious endeavor (other than the visual arts), also involving Gregory the Great's dictum that "the art of arts is the rule of souls." Chaucer was less influenced by the visual arts than by the arts in the wider sense.

79. Lakshmi, Vijay. "The Antiquarian as Literary Analyst: Virginia Woolf on Chaucer." *Osmania Journal of English Studies* 17(1981):19–25. In her essay "The Pastons and Chaucer," Woolf framed an appreciation of Chaucer between the family history of Sir John Paston and his estate, thus creating a new critical approach, informal, inviting, unpretentious.

80. Lanoue, David G. "Musical Imagery in the Poetry of Juan Ruíz, Guillaume de Machaut, and Chaucer: A Comparative Study." *DAI* 42(1981):1141–42A. Medieval musical allusions provide an internationally shared set of signs for allegorical poetry and help unify medieval literature stylistically. Ruíz ironically conflates the fleshly and heavenly aspects of music, and Machaut employs harmony to signify divine order, as does Chaucer in *BD*; in *GP*, *SumT*, and *PardT*, however, Chaucer subverts divine harmony.

81. Leffingwell, William Clare, Jr. "Some Versions of Chaucerian Irony." *DAI* 41(1981):3592A. Chaucerian irony works variously: in *PardT* to show unadmitted brotherhood in sin; in *MLT* to reveal the narrator's limitations; in *KnT* to undercut chivalry; in *TC* to show the self-subversion of courtly love; in *PF* to ridicule the narrator's neglect of the lessons of *Somnium Scipionis* and *De planctu naturae*.

82. Leonard, Frances McNeely. *Laughter in the Courts of Love: Comedy in Allegory from Chaucer to Spenser*. Norman, Okla.: Pilgrim Books, 1981. x, 192 pp. So rarely does medieval poetry combine comedy and allegory that superficially the two modes seem irreconcilable: for some, humor undermines allegory's decorum of high seriousness; for others, it provides (at best) only badly needed comic relief. But the tradition of allegorical love poetry in English from Chaucer to Spenser offers instructive examples in which comic action is integral to purported

allegorical significance. Comedy quickens and animates abstract figurative meaning, whether through satire, irony, or simple joyous delight. Perceptually, it lends
its own peculiar double focus (on what is, on what should be) to the double focus of
allegory (on *figura* and referent).

83. Lindahl, Carl. "Chaucer the Storyteller: Folkloric Patterns in the *Canterbury Tales*." *DAI* 41(1981):5204A. Records of medieval pilgrimages and parish
guilds indicate that groups like that of *CT* actually gathered; thus the frame may
have been modeled on the contemporary scene rather than a literary source. The
pilgrim churls' mutual insults follow a pattern of observing ritual taboos.

84. Martin, Wallace, and Nick Conrad. "Formal Analysis of Traditional Fic-
tions." *PLL* 17(1981):3–22. The Levi-Strauss formula for the structure of myth can
be applied to analogues of *ShT* to illuminate disputed interpretations. In a list of
similar actions in columns, not chronological, the *ShT* shows eight implications of
the Levi-Strauss formula.

85. McCall, John P. *Chaucer Among the Gods: The Poetics of Classical Myth*.
University Park: Pennsylvania State University Press, 1979. 200 pp. Discusses the
ways in which Chaucer uses classical materials in comedy, tragedy, and allegory; in
theme, action, and character, to make available the world of Virgil, Ovid, and
Lucan—sometimes through Dante, Graunson, Boccaccio, and Froissart. See also
no. 298.

86. McGann, Jerome J. "The Text, The Poem, and the Problem of Historical
Method." *NLH* 12(1981):269–88. William Blake avoided the normal publisher-
author relationship. "To know the publishing options taken (and refused) by
Chaucer. . .enables the critic to explain the often less visible, but more fundamental, social engagements which meet in and generate the work in question."

87. Minnis, Alastaire J. "Chaucer and Comparative Literary Theory." In *New
Perspectives* (ACB, *SAC* 5[1983], no. 103), pp. 53–69. In answer to Bloomfield
(no. 51 above), Minnis distinguishes between the "alterity" and the "modernity" of
medieval literature, arguing that medieval theories of literature should be applied
to Chaucer.

88. ———. "The Influence of Academic Prologues on the Prologues and
Literary Attitudes of Late-Medieval English Writers." *MS* 43(1981):342–83. The
academic prologue, which introduced commentaries on *auctores*, developed an
Aristotelian form in the thirteenth century. Chaucer did not employ any of the
traditional prologue paradigms, but many of his literary attitudes seem to have
been influenced by the academic literary prologue, as when he discusses the
mateere, *manere*, and *entente* of a literary work, especially in *MkT*, *Mel*, *NPT*,
and *TC*.

89. Muscatine, Charles. "'What Amounteth Al This Wit?'—Chaucer and
Scholarship." *SAC* 3(1981):3–11 (Presidential address to the New Chaucer Soci-

ety). Chaucerians must engage undergraduate minds, going beyond source studies, textual studies, and narrow explications into cultural history, sociology, historiography, and ethnography.

90. Neuss, Paula. "Images of Writing and the Book in Chaucer's Poetry." *RES* 32(1981):385–97. For Chaucer poetry and love are closely related: both are creative arts to which the verb "make" is applied. Chaucer uses writing and book imagery to symbolize a creative love act.

91. Olson, Glending. "Making and Poetry in the Age of Chaucer." *CL* 31 (1979):272–90. Chaucer's distinction between "makere" and "poete" is found elsewhere in medieval writings. Serving both to separate classical from contemporary and to distinguish artistic quality from moral seriousness, the distinction suggests the relationship between vernacular versifiers and Latin Christian humanists.

92. Orme, Nicholas. "Chaucer and Education." *ChauR* 16(1981):38–59. Chaucer's references to education are scattered, unpredictable, and peripheral, except in the *WBT* and *SqT*, where the education theme is central.

93. Payne, F. Anne. *Chaucer and Menippean Satire*. Madison: University of Wisconsin Press, 1981. xii, 290 pp. A difficult form requiring of the reader a complex consciousness and thus hitherto largely neglected by critics, Menippean satire provides a meaningful context for Chaucer. The works of the third century B.C. satirist, themselves being lost, come to us through Lucian, as a highly elaborate satiric form, questioning not only deviations from the ideal but also even the possibility of any ideal — a questioning attitude couched nevertheless in a tone of enormous good humor and courtesy. Payne explicates Boethius's *Consolation of Philosophy* as Menippean satire and then proceeds to set the chief works of Chaucer showing Boethian influence in the same context, devoting two chapters to each: *TC*, pp. 86–158; *NPT*, pp. 159–206; *KnT*, pp. 207–58. Of these, *KnT*, itself a parody of the genre, is the most complex.

94. Pearsall, Derek. "Chaucer and the Modern Reader: A Question of Approach." *DQR* 11(1981):258–66. Modern readers must resist the limitations of twentieth-century literary-critical approach and interpret Chaucer in the traditional critical context: studies of manuscript tradition, text, and lexical context.

95. ———. *Old English and Middle English Poetry*. London and Boston: Routledge & Kegan Paul, 1977. Covers the first nine hundred years of English poetry. Includes treatment of Chaucer, his circle of friends, his choice of English as a literary language, his foreign influences.

96. Perry, Sigrid Pohl. "Trewe Wedded Libbynge Folk: Metaphors of Marriage in *Piers Plowman* and the *Canterbury Tales*." *DAI* 42(1981):2125A. In Chaucer, as in patristic writings, true marriage proceeds from physical to psychological to spiritual union, even emblematizing the relationship of God to church or soul. Analysis of marriage in *CT* further reveals sexual politics.

97. Reiss, Edmund. "Chaucer's Thematic Particulars." In *Signs and Symbols* (ACB, *SAC* 5[1983], no. 73), pp. 27–42. Symbolic details in Chaucer may also be thematic, e.g., the five etymologies of Saint Cecilia's name in *SNT*, and certain features of *GP*, *MerT*, *FranT*, others of the *CT*, and *TC*. Words and phrases also are often thematic.

98. Ridley, Florence H. "Questions Without Answers—Yet or Ever? New Critical Modes and Chaucer." *ChauR* 16(1981):101–106. Chaucerians should welcome the new critical techniques, which will help them determine what it is in the words that causes us to respond as we do. The application of these methods will transcend cultural differences that separate us from Chaucer.

99. ————. "A Response to 'Contemporary Literary Theory and Chaucer.'" In *New Perspectives* (ACB, *SAC* 5[1983], no. 103), pp. 37–51. Descriptive rather than interpretative approaches are preferred for Chaucer literary studies, according to Bloomfield, but we need to know *how* the poet constructed his work; thus semantics, the philosophy of speech acts, sociology, etc., are central to literary study.

100. Robertson, D. W., Jr. "Chaucer and the 'Commune Profit': The Manor." *Mediaevalia* 6(1980):239–59. Aware of the ethics of "commune profit," Chaucer condemns the self-seeking Franklin, Miller, Reeve, and Wife of Bath, while commending the other-centered Parson and Plowman.

101. ————. "Simple Signs from Everyday Life in Chaucer." In *Signs and Symbols* (ACB, *SAC* 5[1983], no. 73), pp. 11–26. Concerned with the practical and beneficial impact of his work, Chaucer drew figurative language from everyday sources, e.g., the visual arts. Knowledge of these sheds light on *GP*, *WBT*, and *RvT*.

102. Rollinson, Philip (appendix on primary Greek sources by Patricia Matsen). *Classical Theories of Allegory and Christian Culture*. Duquesne Studies in Language and Literature Series, vol. 3. Pittsburgh, Pa.: Duquesne University Press; London, Harvester Press, 1981. xx, 175 pp. Classical and medieval theories of allegory profoundly affected the interpretation and creation of medieval allegorical literature. The medieval audience believed that all worthwhile writing represented some truth, not necessarily Augustinian *caritas*. Appendix contains Englished excerpts from many of the authors in *Rhetores Graeci*.

103. Rose, Donald M., ed. *New Perspectives in Chaucer Criticism*. Norman, Okla.: Pilgrim Books, 1981. 248 pp. Commissioned originally to be read at the Second International Congress of the New Chaucer Society, these thirteen essays demonstrate the validity of recent critical trends in Chaucer. Several essays on historical approaches to Chaucer suggest new strategies; others cover Chaucer and Langland, twentieth-century critical theories applied to Chaucer, the arts and Chaucer, textual analyses, and French influence. See nos. 18, 39, 51, 65, 66, 76, 78, 87, 99, 109, 114, 199, 212.

104. Rosenberg, Bruce A. "The Oral Performance of Chaucer's Poetry." *Forum* 13(1980):224–37. The paucity of readers in the fourteenth century and explicit statements throughout Chaucer's works indicate that his poetry was recited aloud to a live audience, at least part of the time. Oral readings are most usefully appreciated by criteria one would apply to drama and oral performances.

105. Rudat, Wolfgang E. H., and Patricia Lee Youngue. "From Chaucer to Whitman and Eliot: Cosmic Union and the Classical/Christian Tradition." *DVLG* 55(1981):19–43. The Virgilian *Iuppiter descendens* in *CT* combines the sacred and the profane. Sexual motivation governs the behavior and storytelling of some of the pilgrims. Medieval man was able to integrate the serious with the comical because he possessed a Christian-Classical vision that embraced both physicality and spirituality.

106. Ruud, Jay Wesley. "Tradition and Individuality in Chaucer's Lyrics." *DAI* 42 (1981):2146A. Chaucer's lyric mode developed from the conventional toward the original, from everyman-speaker toward individual voice, from vague to concrete, from realist toward nominalist in philosophical outlook.

107. Salter, Elizabeth, and Derek Pearsall. "Pictorial Illustration of Late Medieval Poetic Texts: The Role of the Frontispiece or Prefatory Picture." In *Medieval Iconography and Narrative: A Symposium*. Ed. Flemming G. Andersen, Esther Nyholm, Marianne Powell, and Flemming Talbo Stubkjaer. Odense: Odense University Press, 1980, pp. 100–23. The study of the relationship of text to picture in medieval manuscripts is worthwhile, but seldom performed for Middle English texts, especially Chaucer, except for the *Troilus* frontispiece in Corpus Christi College Cambridge MS 61. It is important, both for what it tells us, enigmatically, of Chaucer's audience and for its reflection of the content of *TC*.

108. Shikii, Kumiko. "Chaucer and Catholicism." *Shirayuri Joshi Daigaku Eibungakka*. Shirayuri English Language and Literature Association (publications) 10(Tokyo, 1981):26–31. In Japanese. Chaucer's optimism, humor, and satire as well can be properly appreciated only in the light of his Catholic view of life. Some typical mistakes in translation are also made from lack of enough knowledge of Catholicism: the doctrines, liturgies, particular devotions, and so on.

109. Shoaf, R. Allen. "Dante's *Commedia* and Chaucer's Theory of Mediation: A Preliminary Sketch." In *New Perspectives* (ACB, *SAC* 5[1983], no. 103), pp. 83–103. Modern literary theory is concerned with the problem of "how language 'refers' in the critical text that has lost faith in the communion between language and reality." Shoaf observes this faith, which was stronger in the Middle Ages, at work in the *Commedia* and *TC*.

110. Southmayd, David Edward. "Chaucer and the Medieval Conventions of Bird Imagery." *DAI* 41(1981):3596A. Chaucer develops original significances for birds, especially in *HF*, *NPT*, and *PF*. Birds variously represent the bestial in humanity, models for human society, objects of ridicule, and mediators between

God and man. All four can be seen in the complex of patterns relating birds to love in *PF*.

111. Sylvia, Daniel, Donald R. Howard, Beryl Rowland, E. Talbot Donaldson, and Florence Ridley. "Thwarted Sexuality in Chaucer's Works." *Florilegium* 3(1982):239–56. Chaucer repeatedly depicts himself as a poet of love frustrated. Several critics look at the thwarted erotic element in *PF*, *TC* and *CT*, focusing on *PardT*, *WBT*, *ShT*, *MilT*, *MerT*, *MkT*, and *PrT* and the tellers of these tales.

112. Vance, Eugene. "Chaucer, Spenser, and the Ideology of Translation." *CRCL* 8(1981):227–38. Chaucer considers history as a process of translation. For Chaucer to English the Troy legend is to read his culture into that tragic history.

113. Weiss, Alexander. "Chaucer's Early Translations from French: The Art of Creative Transformation." In *Literary and Historical Perspectives of the Middle Ages: Proceedings of the 1981 SEMA Meeting*. Ed. Patricia W. Cummins, Patrick W. Conner, and Charles W. Connell. Morgantown: West Virginia University Press, 1982, pp. 174–82. The success of Chaucer's early translations from French cannot be attributed solely to his knack for finding the *mot juste* or to his "good ear" for English idiom. He drew on the native English poetic tradition for visual concreteness and meaningful rhythms.

114. Wetherbee, Winthrop. "Convention and Authority: A Comment on Some Recent Critical Approaches to Chaucer." In *New Perspectives* (ACB, *SAC* 5[1983], no. 103), pp. 71–81. Modern critical theory demonstrates the radically traditional closed system of medieval poetry. In his negative examples and examples of abuse and falsification, especially in *TC*, Chaucer is also aware of what the classical tradition is *not*.

115. Wilkes, G. A., and A. P. Riemer, eds. *Studies in Chaucer*. Sydney Studies in English. Sydney: University of Sydney, 1981. Essays by various hands. See nos. 115, 157, 166, 181, 197.

116. Wilkins, Nigel, *Chaucer Songs*. Cambridge: D. S. Brewer, 1980. 29 pp. A companion volume to *Music in the Age of Chaucer*. Fourteen of Chaucer's lyrics on the French model are presented in a performing edition with musical settings derived from contemporary songs by Machaut, Senleches, Solage, Andrieu, and the French-Cypriot repertory. The main justification for this exercise in *contrafactum* is Chaucer's observation in the *PF* that the musical setting for the roundel of the birds "maked was in France"; further strong links between Chaucer's lyrics and the French musical and poetic background are established.

117. ———. *Music in the Age of Chaucer*. Cambridge: D. S. Brewer, 1979. 174 pp. A general guide to fourteenth-century music in France, Italy, and Britain. The main composers, musical forms, and centers of musical activity are surveyed and illustrated in facsimiles, pictures, and music examples. Musical references in Chaucer's works show that, while not a practicing musician, he had an uncommon

interest in and sympathy for music. Gives a detailed study of minstrelsy and a general introduction to instruments.

Teaching Chaucer

118. Gibaldi, Joseph, ed. *Approaches to Teaching Chaucer's Canterbury Tales.* Approaches to Teaching Masterpieces of World Literature. Ed. Florence H. Ridley. New York: Modern Language Association, 1980. 175 pp. A collection of pedagogical articles from diverse perspectives—general overviews and approaches as well as specific approaches—by well-known Chaucerians, including John Fisher, Emerson Brown, Robert M. Jordan, William Provost, and Thomas W. Ross. See also no. 282.

119. Sato, Tsutomu. *An Approach to Chaucer.* Tokyo: Seibido, 1982. 150 pp. In Japanese. A primer on Chaucer, introducing Japanese students to Chaucer the poet, his age, his language, and other basic aspects related to Chaucer's world.

The Canterbury Tales — General

120. Allen, Judson Boyce, and Theresa Anne Moritz. *A Distinction of Stories: The Medieval Unity of Chaucer's Fair Chain of Narratives for Canterbury.* Columbus: Ohio State University Press, 1981. xi, 258 pp. Medieval literary theory in general, and commentary on Ovid's *Metamorphoses*, the tales-in-a-frame book most certainly important to Chaucer, suggest that *CT* can best be understood when grouped in four kinds: natural, magical, moral, and spiritual. When Chaucer's established fragments are reordered, under the guidance of this medieval precedent, as I, VIII, V, III, VI, II, IV, IX, VII, X, a structure emerges of four groups of tales. In each group—*KnT* to *CkT*, *SNT* to *PardT*, *MLT* to *ShT*, *PrT* to *ParsT*—the tales come in a logically descending order. Although marriage is in some sense paradigmatic for the whole collection, the third, moral, group is a newly proposed marriage group. The tales are put into a fresh order that stimulates new ideas.

121. Benson, Larry D. "The Order of *The Canterbury Tales*." *SAC* 3(1981): 77–120. By analysis of manuscript traditions Benson argues that there were at most two early orderings of *CT*. All later orderings in manuscripts are scribal rearrangements or distortions of these two. Both orders, one of which is the Ellesmere order, probably originated with Chaucer and differ only in the placement of the G fragment. But the Ellesmere represents Chaucer's "own final arrangement."

122. Blake, N. F. "Critics, Criticism and the Order to the *Canterbury Tales*." *Archiv* 218(1981):47–58. None of the structural orders that critics have strained to produce are totally satisfactory for a poem in such an obviously fragmentary state as *CT* by an author whose plans and intentions are as enigmatic as Chaucer's.

241

123. Buffoni, Franco. *Chaucer Testone Medievale*. Università degli Studi di Trieste, Facoltà di Economia e Commercio, Istituto di Lingue Straniere Moderne, vol. 10. Trieste: Nuova Del Bianco Industrie Grafiche, 1981. The *CT* are seen as a single unit. In particular, *Mel* and *MLT* are analyzed in the light of Marsilio of Padua's *Defensor Pacis* and Wyclif's religious position.

124. Duder, Clyburn. "Thematic Relationships Between Hagiographical References and the *Canterbury Tales*." *DAI* 41(1981):4707A. Contains a glossary of all saints referred to in *CT*, with notes relating them to medieval art, plus commentary on fourteen as associated with Reeve, Wife of Bath, and Pardoner or named in *FrT*, *SumT*, and *CYT*.

125. Edsall, Donna Marie. "Chaucer and the Chivalric Tradition." *DAI* 42(1981):2663A. The fourteenth century accepted literary conventions of the love code and approved warfare with honor and profit conjoined. Chaucer understands chivalry without attacking it: Theseus, in *KnT*, is an idealized knight modeled on Edward III; *Th* ridicules bourgeois misunderstanding of chivalry.

126. Giaccherini, Enrico. *I "Fabliaux" di Chaucer: Tradizione e innovazione nella narrativa comica chauceriana*. Pisa: ETS Universita 12, 1980. *MilT*, *RvT*, *FrT*, *SumT*, *ShT*, *MerT* can be called fabliaux if this term is taken in a typological, rather than strictly historical, acception. Their homogeneity is, however, only apparent. The six tales from *CT* are divided into three categories—students and bourgeois, religion and the religious, and monks and merchants.

127. Holloway, Julia Bolton. "Medieval Liturgical Drama: *The Commedia*, *Piers Plowman*, and the *Canterbury Tales*." *ABR* 32(1981):114–21. Recent Princeton performances of the *Officium Peregrinorum* (from Luke 24) reveal probable echoes in *CT* of the liturgical drama of Christ's pilgrimage to Emmaus in the pilgrimage frame itself, in the poet who like Christ uses "lying" fables to present truth, and in the motif of the naïve narrator.

128. Howard, Donald R. *Writers and Pilgrims: Medieval Pilgrimage Narratives and Their Posterity*. Berkeley: University of California Press, 1980. x, 133 pp. In the chapter on Chaucer, Howard links and compares medieval pilgrim narratives with *CT*. See also no. 287.

129. Kahlert, Shirley Ann. "The Breton Lay and Generic Drift: A Study of Texts and Contexts." *DAI* 42(1981):1629A. The Breton lay evolved from Celtic tradition to generic identity with Marie de France to art form in Chaucer's *WBT* and *FranT*. Most clearly characterized by the *merveilleux*, it has crossed cultural boundaries in such a way as to lose its motives but retain its marvels.

130. Lawler, Traugott. *The One and the Many in* The Canterbury Tales. Hamden, Conn.: Archon, 1980. 199 pp. The relations between diversity and unity, and between particular and general, are a major issue in *CT*, and emerge especially in the emphasis on profession, the sexes, and the relation of individual

experience to normative authority. Emphasis on profession, strong in *GP*, re-emerges in the fabliaux, and is exploited most richly in the "professional" confessions of the Wife, Pardoner, and Canon's Yeoman; the entire *CT* is a "meta-fabliau." Male and female stereotypes are established in the contrasting portraits of Wife and Parson in *GP*, and are reinforced by the notion of "auctoritee." Despite the value clearly granted to diversity, there is thus a certain "thrust toward unity" in the poem, which is seen also in a strong closural drive in *CYT* and *ParsT*—and in *Ret*. See also no. 292.

131. Morgan, Gerald. "Rhetorical Perspectives in the *General Prologue* to the *Canterbury Tales*." *ES* 62(1981):411–22. The portraits of *GP*, which depict types, belong to the tradition of rhetorical description, not of satire. Epideictic rhetoric provides for representation of virtue and vice alike and aims at the unity of perspective that we find in the descriptions of the pilgrims. It still accommodates irony, as in the presentation of the Prioress.

132. Pazdziora, Marian. "The Sapiential Aspect of *The Canterbury Tales*." *KN* 27(1980):413–26. *CT* is filled with proverbs, maxims, and witticisms included consciously by Chaucer for entertainment combined with instruction. The sapiential material in *CT* falls into four thematic groups: time, transience and death; god, destiny and fortune; love and marriage; and sin and salvation.

See also nos. 8, 11, 18, 19, 22, 45, 46, 49, 52, 57, 62, 67, 72, 76, 81, 83, 96, 97, 105, 111, 118, 252.

CT—The General Prologue

133. Goodall, Peter. "Chaucer's 'Burgesses' and the Aldermen of London." *MÆ* 50(1981):284–91. Examines *GP* 369–84 in light of the guild feud in London in the 1370s and 1380s, reviewing opinions of Kuhl and Fullerton, and Skeat. "In his attitudes toward the gildsmen . . . the pilgrim Chaucer shows himself as more petty-bourgeois than bourgeois."

See also nos. 6, 18, 39, 66, 80, 81, 97, 100, 101, 111, 130, 131, 138, 154, 174.

CT—The Knight and His Tale

134. Ciavolella, M. "Medieval Medicine and Arcite's Love Sickness." *Florilegium* 9(1979):222–41. In *KnT*, Chaucer presents Arcite's love sickness in scientific terms. Boccaccio reveals Arcite to be changed into a savage-looking creature, whereas Chaucer's description recreates the ideal world of chivalry.

135. Green, Richard Firth. "Arcite at Court." *ELN* 18(1981):251–57. Chaucer's digression from Boccaccio concerning Arcite's career at court should be interpreted not biographically but rather in the context of the career of Havelock the Dane. Both tales show the social stigma of being a page; Arcite's role emphasizes his subservience to love, and his rise to squire idealizes the Athenian court, where true merit is rewarded.

136. Hallissy, Margaret. "Poison and Infection in Chaucer's Knight's and Canon's Yeoman's Tales." *EAS* 10(1981):31–39. Chaucer draws on the medical and literary traditions about poison current in his day. In *KnT*, Arcite's love for Emelye is pictured as a deadly infection.

137. Jones, Terry. *Chaucer's Knight: The Portrait of a Medieval Mercenary.* Baton Rouge: Louisiana State University Press, 1980. Ranging through the history of the Crusades, Jones attempts to prove that Chaucer's Knight is a venal mercenary. See also no. 289.

138. Lester, G. A. "Chaucer's Knight and the Earl of Warwick." *N&Q* 28(1981):200–202. Similarities between Chaucer's description of the knight and the descriptions in *Warwick Pageant*, a fifteenth-century complimentary biography of the Earl of Warwick, indicate that Chaucer's description contains not irony but praise.

139. Olson, Paul. "Chaucer's Epic Statement and the Political Milieu of the Late Fourteenth Century." *Mediaevalia* 5(1979):61–87. *KnT* offers a reflection of several problems in late fourteenth-century society and of a judge and commentator, Theseus, who is free because he can rationally interpret history. Through *KnT* and its inversion in *MilT*, Chaucer offers a mythos of peace applicable to the historical conflicts of his time.

140. Schweitzer, Edward C. "Fate and Freedom in *The Knight's Tale*." *SAC* 3(1981):13–45. Precise astrological material and medical details pertaining to the disease *amor hereos* support the theory that Saturn and the fury that startles Arcite's horse dramatize the consequences of human choice rather than fatalism. Chaucer uses Boethius's *Consolation* to turn apparent contradictions between universal order and particular disorder into significant paradox.

141. Yamanaka, Toshio. "Theseus in *The Knight's Tale*." *Sophia English Studies* 4(1979):11–22. In Japanese. The keywords to determine Theseus's roles in *KnT* are "lord," "governour," "conquerour," "hunter," "servant," and "judge." Theseus has analogy with Mars, Venus, and Diana, as "conquerour," "servant," and "hunter," symbolized in his construction of the three temples.

See also nos. 18, 32, 39, 50, 55, 60, 62, 81, 93.

CT—The Miller and His Tale

142. Martin, B. K. "The Miller's Tale as Critical Problem and Dirty Joke." In *Studies in Chaucer* (ACB, *SAC* 5[1983], no. 115), pp. 86–120. Analyzes plot and content to show that *MilT* is a popular tale, not a bookish one, and is based on twelve "joke motifs."

143. Nicholson, Lewis E. "Chaucer's 'Com pa me': A Famous Crux Reexamined." *ELN* 19(1981):98–102. Despite recent scholarship of *MilT* that equates Alison's "pa" (line 3709) with the Wife of Bath's "ba" (*WBT*, line 433), the two words should be distinguished. "Pa" seems to be a shortening of *pax*, the liturgical embrace of Christian love. In light of the ironic pattern of allusion to the Canticle "pa" is especially fitting.

144. Nitzsche, Jane Chance. "'As swete as is the roote of lycorys, or any cetewale': Herbal Imagery in Chaucer's *Miller's Tale*." *Chaucer Newsletter* 2, 1(1980):6–8. Chaucer uses herbal imagery of licorice and cetewale, breath sweeteners associated with love in *MilT*, to establish the theme of character dependence on them. Cetewale is aphrodisiac; licorice quenches thirst; love is reduced to the physical and ephemeral.

145. Plummer, John F. "The Woman's Song in Middle English and Its European Backgrounds." In *Vox Feminae: Studies in Medieval Woman's Songs*. Ed. John F. Plummer. Studies in Medieval Culture, vol. 15. Kalamazoo: Medieval Institute, Western Michigan University, 1981, pp. 135–54. In the character of Absolon in *MilT*, Chaucer exploits the literary fact that "the minor orders were not taken seriously as lovers, but were found precisely in the burlesque world of the *fabliau*." The willfulness and sexual appetite of the Wife of Bath derive directly from antifeminist traditions.

146. Ross, Thomas W. "*Astromye* in the Miller's Tale Again." *N&Q* 28(1981):202. *Astromye* is neither a scribal error nor an acceptable variant for *astronomye* but a malapropism that probably appeared originally as *arstromye*, containing a pun in the first syllable.

147. Stevens, John. "Angelus ad virginem: the History of a Medieval Song." In *Medieval Studies for J. A. W. Bennett* (ACB, *SAC* 5[1983], no. 74), pp. 297–328. A valuable edition based on British Library Arundel 248 with variants from other texts of the late-thirteenth-century Latin song sung by "hende Nicolas" in *MilT*. In addition to its sources, Stevens discusses it as a type of canto that eventually found a place in the liturgy as part of the masses of Our Lady especially during Advent.

148. Williams, David. "Radical Therapy in the *Miller's Tale*." *ChauR* 15(1981): 227–35. John of Arderne's *Fistula in ano* and the *Book of Quinte Essence* provide insight into the illness references in the tale.

See also nos. 18, 45, 60, 69, 111, 126, 139, 187.

CT—The Reeve and His Tale

149. Clark, Cecily. "Another Late-Fourteenth-Century Case of Dialect-Awareness." *ES* 62(1981):504–505. The use of regional dialects in *RvT* and the *Second Shepherd's Play* indicates a sporadic literary exploitation of dialect differences in the fourteenth century and implies an ability, at least among the educated, to classify the different dialects heard.

150. Higuchi, Masayuki. "Verbal Exploitation in the *Reeve's Tale*." *HSELL* 25(1980):1–12. Distinctions made between "expression-oriented" and "content-oriented" texts serve as a framework for demonstrating the interrelated nature of language in *RvT*. Philological tracings of word associations set up lexical chains that illustrate semantic links in the language used in the tale.

See also nos. 6, 18, 39, 66, 68, 101, 124, 126, 187.

CT—The Man of Law and His Tale

151. Clogan, Paul M. "The Narrative Style of the Man of Law's Tale." *M&H* n.s. 8(1977):217–33. The narrative of *MLT* depends less on organic structure to develop the story than on exemplary episodic narrative sequence. Lack of descriptive detail is an effect of the narrator's interest in action, and the mode of presentation and the style of the persona of the narrator are deliberate effects of the style of hagiographic romance.

152. Harty, Kevin J. "Chaucer's Man of Law and the 'Muses that men clepe Pierides.'" *SSF* 18(1981):75–77. The Man of Law's allusion to the story of the nine daughters of Pierus, as presented in *Metamorphosis* 5, is viewed as literary criticism that emphasizes the fact that the Man of Law is reluctant to be compared to the daughters—who lost their singing contest—because he wishes to win the storytelling contest in which he is engaged.

153. Hinton, Norman. "Lucan and the Man of Law's Tale." *PLL* 17(1981): 339–46. The disparity between Chaucer's allusion to Lucan in *MLT* 400–403 and the actual passage in Lucan might be explained by commentaries that Chaucer might have known. The *Pharsalia* shares thematic parallels with Chaucer's story, and may reflect his knowledge of contemporary glosses.

154. Wentersdorf, Karl P. "The *Termes* of Chaucer's Sergeant of the Law." *SN* 53(1981):269–74. After discussing various readings for the phrase, "In termes hadde he cas and doomes alle..." (*GP* 323), Wentersdorf argues that *term* is equivalent to a court session: thus, when courts were in session, this man of law had at his disposal all the legal precedents pertaining to the case he was arguing.

See also nos. 30, 81, 123.

CT—The Wife of Bath and Her Tale

155. Atkinson, Michael. "Soul's Time and Transformations: The Wife of Bath's Tale." *SoRA* 13(1980):72–78. *WBT* is a tale of transformations best understood by applying to it Jung's anima. The knight's quest is really a search for understanding of his inner self, the feminine psyche. The transformation of the hag at the end mirrors his own inner transformation as he accepts submission and affirms the power of the feminine psyche.

156. Puhvel, Martin. "The Wyf of Bath and Alice Kyteler—A Web of Parallelism." *SN* 53(1981):101–106. Similarities in the career of Alice Kyteler of Kilkenny, Ireland, and Chaucer's Alice suggest that the case against the former may have influenced Chaucer's portrait. Alice Kyteler was married four times and was accused of carnal relations with a devil ("Robinus filius Artis"), and of practicing magic.

157. Singer, Margaret. "The Wife of Bath's Prologue and Tale." In *Studies in Chaucer* (ACB, *SAC* 5[1983], no. 115), pp. 28–37. Tries to reconcile the change from the naturalism of the *Prologue* to the abstract quality of the tale. Gives an extended definition of *gentilesse*.

158. Storm, Melvin. "Alisoun's Ear." *MLQ* 42(1981):219–26. The deafness of the Wife of Bath is viewed as an iconographic reflection of her unbalanced intellectual and spiritual position. Hearing as she does with only one ear, the Wife's views are skewed to improper attention to the present—to the things of this world—at the expense of the things of the next.

See also nos. 55, 64, 69, 92, 101, 111, 124, 129, 143, 145.

CT—The Friar and His Tale

See nos. 40, 66, 124, 126.

CT—The Summoner and His Tale

159. Jungman, Robert E. "'Covent' in the *Summoner's Tale*." *MissFR* 14(1980):20–23. In *SumT* "covent" refers not only to the Friar's house, but also to witches' "coven," as indicated by various references to witchcraft or demonology—thus suggesting that the friar is a witch.

160. Lancashire, Ian. "Moses, Elijah and the Back Parts of God: Satiric Scatology in Chaucer's *Summoner's Tale*." *Mosaic* 14(1981):17–30. Chaucer employs scriptural allusions in Thomas's gift and its codicil; typological exegesis demon-

strates that, if Jankin's division of the fart suggests Pentecost, Thomas's first gift recalls the events in the lives of Moses and Elijah that Pentecost fulfills. *SumT* can be seen as an intentional perversion of scriptural history.

See also nos. 57, 66, 80, 124, 126.

CT — The Clerk and His Tale

161. Wilcockson, Colin. " 'Thou' and 'Ye' in Chaucer's Clerk's Tale." *Use of English* 31(1980):37–43. The Marquis in *C/T* addresses Janicola with the formal "ye" and, at certain points, Griselda as "thou," the intimate or insulting form. In keeping with her unfailing humility, Griselda never deviates from the formal "ye" when addressing Walter.

162. Wimsatt, James I. "The Blessed Virgin and the Two Coronations of Griselda." *Mediaevalia* 6(1980):187–207. The parallel between Griselda and Mary, from preelection and marriage through maternal suffering to final coronation, is integral and pervasive in *C/T*. Mary embodies the canonical myth of the life of the Christian soul from baptism to heaven; Griselda humanizes the myth, but retains mythic force.

See also nos. 18, 55.

Source Studies

163. Bornstein, Diane. "An Analogue to Chaucer's *Clerk's Tale*." *ChauR* 15(1981):322–31. Christine de Pizan uses the Griselda tale to illustrate the virtues of patience and constancy in her *Livre de la Cité des Dames*, derived from a French prose version by Philippe de Mézières, perhaps also consulting the anonymous French prose translation, Chaucer's main source.

164. Kadish, Emilie P. "Petrarch's *Griselda*: An English Translation." *Mediaevalia* 3(1977):1–24. According to the introduction, Petrarch's version of the tale — the immediate source of Chaucer's *C/T* — brings Griselda to the fore and attains the maximum effect from the story's potential for pathos.

CT — The Merchant and His Tale

165. Annunziata, Anthony. "Tree Paradigms in the *Merchant's Tale*." *Acta* 4(1977):125–35. Tree as word and image is a structural device in the *MerT*. Etymologically, "tree" and "true" are connected. Paradigmatic trees, including the

Tree of Jesse, the Tree of Knowledge, and the Tree of Vices, offer symbolic counterpoints to the actions of January and May culminating in the self-erected Rood Tree of January.

166. Rogers, H. L. "The Tales of the Merchant and the Franklin: Text and Interpretation." In *Studies in Chaucer* (ACB, *SAC* 5[1983], no. 115), pp. 3–27. An explication of the *MerT* and *FranT* using the Hengwrt manuscript order, the article surveys some critical interpretations of the two tales, concerning the clerical or secular nature of the tellers.

167. Schwartz, Robert B. "The Social Character of May Games: A Popular Background for Chaucer's *Merchant's Tale*." *ZAA* 27(1979):43–51. Damyan is seen as a type of fourteenth-century Robin Hood, who presided over May revels and mated with the May queen, and who was prosecuted under vagrancy laws which Chaucer may have enforced.

See also nos. 14, 34, 57, 60, 68, 74, 97, 111, 126.

Source Studies

168. DiMarco, Vincent. "Richard Hole and the *Merchant's* and *Squire's Tales*: an Unrecognized Eighteenth-Century (1797) Contribution to Source and Analogue Study." *ChauR* 16(1981):171–80. Hole's *Remarks on the Arabians Nights' Entertainments* contains speculations about the sources of the pear-tree motif and the magical objects in the two tales. While many of his guesses are without substantiation, he does suggest a pear-tree analogue to be found in the *Bahar-i Danish* of Inayat Allah Kanbu (1608–71). A likely source for the healing-sword motif is Pliny's *Natural History*.

CT — The Squire and His Tale

Source Studies

169. Dimarco, Vincent. "Canacee's Magic Ring." *Anglia* 99(1981):399–405. The legend of Moses' magic, alluded to in *SqT* 247–51, first occurs in Peter Comestor's *Historia scholastica*. Nicholas Trevet and Gower also mention this motif, but probably Chaucer's source for the allusion is Roger Bacon's *Opus maius*.

On *The Squire and His Tale*, see also nos. 14, 92, 168.

CT—The Franklin and His Tale

170. Carruthers, Mary J. "The Gentilesse of Chaucer's Franklin." *Criticism* 23(1981):283–300. The Franklin is a gentleman with old-fashioned but praise-worthy standards. *FranT* treats the fourteenth-century interdependent virtues of "trouthe and honour, fredom and curteisie (A46)"—moral values in ambiguous wrappings.

171. Miller, Robert P. "Augustinian Wisdom and Eloquence in the F-Fragment of the *Canterbury Tales*." *Mediaevalia* 4(1978):245–75. Cicero's ideal rhetorical style, which combined wisdom and eloquence, was redefined in Christian terms by Saint Augustine. Chaucer's Franklin, who pretends to follow Augustinian rhetorical ideals, in fact defines wisdom and eloquence in a worldly manner, as the Epicurean Chaucer proclaims him to be.

172. ———. "The Epicurean Homily on Marriage by Chaucer's Franklin." *Mediaevalia* 6(1980):151–86. The Franklin revises the law of the sacrament of marriage according to the medieval understanding of Epicurus. Ironically, echoing Amis and la Vielle from the *Roman de la Rose*, the Franklin advocates the pursuit of "ese" and "delit" and the substitution of the law of nature for Christian freedom.

173. Schuman, Samuel. "Man, Magician, Poet, God—An Image in Medieval, Renaissance, and Modern Literature." *Cithara* 19(1980):40–54. Discusses the function of the Briton clerk's predinner magical scene (*FranT* 1189–1207) and compares it with the masque of Ceres in act 4 of Shakespeare's *The Tempest*.

174. Specht, Henrik. *Chaucer's Franklin in* The Canterbury Tales: *The Social and Literary Background of a Chaucerian Character*. Publications of the Department of English, University of Copenhagen, vol. 10. Copenhagen: Akademisk Forlag, 1981. 206 pp. Discusses the franklin "class" of late-medieval England: etymology, legal status, land tenure, wealth, rank, and social position. Adducing contemporary evidence, some of which is here discussed for the first time, the author explores the clues contained in Chaucer's description of the Franklin in *CT*, establishing his social identity, and questioning hitherto proposed models for this character. The results are applied in a reconsideration of Chaucer's literary aims with respect to the Franklin's character, behavior, and tale, to place the Franklin and his tale near the heart of the "Chaucerian ethos."

175. Watanabe, Ikuo. "*The Franklin's Tale*: A Narrative." *Journal of Tenri University* (1981):91–109. In Japanese. In spite of an appearance as a tragedy, the tale by the sanguine Franklin quickly arrives at the conclusion of a happy ex-emplum. It is the narrator himself who most keenly enjoys the tale.

See also nos. 14, 15, 60, 97, 129, 166.

CT—The Physician and His Tale

175A. Baird, Lorrayne Y. "The Physician's 'urynals and jurdones.'" *Fifteenth Century Studies* 2(1979):1–8. The Host's reference to the standard emblems of the physician may be a naïve-ironic insult.

176. Delany, Sheila. "Politics and the Paralysis of the Poetic Imagination in the Physician's Tale." *SAC* 3(1981):47–60. In contrast to other analogues to *PhysT*, Chaucer "systematically obliterates social content" to deprive the characters of plausible motives. This "bad piece of work" is "pornographic or free-floating sadistic sensationalism, with murder as its only real centre."

See also no. 71.

CT—The Pardoner and His Tale

177. Beidler, Peter G. "Noah and the Old Man in the *Pardoner's Tale*." *ChauR* 15(1981):250–54. Although thought immortal and evil, the Old Man in *PardT* is mortal in his longing for death, and, furthermore, good, patient, and kind. Chaucer's audience might have seen a parallel with Noah, the incredibly old survivor of a worse "plague," the Flood.

178. Gill, Richard. "Jung's Archetype of the Wise Old Man in Poems by Chaucer, Wordsworth, and Browning." *Journal of Evolutionary Psychology* 2(1981):18–32. Ambiguous old men in English poetry, including the one in *PardT*, can be illuminated by the psychological archetype of the *wise old man* that Jung describes in "The Phenomenology of the Spirit in Fairy Tales."

179. Ginsberg, Warren. "Preaching and Avarice in the *Pardoner's Tale*." *Mediaevalia* 2(1976):77–99. References to medieval treatises and exegetical tradition suggest that the Pardoner's connection with ale, dove, and tree indicates that, through avarice, he is too literal to preach God's word. The Old Man, taken literally by the Pardoner, signifies the effects of avarice. The Old Man is repentant, but the Pardoner is not.

180. Kuntz, Robert Allen. "The Pardoning of the Pardoner: Critical Approaches to the Morality of Chaucer's Pardoner." *DAI* 42(1981):1141A. Critical views of the Pardoner range from total condemnation to interpretations of him as Christlike, with current views seeing him as evil. Interpretations can be immediate, direct, and simple, or complicated sociopsychologically or patristic-exegetically.

181. Lawton, D. A. "The Pardoner's Tale: Morality and Its Context." In *Studies in Chaucer* (ACB, *SAC* 5[1983], no. 115), pp. 38–63. Explicates *PardT* with a concern for the division between the tale proper (lines 463–903) and its frame. The

tale is structurally a digression, theologically orthodox, but unconventional in "tone," and is to be taken seriously.

182. Nitecki, Alicia K. "The Convention of the Old Man's Lament in the *Pardoner's Tale.*" *ChauR* 16(1981):76–84. Although the major sources of the Old Man figure have long been known, the existence of the figure in alliterative and lyric poetry shows how Chaucer transforms the tradition. His Old Man is a trope for man's desire for transcendence.

183. Sato, Noriko. "The Old Man in *The Pardoner's Tale.*" *Thought Currents in English Literature* 54(1981):11–36. Tokyo: English Literary Society of Aoyama Gakuin University. The Old Man in *PardT* represents a fusion of divine force with the sense of futility and remorse that accompany physical aging — a motif found in medieval lyrics, Villon, and in later writers.

184. Scheps, Walter. "Chaucer's Numismatic Pardoner and the Personification of Avarice." *Acta* 4(1977):107–23. Avarice and sterility, as seen in the Pardoner's unnatural multiplication of money and his abnormal sexuality, are connected verbally, iconographically, and symbolically through his main interest — money. The inscription and the cross on the florin relate to the Pardoner and his tale; he personifies all aspects of avarice in his physical appearance and practices.

185. Standop, Ewald. "Chaucers Pardoner: das Charakterproblem und die Kritiker." In *Geschichtlichkeit und Neuanfang im sprachlichen Kuntswerk. Studien zur englischen Philologie zu Ehren von Fritz W. Schulze.* Ed. Peter Erlebach, Wolfgang G. Müller, Klaus Reuter. Tübingen: Gunter Narr Verlag, 1981, pp. 59–69. All attempts by critics to ascribe psychological implications to conventional self-revelations of a fictional character such as Chaucer's Pardoner lead to a false evaluation. The text does not contain the slightest suggestion that the Pardoner is a sexual deviate whose offer to the Host disguises a coarse jest.

See also nos. 34, 39, 45, 61, 80, 81, 111, 124.

CT—The Shipman and His Tale

186. Coletti, Theresa. "The *Mulier Fortis* and Chaucer's Shipman's Tale." *ChauR* 15(1981):236–49. In *ShT*, Chaucer may have used the well-known text of Proverbs 31.10–31, which praises the valiant woman, in ironic fashion. The scriptural *mulier fortis* is praised for her "huswifery," her provision of food and clothing, her "rendering" to her husband — qualities ironically inverted by the wife of St. Denis.

187. Gibson, Gail McMurray. "Resurrection as Dramatic Icon in the Shipman's Tale." In *Signs and Symbols* (ACB, *SAC* 5[1983], no. 73), pp. 102–12. In the Noah's Flood motif of *MilT*, the audience delightedly and ruefully recognizes the

consequences of the perversion of God's order. In addition to visual or other sensory images (the runaway mare in *RvT*) Chaucer employs also dramatic icons, as in *ShT*, a "parodic enactment of Christ's Resurrection appearance to Mary Magdalen."

188. Nicholson, Peter. "The Medieval Tales of the Lover's Gift Regained." *Fabula* 21(1979):200–22. J. W. Spargo has not proved the existence of an extraliterary tradition among texts written by Chaucer and Boccaccio. The oral circulation of the tale does not support the hypothesis that Chaucer and Boccaccio had a common source.

189. Stock, Lorraine Kochanske. "The Meaning of 'Chevyssaunce': Complicated Word Play in Chaucer's *Shipman's Tale*." *SSF* 18(1981):245–49. Suggests that in three places in the *ShT*—lines 1519-21, 1536-37, 1581—Chaucer exploits two denotations of "chevyssaunce." In addition to the specific denotation "usury," the word has a more general denotation—*MED* meaning 2—which, when applied, solves the problem of why Chaucer departed from his analogues.

See also nos. 18, 84, 111, 126.

CT—The Prioress and Her Tale

190. Ferris, Sumner. "Chaucer at Lincoln (1387): *The Prioress's Tale* as a Political Poem." *ChauR* 15(1981):295-321. As all five saints of *PrT* had Lincoln associations in Chaucer's day, so the poem was intended for Lincoln. *PrT* commemorates the visit to Lincoln Minster, on March 26, 1387, of Richard II, who sought by its means the political support of John Buckingham, Bishop of Lincoln, against the faction of Thomas, Duke of Gloucester; and Chaucer read it aloud there on that occasion.

191. ———. "The Mariology of the *Prioress's Tale*." *ABR* 32(1981):232-54. Theologically, the Blessed Virgin is highly venerated, with *hyperdulia*, but she is nevertheless only a means to the one mediator, Christ (1 Tim. 2.5), who is worshiped with *latria*. This distinction, most unusual for a work of literature, is a major theme of *PrT*.

192. Gabrieli, Vittorio. "Magia e Miracolo in Due Favole Medievali." *La Cultura* 17(1980):90-104. Petrarch's account of a gemstone ring that, under the tongue of a beautiful corpse, drove Charlemagne mad with passion (*Familiares* 1.1.4) may have been known to Chaucer. The legend provides a suggestive analogue for the motif of the "grain" in the *PrT*.

193. Shikii, Kumiko. "Chaucer's Prioresse Re-considered." *Soundings* 7 (Tokyo, 1981):11-24. In Japanese. Chaucer's Prioress is said to be a miniature of *CT*. Just as Madame Eglantine is a religious with fairly secular characters, so *CT* shows all kinds of people, with their sublime and indecent faces, their beauty, and their ugliness.

194. Wood, Chauncey. "Chaucer's Use of Signs in His Portrait of the Prioress." In *Signs and Symbols* (ACB, *SAC* 5[1983], no. 73), pp. 81–101. Chaucer uses signs playfully, *in bono*, *in malo*: tears cited by the Parson are signs of contrition; the Prioress weeps for dead mice and whipped dogs. Chaucer is original in his treatment of her features, all of which point to worldliness.

See also nos. 39, 111, 131.

CT—The Tale of Sir Thopas

See nos. 50, 63, 125.

CT—Melibeus

See nos. 50, 55, 72, 88, 123.

CT—The Monk and His Tale

See nos. 69, 88, 111.

Source Studies

195. Fleming, John V. "Daun Piers and Dom Pier: Waterless Fish and Unholy Hunters." *ChauR* 15(1981):287–94. For his portrait of the Monk in *GP*, Chaucer probably recalled Dante *Paradiso* 21.118–20, 127–35, an encomium of Peter Damian, and Damian's own words regarding "unholy hunters, cloisterless monks, and waterless fish." "Palfrey" may be an echo of Dante's *palafreni*. Daun Piers may even recall Dom Pier, Peter Damian himself.

196. Waller, Martha S. "The Monk's Tale: Nero's Nets and Caesar's Father—An Inquiry into the Transformations of Classical Roman History." *Indiana Social Studies Quarterly* 31(1978):46–55. The uniquely English tradition of Julius Caesar's humble birth conflates other supposed bases for insult (baldness, homosexuality, or weakness) with misinterpretation of his relationship to Augustus.

CT—The Nun's Priest and His Tale

197. Knight, Stephen. "Form, Content and Context in The Nun's Priest's Tale." In *Studies in Chaucer* (ACB, *SAC* 5[1983], no. 115), pp. 64–85. An

explication of *NPT*, analyzing it within its historical context.

198. Schauber, Ellen, and Ellen Polsky. "Stalking a Generative Poetics." *NLH* 12(1981):397–413. Readers resolve conflicts by readjusting genre expectations. *NPT* is a beast fable "told in the rhetoric of epic. The homely moral of the tale is comically inconsistent with the implications of high seriousness in the language."

See also nos. 18, 34, 61, 71, 88, 93, 110.

CT—The Second Nun and Her Tale

199. Kolve, V. A. "Chaucer's Second Nun's Tale and the Iconography of Saint Cecilia." In *New Perspectives* (ACB, *SAC* 5[1983], no. 103), pp. 137–74. Although Chaucer was not a "painterly" poet, he was, like most other serious writers of the time, an iconographic poet. Examines a number of medieval images appropriate to Chaucer's life of Saint Cecilia and includes twenty reproductions in black and white.

See also nos. 55, 69, 97.

CT—The Canon's Yeoman and His Tale

See nos. 14, 69, 124, 130.

CT—The Manciple and His Tale

200. Westervelt, L. A. "The Medieval Notion of Chaucer's *Manciple's Tale*." *SoRA* 14(1981):107–15. The focus of *ManT* is not adultery and murder but rather talebearing. Chaucer returns to Ovid for janglery as a serious crime. If janglery causes murder, the janglerer is as guilty as the murderer because he is the cause of the crime.

201. Wood, Chauncey. "Speech, the Principle of Contraries, and Chaucer's Tales of the Manciple and the Parson." *Mediaevalia* 6(1980):209–29. The principle of contraries provides a method for relating pairs of tales. *ManT* and *ParsT* offer paradigms for improper and proper use of speech. The Manciple uses and misglosses the tale of Phoebus and the Crow, while the Parson speaks the truth without an "ennucleating story."

See also no. 71.

CT—The Parson and His Tale

202. Correale, Robert M. "The Sources of Some Patristic Quotations in Chaucer's The Parson's Tale." *ELN* 19(1981):95–98. Five patristic quotations in *ParsT* have not been noted: one originates in Pseudo-Augustine, a second in Isidore of Seville, and another in St. Jerome, and two others can be traced to St. Gregory.

203. Shimogasa, Tokuji. "Chaucer's Colloquial Style in *The Parson's Tale*." *Era*, n.s. 2(Hiroshima, 1981):41–61. In English. Frequently used in *ParsT*, colloquial anaphora enhances the homiletic style in such repetitious expressions as "Now Comth...," "Look forther...," "Certes...," and "Soothly,...."

204. Wurtele, Douglas. "The Penitence of Geoffrey Chaucer." *Viator* 11 (1980):335–61. Neither Gascoigne's comments on Chaucer's deathbed repentence nor the retraction at the end of *ParsT* should be read too strongly. Rather *Ret* should be connected to the *ParsT* more clearly and seen in relationship to remarks on repentence in *ParsT* 93–94.

See also nos. 18, 30, 55, 130, 201.

CT—Retraction

See nos. 121, 130, 204.

Anelida and Arcite

205. Norton-Smith, John. "Chaucer's *Anelida and Arcite*." In *Medieval Studies for J. A. W. Bennett* (ACB, *SAC* 5[1983], no. 74), pp. 81–99. As suggested by the manuscripts, *Anel* is a complete, finished poem (with the omission of an unchaucerian final stanza). It is concerned with the theme of poetry as an art functioning as a record of history. Its closest affiliations are with the Theban material of *TC*, book 5, and with *LGW*.

See also nos. 7, 10, 12, 49, 69.

Astrolabe

206. Owen, Charles A., Jr. "A Certein Nombre of Conclusions: The Nature and Nurture of Children of Chaucer." *ChauR* 16(1981):60–75. Chaucer shows a keen awareness of children's nature, their relationship with their parents, and their limitations: they are not viewed as miniature adults. *Astr*, a popular piece, not

simply a book of instructions to accompany the gift of the instrument to his son, shows the poet's understanding of a child of ten.

Boece

207. Caretta, Vincent. *"The Kingis Quair* and *The Consolation of Philosophy."* *SSL* 16(1981):14–28. *The Kingis Quair* has been interpreted as autobiographical and as Boethian. If, however, James I understood Boethius as Chaucer did, both interpretations are incorrect. James discredits his narrator persona by using the Chaucerian Boethius as a standard that he cannot attain.

See also no. 57.

The Book of the Duchess

208. Dinzelbacher, Peter. *Vision und Visionsliteratur im Mittelalter*. Monographien zur Geschichte des Mittelalters, vol. 23. Stuttgart: Hiersemann, 1981. Deals with both real ecstatic visions and fictional literary visions and gives criteria to discern them. Thus it provides the background for Chaucer's dream poetry as well, quoting Langland, *BD*, *HF*, *LGW*, *PF*, etc.

209. Kaiser, Ulrike. "Die 'Schwurzene' in Chaucers *Book of the Duchess."* *Euphorion* 75(1981):110–17. An examination of the source, Machaut's *Jugement dou Roy de Behaingne*, proves that the Knight's and the Dreamer's mutual lack of understanding — which serves a powerful dramatic purpose — stems from differences in social background and rank.

210. Morse, Ruth. "Understanding the Man in Black." *ChauR* 15(1981): 204–208. Chaucer's audience would not have come to *BD* with our preconceptions (that the Man is John of Gaunt and that his song is personal). Rather, they would have experienced the gradual revelations as they are unfolded and would have concerned themselves with the Man rather than with the Dreamer.

211. Neaman, Judith S. "Brain Physiology and Poetics in *The Book of the Duchess."* *Res Publica Litterarium* 3(1980):101–13. The narrator, Alcyone, and the Black Knight suffer from melancholy. Brain functions and anatomy, progress, and treatment of the illness are linked chronologically, and the time shifts are analogous to the order and process of brain physiology as understood in the Middle Ages.

212. Nolan, Barbara. "The Art of Expropriation: Chaucer's Narrator in *The Book of the Duchess."* In *New Perspectives* (ACB, *SAC* 5[1983], no. 103), pp. 203–22. In *BD* Chaucer skillfully breaks with French poetic practice to produce a new kind of poetry. The enigmatic narrator does not participate in established

conventions; an insomniac amateur reader, he does not fully understand the matter he presents.

213. Philips, Helen. "Structure and Consolation in the *Book of the Duchess.*" *ChauR* 16(1981):107–18. Critics differ in their assessment of the structure and the nature of the consolation in *BD*. Chaucer uses juxtaposition as his structural principle. The consolation is Boethian, transcending the intensity of human grief, but Chaucer insists upon the reality of the grief as well.

214. Shoaf, R. A. " 'Mutatio Amoris': 'Penitentia' and the Form of *The Book of the Duchess.*" *Genre* 14(1981):163–69. *BD*'s central theme is that change is necessary and inevitable and must be but graciously accepted. Initially the Black Knight avoids change; by the end of *BD* he is reconciled with, and embraces, change. In *BD*, Chaucer succeeds in his portrayal of arguments as a theological poet.

215. Thoms, John Clifton. "Looking at Death: A Study in the Literary and Historical Background of Chaucer's *Book of the Duchess.*" *DAI* 42(1981):208A. The narrator's eight-year sickness may refer to the last illness of Henry, Duke of Lancaster. The portrait of Lady White departs significantly from that of Machaut's lady in *Jugement dou Roy de Behaingne* to reconcile courtly with Christian love.

216. Wimsatt, James I. "*The Book of the Duchess*: Secular Elegy or Religious Vision?" In *Signs and Symbols* (ACB, *SAC* 5[1983], no. 73), pp. 113–29. Reconciles Wimsatt's other writings on *BD*—one emphasizing the closeness of *BD* to fourteenth-century French love poetry, the other studying the religious significance of the poem in the context of Christian tradition—which produce quite different readings.

See also nos. 7, 10, 12, 20, 29, 49, 52, 62, 69, 71, 74, 80.

The House of Fame

217. Braswell, Mary Flowers. "Architectural Portraiture in Chaucer's House of Fame." *JMRS* 11(1981):101–12. Far from being "entirely tropological" or imaginative, the descriptions of the Temple of Venus and the House of Fame and Rumor accurately reflect the forms and details of contemporary structures. As Clerk of the Works and perhaps an acquaintance of Henry Yevele, Chaucer would have had opportunity to observe fourteenth-century architecture.

218. Buckmaster, Elizabeth Marie. " 'Caught in Remembraunce': Chaucer and the Art of Memory." *DAI* 42(1981):2136A. *HF* classifies memory as an aspect of Prudence, as reflected in its three-part structure and reinforced by its thematic meditation on fame. *GP* portraits develop with details of "artificial" memory, as do the pilgrimage itself and the game. *KnT* builds on the memory image of the tournament theater, and the two following tales build on *KnT*.

219. Dane, Joseph A. "Chaucer's Eagle's Ovid's Phaethon: A Study in Literary Reception." *JMRS* 11(1981):71–82. In having the Eagle retell the story of Phaethon from Ovid and from medieval interpretations of Ovid, Chaucer oversimplifies and creates conflicts or deficiencies of meaning; this allusive and contradictory treatment of literary tradition in *HF* signals Chaucer's method in his later poetry.

220. ————. "Yif I 'Arma Virumque' Kan: Note on Chaucer's *House of Fame* Line 143." *AN&Q* 19(1981):134–35. Just as the theme of memory pervades *HF*, so Chaucer's recounting of the *Aeneid* in book 1 begins with both detail and accuracy and ends in hasty paraphrase. Chaucer's lines 143–48 translate the opening sentence of the *Aeneid* accurately, save for the interpolated "yif I kan," the last word of which phrase may echo Virgil's *cano*.

221. Isenor, Neil, and Ken Woolner. "Chaucer's Theory of Sound." *Physics Today* 3(1980):114–16. *HF* 782–834 displays an uncanny foreknowlege of details of the modern theory of sound and wave motion, especially in lines 809–13, where, in a great creative leap of scientific imagination, the motion of water waves is transferred to the propagation of sound waves.

222. Newman, Francis X. " 'Partriches Wynges': A Note on *Hous of Fame*, 1391–92." *Mediaevalia* 6(1980):231–38. The "partridge wings" at the end of the *pictura* of Fame result not from error but from Chaucer's following the commentary on the *Metamorphoses* in *Ovide moralisé*, where Perdix (partridge) represents a clever but deceitful craftsman and Daedalus the type of the wise man. "Partriches wynges" is a precise iconographic gesture, implying the emptiness of Fame and the verbal arts.

223. Rowland, Beryl. "The Art of Memory and the Art of Poetry in the *House of Fame*." *RUO* 51(1981):163–71. Chaucer's address to Thought in the Invocation to book 2 stresses the function of memory in his art. Love tidings are words from old books. Books are still the activator of new poems, even though "auctorite" may be enriched by "experimentum." The poet's task is to translate words into images, which must then be transmuted into a new poem.

See also nos. 7, 10, 49, 52, 56, 57, 62, 69, 110, 208.

The Legend of Good Women

224. Kolve, V. A. "From Cleopatra to Alceste: An Iconographic Study of *The Legend of Good Women*." In *Signs and Symbols* (ACB, *SAC* 5[1983], no. 73), pp. 130–78. In *LGW*, Chaucer suppressed most of the Cleopatra tradition (asps, etc.) to make her a medieval "good woman," who builds a shrine for Anthony and enters a snake pit to dramatize the grave-worm *topos*. Alceste transcends the grave — the thematic impulse of *LGW*.

259

225. Shigeo, Hisashi. "Chaucer's Idea of 'Love' and 'Goodness' in *The Legend of Good Women* (4)." *Meiji Gakuin Review* 323(Tokyo, 1981):29–45. In Japanese. Some characteristics of the legend of Philomene, Phyllis, and Hypermnestra are discussed. The brief conclusion proves that the poet's attitude toward *LGW* is ambivalent; he seems to be mocking, satirical, and at the same time serious and even religious.

See also nos. 7, 8, 12, 23, 34, 45, 49, 52, 56, 57, 69, 71, 205, 208.

The Parliament of Fowls

226. Aers, David. "The *Parliament of Fowls*: Authority, the Knower and the Known." *ChauR* 16(1981):1–17. It has been argued that the poem exhibits multiplicity and disharmony, though the poet shows a commitment to traditional forms of culture. There is no such commitment in *PF*. The multiplicity of authority and the "continuous self-reflexivity" does not permit the poem to be subsumed into a pattern of orthodox theodicy.

227. Benson, Larry D. "The Occasion of *The Parliament of Fowls*." In *The Wisdom of Poetry*. Ed. Larry D. Benson and Siegfried Wenzel. Kalamazoo, Mich.: Medieval Institute Publications, 1982, pp. 123–44. Offers new support for the old theory that *PF* represents Anne of Bohemia as the "formel eagle" and King Richard, Charles of France, and Friedrich of Meissen as her three suitors, presenting new arguments for dating the poem in 1380 and new evidence that both Charles and Friedrich were actual rivals for Anne's hand.

228. Ferster, Judith. "Reading Nature: The Phenomenology of Reading in the *Parliament of Fowls*." *Mediaevalia* 3(1977):189–213. Responding to the growing custom of reading silently, Chaucer focuses on the dilemma that there can be no interpretation without will but that the use of will can lead to prejudiced, subjective interpretations. The birds cannot communicate, but the narrator represents an affirmative solution through his loving relationship with literary texts.

229. Oruch, Jack B. "St. Valentine, Chaucer, and Spring in February." *Speculum* 56(1981):534–65. Although Charles d'Orleans first described an actual Valentine's Day lottery, it was apparently Chaucer who, in *PF* and *Mars*, first associated Saint Valentine's Day with love, both in its ornithological simplicity and in its human complexity. His innovation was adopted by Gower, Clanvowe, and Oton de Grandson.

230. Quilligan, Maureen. "Allegory, Allegoresis, and the Deallegorization of Language: The *Roman de la Rose*, the *De planctu naturae*, and the *Parlement of Foules*." In *Allegory, Myth, and Symbol*. Ed. Morton W. Bloomfield. Harvard English Studies, vol. 9. Cambridge, Mass.: Harvard University Press, 1981, pp.

163–83. Distinguishing the process of allegory from the nature of allegoresis, Chaucer deallegorizes his sources. He addresses not a reader but an "auditor," who is not asked to judge his own interpretive procedures. Jean de Meun defends the use of slang for explaining the truth; Chaucer bases his defense on verisimilitude. *PF* is deliberately unallegorical.

231. Sklute, Larry M. "The Inconclusive Form of the *Parliament of Fowls.*" *ChauR* 16(1981):119–28. Unlike his earlier dream visions, Chaucer's *PF* exhibits no structural confusion. Rather, the poet poses the possibility of variable pluralisms and leaves the poem inconclusive. The narrator is relatively uninvolved in the action, which permits Chaucer a calmer tone and a more assured, linear progression of events.

See also nos. 7, 8, 10, 12, 49, 52, 57, 62, 69, 81, 110, 111, 116, 208.

Romaunt of the Rose

232. Hira, Toshinori. "*The Romaunt of the Rose* (Fragment A), Translated into Japanese." *Bulletin of the Faculty of Liberal Arts, Nagasaki University, Humanities* 21, 2(1981):75–88.

See also no. 49.

Troilus and Criseyde

233. Barney, Stephen, ed. *Chaucer's Troilus: Essays in Criticism*. Hamden, Conn.: Archon Books, 1980. x, 323 pp. Contains seventeen articles ranging from classics by George Lyman Kittredge and C. S. Lewis to recent criticism and includes retrospective comments by established scholars. The later essays emphasize structuralist approaches and the narrator.

234. Bestul, Thomas H. "Chaucer's *Troilus and Criseyde*: The Passionate Epic and Its Narrator." *ChauR* 14(1980):366–78. Like other late medieval art, *TC* exhibits a growing concern with the portrayal of emotions, especially through the shifting role of the narrator. He sometimes resorts to *occupatio*, claiming inability to describe an emotional state, and eventually in Book V he, along with Troilus, recognizes that the passions in the poem are ephemeral, but nevertheless real.

235. Bishop, Ian. *Chaucer's Troilus and Criseyde: A Critical Study*. Bristol: University of Bristol Academic Publications, 1981. 116 pp. The poem's central interest lies in the attempt by two human souls to establish the deepest and most testing of relationships. The representation of this relationship involves more than

a dialogue: it insinuates a dialectical process that worries out the true natures of the lovers. Although their voices blend in the "love duet" in Book III, they are heard in almost acrimonious debate in the concluding scene of Book IV. The contrast between these scenes is itself part of a wider dialectic that induces a searching anatomy of love. The generalized notion of love is diffracted into a living spectrum of merging attitudes embodied in the *dramatis personae*, and the narrative of human intercourse is poised between a Prologue that declares allegiance to the cult of Cupid and an Epilogue that affirms the only true source of love to be the religion of Christ.

236. Björk, Lennart A. "Courtly Love or Christian Love: Animal Imagery in Book I of Chaucer's *Troilus and Criseyde.*" In *Studies in English Philology, Linguistics, and Literature Presented to Alarik Rynell 7 March 1978.* Ed. Mats Rydén and Lennart A. Björk. Stockholm Studies in English, vol. 46. Stockholm: Almqvist & Wiksell International, 1978, pp. 1–20. The courtly love interpretations of *TC* are not plausible; *TC* offers a burlesque of courtly love. In support of the exegetical promotion of *caritas*, serious flaws in Troilus's character are revealed in animal imagery.

237. Brewer, D. S. "Observations on the Text of *Troilus.*" In *Medieval Studies for J. A. W. Bennett* (ACB, *SAC* 5[1983], no. 74), pp. 121–38. *TC* 1.502, 85, 458, 89 are discussed on the basis of manuscript evidence, and the relevance of each variant to the meaning of a particular passage is pointed out. The case of *TC* 1.85 might call into question Root's theory of revision of *TC* by Chaucer.

238. Bruckmann, Patricia. "*Troilus and Criseyde*, III, 1226–32: A Clandestine Topos." *ELN* 18(1981):166–70. Although the tree-vine *topos* with which Chaucer describes the embrace of Troilus and Criseyde is a literary commonplace, it usually describes a relationship that is either destructive or supportive. In *TC* the *topos* is ambiguous and highlights the ambiguity of the clandestine marriage.

239. Dean, Christopher. "Chaucer's Play on the Word *Beere* in *Troilus and Criseyde.*" *ChauR* 15(1981):224–26. Middle English "beere" could mean "bear," "bier," or "pillow." The first of these is impossible in the context of *TC* 2.1638, but both other meanings are probably there: Pandarus ironically foreshadows Troilus's death, and he also foresees the hero in bed with Criseyde, his "pillow."

240. Eldredge, Laurence. "Boethian Epistemology and Chaucer's Troilus in the Light of Fourteenth-Century Thought." *Mediaevalia* 2(1976):49–75. Boethian epistemological hierarchy allows for movement from the earthbound faculties to the higher, abstractive, freer faculties. Troilus's early confusion and final ascent to the eighth sphere parallel the Boethian hierarchy and are crucial to the moral aspect of the Epilogue.

241. Fish, Varda. "From 'Benigne Love' to the 'Blynde and Wynged Sone': *Troilus and Criseyde* as a Literary Critique of *Filostrato* and the Tradition of Courtly

Love Poetry." *DAI* 42(1981):1628–29A. Comparison of Chaucer's poem with Boccaccio's reveals the narrator in conflict with the story as Chaucer himself both came into conflict with the ideas and ideals represented and also understood his role as poet. As lovers are seduced by a seemingly divine passion, poet and audience may be seduced by love poetry.

242. Green, D. H. *Irony in the Medieval Romance*. New York: Cambridge University Press, 1979. 441 pp. Examines various Continental and English works, including *TC*. See also no. 283.

243. Hanning, R. W. "The Audience as Co-Creator of the First Chivalric Romances." *YES* 2(1981):1–28. Extrinsic models for twelfth-century audiences of chivalric romances (Duly, Bezzola, Legge) should be complemented by indirect evidence that defines such audiences as literary virtuosos, humanists able to evaluate romances to discover the poet and his aims. Chaucer's *TC* reevokes such an audience.

244. Hart, Thomas Elwood. "Medieval Structuralism: 'Dulcarnoun' and the Five-Book Design of Chaucer's *Troilus*." *ChauR* 16(1981):129–70. Number is an aesthetic basis for *TC*. The architectural metaphor of Geoffrey of Vinsauf and Euclid's theorem on proportion in triangles can be used to demonstrate proportions (involving line numbers) in *TC*.

245. Huppé, Bernard F. "The Unlikely Narrator: The Narrative Strategy of the *Troilus*." In *Signs and Symbols* (ACB, *SAC* 5[1983], no. 73), pp. 179–94. Inconsistencies are found in the poems, in the tone of the narrator, and in the discrepancy between the comic mode of *TC* and the seriousness of the conclusion. The design of the poem either "employs inconsistency and incongruity, or conversely is marred by them." Apparent discrepancies serve a function in overall design, especially in the character of the narrator.

246. Johnson, L. Staley. "The Medieval Hector: A Double Tradition." *Mediaevalia* 5(1979):165–82. The Middle Ages provided two contrasting traditions in the characterization of Hector, one celebrating his heroism, the other viewing him as possessed of physical flaws and spiritual debilities. In *TC*, Chaucer combines the two traditions in his characterization.

247. Osberg, Richard H. "Between the Motion and the Act: Intentions and Ends in Chaucer's *Troilus*." *ELH* 48(1981):257–70. *TC* is a thoroughly Christian poem in which characters of a pagan past bring about through their actions the contrary of their expectations, whereas the narrator achieves his purpose exactly, despite his seemingly varied tones. Thus the palinode operates not as contradiction but as logical outcome of the narrator's Christian intent.

248. Renoir, Alain. "Bayard and Troilus: Chaucerian Non-Paradox in the Reader." *OL* 36(1981):116–40. *TC*'s first three images (peacock, stairs, Bayard) assume an affective function and create a context for reader response. Passages from

the *Iliad*, the *Aeneid*, and *Chanson des quatre fils Amyon* explain the strong affective element of the allusion to Bayard, and all affective elements support Donaldson's view of Chaucer's narrative technique.

249. Rowland, Beryl. "Chaucer's Speaking Voice and Its Effect on His Listeners' Perception of Criseyde." *ESC* 7, 2(1981):129–40. The narrator establishes a relationship with the audience to give the impression that they are jointly and empirically exploring human nature. His continuous presence and the mode of oral delivery enables the narrator to impose his views on the audience, especially his view of Criseyde.

250. Rutherford, Charles S. "Troilus' Farewell to Criseyde: the Idealist as Clairvoyant and Rhetorician." *PLL* 17(1981):245–54. Troilus's final speech in Book IV includes three of the only four proverbs he uses, suggesting a new-found "auctoritee." Troilus casts off idealism, speaking for the first time as a cynic and unhappy prophet. The Troilus who allows Criseyde to depart is the more self-aware Troilus who will eventually become the tragic, heroic figure of Book V.

251. Salemi, Joseph S. "Playful Fortune and Chaucer's Criseyde." *ChauR* 15(1981):209–23. Although the frame of *TC* is Boethian determinism, within it works the playful hand of Fortune (and the word "play" occurs frequently, with a variety of senses). The three major personages represent different attitudes toward freedom of choice and Fortune; only Criseyde succeeds in transcending Fortune, however briefly.

252. Tavormina, M. Teresa. "The Moon in Leo: What Chaucer Really Did to *Il Filostrato*'s Calendar." *BSUF* 22(1981):14–19. The lunar calendar and imagery of *TC* 4, though inspired by a similar device in *Filostrato*, are far more elaborate than those in the source. The title characters are often directly correlated to these images, which deepens their development.

253. Wentersdorf, Karl P. "Some Observations on the Concept of Clandestine Marriage in *Troilus and Criseyde*." *ChauR* 15(1980):101–26. A clandestine "marriage" was not fornicatory but simply unlawful, since the church insisted on an eventual ceremony. Chaucer adds the troth plight to his source, thus raising the story above amorous intrigue and heightening the poignancy of Criseyde's unfaithfulness.

See also nos. 8, 9, 17, 21, 24, 28, 30, 34, 39, 49, 52, 55–57, 68, 69, 72, 81, 88, 93, 97, 107, 109, 111, 114, 205, 259.

Source Studies

254. Benson, C. David. *The History of Troy in Middle English Literature: Guido delle Colonne's "Historia destructionis Troiae" in Medieval England.*

Cambridge: D. S. Brewer; Totowa, N.J.: Rowman & Littlefield, 1980. 174 pp. The last chapter, dealing with the degeneration of the history of Troy matter, emphasizes tragic ignorance rather than moral weakness in *TC*. See also no. 265.

255. Clogan, Paul M. "Two Verse Commentaries on the Ending of Boccaccio's *Filostrato*." *M&H*, n.s. 7(1976):147–52. Of the six additional new manuscripts of Boccaccio's *Filostrato*, three contain verse commentaries on the ending of Boccaccio's poem. The two texts of the verse commentaries, edited here for the first time, may shed new light on the ending of Boccaccio's poem and the disowning of pagan and earthly love in *TC* 5.1835–55.

256. Collins, David G. "The Story of Diomede and Criseyde: Changing Relationships in an Evolving Legend." PAPA 7(1981):9–30. As the figure of Briseida, Criseyd, Cressida moved from Benoît de Sainte-Maure (ca. 1160) and Guido della Colonne (1287), through Boccaccio (1336) and Chaucer (ca. 1385), to Shakespeare (1601–1602) and Dryden (1679), her portrait becomes increasingly sympathetic, while Diomede becomes increasingly vicious.

257. Matthews, Lloyd J. "*Troilus and Criseyde*, V.743–749: Another Possible Source." *NM* 82(1981):211–13. The lines of Matteo Frescobaldi's "Canzone XI" provide the nearest analogue for Chaucer's description of Prudence wth "eyen thre." As bankers to the crown, the Frescobaldi had direct links with fourteenth-century England, and the verbal parallels make this a much more likely source for *TC* 5.743–49 than Dante.

See also nos. 241, 252, 253.

Lyrics, Short Poems

A Complaint to His Lady

258. Clogan, Paul. "The Textual Reliability of Chaucer's Lyrics: *A Complaint to His Lady*." *M&H*, n.s. 5(1974):183–89. The extensive emendations in the text of *Lady* are unjustified. The poem is a series of unfinished metrical innovations, showing Chaucer experimenting and practicing his art. The search for metrical regularity has in this lyric deprived the poem of its distinctive style and versification.

The Complaint of Mars

259. Amsler, Mark E. "Mad Lovers and Other Hooked Fish: Chaucer's *Complaint of Mars*." *Allegorica* 4(1979):301–14. *Mars* is placed within Christian moral interpretation when Mars refers to lovers as fish caught on a hook. Asking why God

made human love enticing, Mars inverts the "hierarchy of human and divine lovers." For him the love bait on the hook is not divine. The two kinds of love are central also in *TC*.

260. Parr, Johnstone, and Nancy Ann Holtz. "The Astronomy-Astrology in Chaucer's *The Complaint of Mars*." *ChauR* 25(1981):255–66. Recently computerized astrological tables permit faster and more accurate computation. Chaucer describes events that took place in 1385, but the unusual planetary configurations would undoubtedly have been predicted before that date; hence one cannot with assurance date the poem on this basis.

The Envoy to Scogan

261. Hallmundsson, May Newman. "Chaucer's Circle: Henry Scogan and His Friends." *M&H*, n.s. 10(1981):129–39. Draws upon Chaucer's *Scog* to try to establish a picture of Scogan himself. Scogan is the subject of the article rather than Chaucer.

On the various lyrics and short poems, see also nos. 7, 8, 10, 12, 16, 30, 33, 49, 50, 56, 57, 71, 72, 106, 116.

Chaucer Apocrypha

262. Jenkins, Anthony, ed. *The Isle of Ladies or the Isle of Pleasaunce*. New York: Garland Publishers, 1980. 195 pp. Faithfully reproduces the Longleat MS 256 of *The Isle of Ladies* (included in Speght's edition of Chaucer). Provides glossary, introduction, notes. See also no. 288.

See also no. 41 on *The Plowman's Tale*.

Book Reviews

263. Aers, David. *Chaucer, Langland, and the Creative Imagination* (ACB, *SAC* 3[1981], no. 1). Rev. *Choice* 17(1980):668; Jill Mann, *Encounter* (1980): 60–64; J. J. Anderson, *CritQ* 23(1981):82–83; Elton D. Higgs, *SAC* 3(1981): 121–24.

264. Baird, Lorrayne Y. *Bibliography of Chaucer, 1964–73* (ACB, *SAC* 2[1980], no. 1). Rev. Thomas A. Kirby, *ES* 62(1981):383–85.

265. Benson, C. David. *The History of Troy in Middle English Literature: Guido delle Colonne's "Historia destructionis Troiae" in Medieval England* (ACB,

SAC 5[1983], no. 254). Rev. Lois Ebin, *Speculum* 56(1981):848–50; Jill Mann, *Encounter* (1980):60–64; McKay Sundwall, *SAC* 3(1981):124–28.

266. Benson, Robert G. *Medieval Body Language: A Study of the Use of Gesture in Chaucer's Poetry* (ACB, *SAC* 5[1983], no. 49). Rev. Edmund Reiss, *SAR* 46(1981):100–101.

267. Blake, N. F., ed. *Geoffrey Chaucer: The Canterbury Tales* (ACB, *SAC* 5[1983], no. 14). Rev. John H. Fisher, *Analytical and Enumerative Bibliography* 5(1981):160–61; L. Chaskalson, *Unisa English Studies* 19(1981):36–38.

268. Boyd, Beverly. *Chaucer According to William Caxton: Minor Poems and "Boece"* (ACB, *SAC* 2[1980], pp. 151–53). Rev. Traugott Lawler, *Speculum* 55(1980):861.

269. Brewer, Derek. *Chaucer and His World* (ACB, *SAC* 2[1980], no. 9). Rev. R. T. Davies, *MLR* 75(1980):357–58.

270. Brewer, Derek S., ed. *Chaucer: The Critical Heritage.* 2 vols. (ACB, *SAC* 4[1982], no. 168). Rev. *Choice* 15(1979):1662; J. M. Maguin, *CahiersE* 19(1981): 101; Derek Pearsall, *MLR* 76(1981):158–59.

271. Brewer, Derek. *Symbolic Stories* (ACB, *SAC* 5[1983], no. 54). Rev. W. R. J. B., *CritQ* 23(1981):92.

272. Burlin, Robert B. *Chaucerian Fiction* (ACB, *SAC* 2[1980], no. 69). Rev. J. M. Maguin, *CahiersE* 19(1981):99.

273. Burnley, J. D. *Chaucer's Language and the Philosophers' Tradition* (ACB, *SAC* 5[1983], no. 55). Rev. *Choice* 17(1980):526–27; John H. Fisher, *Speculum* 56(1981):448–49; Jill Mann, *Encounter* (1980):60–64; T. A. Shippey, *TLS*, March 7, 1980, p. 272.

274. Caluwé-Dor, Juliette de, trans. *Geoffrey Chaucer: Les Contes de Cantorbéry*, pt. 1. Gand, Belgium: Editions Scientifiques Story-Scientia, 1977. Rev. Roy J. Pearcy, *SAC* 3(1981):128–34.

275. Cooke, Thomas D. *The Old French and Chaucerian Fabliaux: A Study of Their Comic Climax* (ACB, *SAC* 2[1980], no. 90). Rev. Roy J. Pearcy, *Speculum* 55(1980):783–86.

276. Davis, Norman, et al. *A Chaucer Glossary* (ACB, *SAC* 3[1981], no. 5). Rev. J. J. Anderson, *CritQ* 23(1981):82–83; W. Bruce Finnie, *SAC* 3(1981), pp. 134–37.

277. Eisner, Sigmund, ed. *Nicholas of Lynn, Kalendarium.* Trans. Gary MacEoin and S. Eisner. Athens: University of Georgia Press, 1980. Rev. T. A. Shippey, *TLS*, February 27, 1981, p. 236.

278. Fichte, Joerg O. *Chaucer's "Art Poetical": A Study in Chaucerian Poetics* (ACB, *SAC* 5[1983], no. 62). Rev. Alan T. Gaylord, *Speculum* 56(1981):608–11.

279. Fisher, John H., ed. *The Complete Poetry and Prose of Geoffrey Chaucer* (ACB, *SAC* 2[1980], no. 277). Rev. Ralph Hanna III, *Rev* 1(1979):61–71.

280. Fyler, John M. *Chaucer and Ovid* (ACB, *SAC* 3[1981], no. 37). Rev. James J. Wilhelm, *CL* 32(1980):331–33; Richard L. Hoffman, *JEGP* 80(1981):231–34; Phillipa Hardman, *RES* 32(1981):204–205; John H. Fisher, *Speculum* 55 (1980):866.

281. Gardner, John. *The Poetry of Chaucer* (ACB, *SAC* 2[1980], no. 73). Rev. R. A. Shoaf, *MP* 77(1980):317–20.

282. Gibaldi, Joseph, ed. *Approaches to Teaching Chaucer's Canterbury Tales* (ACB, *SAC* 5[1983], no. 118). Rev. John Kelly, *College Literature* 8(Spring, 1981):192.

283. Green, D. H. *Irony in the Medieval Romance* (ACB, *SAC* 5[1983], no. 242). Rev. Paul G. Ruggiers, *SAC* 3(1981):138–42.

284. Green, Richard Firth. *Poets and Princepleasers: Literature and the English Court in the Late Middle Ages* (ACB, *SAC* 5[1983], no. 70). Rev. Diane Bornstein, *Speculum* 56(1981):874–76.

285. Haas, Renate. *Die mittelenglische Totenklage: Realitätsbezug, abend-ländische Tradition und individuelle Gestaltung* (ACB, *SAC* 5[1983], no. 71). Rev. Martin Lehnert, *ZAA* 29(1981):167–68; Wolfgang Schulze, *Vox Latina* 17(1981):454–55.

286. Havely, N. R., ed. *Boccaccio — Sources of "Troilus" and the Knight's and Franklin's Tales* (ACB, *SAC* 5[1983], no. 28). Rev. Gay Clifford, *TLS*, January 16, 1981, p. 80; Valerie Adams, *TLS*, May 29, 1981.

287. Howard, Donald R. *Writers and Pilgrims* (ACB, *SAC* 5[1983], no. 128). Rev. Valerie Adams, *TLS*, March 13, 1981, p. 290; *TLS*, April 10, 1981, p. 409; Paul Strohm, *Criticism* 23(1981):180–81.

288. Jenkins, Anthony, ed. *The Isle of Ladies or The Isle of Pleasaunce* (ACB, *SAC* 5[1983], no. 262). Rev. Vincent Daly, *Speculum* 55(1980):867–68.

289. Jones, Terry. *Chaucer's Knight: Portrait of a Medieval Mercenary* (ACB, *SAC* 5[1983], no. 137). Rev. *Choice* 18(1980):248; *Economist*, January 26, 1980, p. 103; Jill Mann, *Encounter*, July, 1980, pp. 60–64; *Listener*, January 31, 1980, p. 157; *Observer*, February 10, 1980, p. 38; *Spectator*, January 19, 1980, p. 21; *Times Educational Supplement*, February 1, 1980, p. 23; *Wall Street Journal*, April 2, 1980, p. 28.

290. Kaminsky, Alice R., ed. *Chaucer's "Troilus and Criseyde" and the Critics* (ACB, *SAC* 4[1982], no. 114). Rev. Gay Clifford, *TLS*, January 16, 1981, p. 60.

291. Kelly, Douglas. *Medieval Imagination: Rhetoric and The Poetry of Courtly Love*. Madison: University of Wisconsin Press, 1978. Rev. James I. Wimsatt, *SAC* 3(1981):142–48.

292. Lawler, Traugott. *The One and the Many in the Canterbury Tales* (ACB, *SAC* 5[1983], no. 130). Rev. R. B. Burlin, *Speculum* 56(1981):630–31; Valerie Adams, *TLS*, May 29, 1981.

293. Lewis, C. S. *Essays on Medieval and Renaissance Literature*. Collected by Walter Hooper. Cambridge: Cambridge University Press, 1980. Rev. Jill Mann, *Encounter* (1980):60–64.

294. Lewis, Robert E., ed. *Giovanni Lotario de Segni (Pope Innocent III): De miseria condicionis humane*. London: Scolar Press, 1980. Rev. T. A. Shippey, *TLS*, February 27, 1981, p. 236.

295. *Manuscript Tanner 346* (ACB, *SAC* 5[1983], no. 12). Rev. N. F. Blake, *ES* 63(1982):71–73.

296. Maresca, Thomas E. *Three English Epics: Studies of* Troilus and Criseyde, The Faerie Queene, *and* Paradise Lost (ACB, *SAC* 3[1981], no. 153). Rev. M. E. McAlpine, *Speculum* 56(1981):457–58; John M. Steadman, *JEGP* 80(1981): 234–37; Gwenn Davis, *SAC* 3[1981]:156–60.

297. McAlpine, Monica E. *The Genre of Troilus and Criseyde* (ACB, *SAC* 2[1980], no. 228). Rev. Thomas A. Kirby, *ES* 62(1981):560–61; Gerald Morgan, *MLR* 75(1980):619–20.

298. McCall, John P. *Chaucer Among The Gods* (ACB, *SAC* 5[1983], no. 85). Rev. George D. Economou, *SAC* 3(1981):152–56.

299. Miller, Robert P., ed. *Chaucer: Sources and Backgrounds* (ACB, *SAC* 2[1980], no. 50). Rev. J. M. Maguin, *CahiersE* 19(1981):99–100.

300. Morgan, Gerald, ed. *Geoffrey Chaucer: The Franklin's Tale* (ACB, *SAC* 5[1983], no. 15). Rev. Jill Mann, *Encounter* (1980):60–64.

301. Norton-Smith, John, intro. *Bodleian Library MS Fairfax 16* (ACB, *SAC* 5[1983], no. 10). Rev. Donald C. Baker, *SAC* 3(1981), pp. 165–69.

302. Owen, Charles A. *Pilgrimage and Story-Telling in the Canterbury Tales: The Dialectic of "Ernest" and "Game"* (ACB, *SAC* 2[1980], no. 88). Rev. Gerald Morgan, *ES* 61(1980):462–65.

303. Pearsall, Derek. *Old English and Middle English Poetry*. London, Boston: Routledge & Kegan Paul, 1977. Rev. Przemysław Mroczkowski, *ES* 61(1980): 457–62.

304. Petti, Anthony G. *English Literary Hands from Chaucer to Dryden* (ACB, *SAC* 5[1983], no. 27). Rev. Johan Geritsen, *ES* 62(1981):92–93.

305. Quilligan, Maureen. *The Language of Allegory*. Ithaca and London: Cornell University Press, 1979. Rev. Paul Strohm, *SAC* 3(1981):169–71.

306. Robertson, D. W., Jr. *Essays in Medieval Culture*. Princeton: Princeton University Press, 1980. Rev. Valerie Adams, *TLS*, January 9, 1981, p. 38.

307. Rowe, Donald M. *O Love! O Charite!: Contraries Harmonized in Chaucer's Poetry* (ACB, *SAC* 1[1979], no. 194). Rev. R. W. V. Eliott, *ES* 61(1980): 367–69.

308. Ruggiers, Paul, ed. *Geoffrey Chaucer: The Canterbury Tales: A Facsimile and Transcription of the Hengwrt Manuscript, with Variants from the Ellesmere*

Manuscript (ACB, *SAC* 5[1983], no. 11). Rev. George Kane, *Mediaevalia* 5(1979):283–88; William C. McAvoy, *Manuscripta* 25(1981):183–85; N. F. Blake, "Chaucer Manuscripts and Texts," *Rev* 3(1981):219–32.

309. Salu, Mary, ed. *Essays on Troilus and Criseyde* (ACB, *SAC* 4[1982], no. 182). Rev. Lee W. Patterson, *Speculum* 56(1981):912–14; Jill Mann, *Encounter* (1980):60–64; C. David Benson, *SAC* 3(1981):171–76.

310. Sato, Tsutomu. *Sentence and Solaas: Thematic Development and Narrative Technique in* The Canterbury Tales (ACB, *SAC* 3[1981], no. 62). Rev. Thomas W. Ross, *SAC* 3(1981):176–79.

311. Smith, Nathaniel B., and Joseph T. Snow, eds. *The Expansion and Transformations of Courtly Literature* (ACB, *SAC* 4[1982], no. 136). Rev. Douglas Kelly, *Speculum* 56(1981):440–41; H. A. Kelly, *SAC* 3(1981):179–83.

312. Thompson, Ann. *Shakespeare's Chaucer: A Study in Literary Origins* (ACB, *SAC* 2[1980], no. 68). Rev. Thomas McAlindon, *JEGP* 80(1981):237–43; J. M. Maguin, *CahiersE* 19(1981):100–101.

313. Vasta, Edward, and Zacharias P. Thundy, eds. *Chaucerian Problems and Perspectives: Essays Presented to Paul E. Beichner, C.S.C.* (ACB, *SAC* 3[1981], pp. 211–17). Rev. Donald Baker, *ELN* 19(1981):56–59.

314. Wenzel, Siegfried. *Verses in Sermons: "Fasciculus Morum" and Its Middle English Poems.* Cambridge, Mass.: Medieval Academy of America, 1978. Rev. James J. Wilhelm, *SAC* 3(1981):183–85.

315. Young, Charles R. *The Royal Forests of Medieval England.* Philadelphia: University of Pennsylvania Press, 1979. Rev. Sumner Ferris, *SAC* 3(1981):185–88.

Author Index—Bibliography

Abbreviations for Chaucer's Works

ABC	*An ABC*
Adam	*Adam Scriveyn*
Anel	*Anelida and Arcite*
Astr	*A Treatise on the Astrolabe*
Bal Comp	*A Balade of Complaint*
BD	*The Book of the Duchess*
Bo	*Boece*
Buk	*The Envoy to Bukton*
CkT	*The Cook's Tale*
ClT	*The Clerk's Tale*
Compl d'Am	*Complaynt d'Amours*
CT	*The Canterbury Tales*
CYT	*The Canon's Yeoman's Tale*
Equat	*The Equatorie of the Planets*
For	*Fortune*
Form Age	*The Former Age*
FranT	*The Franklin's Tale*
FrT	*The Friar's Tale*
Gent	*Gentilesse*
GP	*The General Prologue*
HF	*The House of Fame*
KnT	*The Knight's Tale*
Lady	*A Complaint to His Lady*
LGW	*The Legend of Good Women*
ManT	*The Manciple's Tale*
Mars	*The Complaint of Mars*
Mel	*The Tale of Melibee*
MercB	*Merciles Beaute*
MerT	*The Merchant's Tale*
MilT	*The Miller's Tale*
MkT	*The Monk's Tale*
MLT	*The Man of Law's Tale*
NPT	*The Nun's Priest's Tale*

PardT	*The Pardoner's Tale*
ParsT	*The Parson's Tale*
PF	*The Parliament of Fowls*
PhyT	*The Physician's Tale*
Pity	*The Complaint unto Pity*
Prov	*Proverbs*
PrT	*The Prioress's Tale*
Purse	*The Complaint of Chaucer to His Purse*
Ret	*Chaucer's Retraction*
Rom	*The Romaunt of the Rose*
Ros	*To Rosemounde*
RvT	*The Reeve's Tale*
Scog	*The Envoy to Scogan*
ShT	*The Shipman's Tale*
SNT	*The Second Nun's Tale*
SqT	*The Squire's Tale*
Sted	*Lak of Stedfastnesse*
SumT	*The Summoner's Tale*
TC	*Troilus and Criseyde*
Th	*The Tale of Sir Thopas*
Ven	*The Complaint of Venus*
WBT	*The Wife of Bath's Tale*
Wom Nob	*Womanly Noblesse*
Wom Unc	*Against Women Unconstant*

Index